COOLFORE, WEST FARNEY AND THE NATIONAL SCHOOL SYSTEM, 1826–1968

COOLFORE,
West Farney and the National School system,
1826–1968

Gerard Fealy

East_wood_

*This book is dedicated to the former pupils and teachers of Coolfore national school,
living and deceased.*

First published in 2023
Eastwood Ltd
A member of the Wordwell Group
Unit 9, 78 Furze Road,
Sandyford Industrial Estate,
Dublin 18
www.wordwellbooks.com

Cover image: Coolfore National School, 1914 (*Image courtesy Monaghan County
Museum*)

ISBN: 978-1-916742-52-9 (Paperback)

British Library Cataloguing-in-Publication Data.
A catalogue record for this book is available from the British Library.

Supported by The Ulster Local History Trust, www.ulht.org.uk/

Typeset in Ireland by Wordwell Ltd
Copy-editor: Heidi Houlihan
Cover design and artwork: Wordwell Ltd
Printed by: SprintPrint, Dublin

CONTENTS

FOREWORD

For the author of a book on history, the painstaking research that is needed takes countless hours, days, weeks, months and in some cases years. It involves numerous visits to archives, libraries and repositories, reading books, journals, newspapers and previous research. It also involves searching the internet, speaking with people, recording conversations, copious note-taking and then pulling it all together into a coherent narrative.

Gerard Fealy's publication *Coolfore, west Farney and the national school system, 1826-1968* was, doubtless, very much a labour of love, researching the primary school that he himself and his siblings attended. In his book Gerard traces the historical and social evolution of the national school system in Ireland, from its inception in 1831 until the widespread closure of rural national schools during the late 1960s.

This book investigates the national school system, its policies and practices, both beneficial and flawed. It explores the hierarchy of school management, what were the dominant factors and who were the dominant players. The author draws on the case of his local national school at Coolfore to weave through the history and development of the national school system. The book also contains a chapter dedicated to the recollections of former pupils of Coolfore, a nostalgic journey with which anybody privileged enough to have received their formative education in a rural national school will identify.

Although Coolfore national school was the impetus for this publication, Gerard has gone beyond Coolfore, to include all the rural national schools in the parish of Magheross from penal times right through to the present time. The book also reaches far beyond Magheross in search of a comprehensive account and understanding of the system of primary education in Ireland, and how Coolfore compared in the grand scheme. Hence, although a local history, the book will resonate with any rural parish across Ireland.

We recommend this book as an interesting and informative read, whether from a local viewpoint or as an insight into the wider national school system in Ireland. We wish Gerard every success with his publication. It was an honour and privilege to receive this publication prior to printing, but for those of us involved in local history and heritage, knowing that this aspect of our local history has been preserved in print made it a pleasure to read.

Bernie Ruth and Mary Frances Kerley
Corduff-Raferagh Heritage Group

PREFACE

The idea for this book originated in conversations that took place in 2018, the year that marked the fiftieth anniversary of the closing of Coolfore national school, the rural school in south Co. Monaghan that is the focus of several chapters of this book. At that time, many former pupils wished to mark the anniversary, and as a former pupil myself, I undertook to write a history of the school, but with the caveat that the writing would have to wait until after I retired, which was in 2021.

In writing the book, I have endeavoured to set the history of Coolfore within its local social and historical contexts and within the wider context of the historical development of the national school system. Hence, the book is about the history of the national school system in Ireland, partly told through the experiences of Coolfore and other rural national schools in the parish of Magheross in south Co. Monaghan. (Note: I use 'Magheross' throughout to denote the civil parish of Magheross and this incorporates the Catholic parish of Carrickmacross). The historical narrative references important developments on the Shirley estate in west Farney and the major political and social changes in Ireland over a period of a century and a half. In this way, I hope that the book offfers new understandings on rural schooling and the related social history of west Farney, alongside a comprehensive account of the evolution of educational policy, classroom practices and the experiences of pupils and their teachers.

In researching the book, I examined an extensive range of historical documents and artefacts, and I consulted relevant published sources. I also conducted oral history interviews with thirteen former pupils and with the last schoolmaster of Coolfore. This was one of the most pleasing aspects of the research since it brought me back to a time and a place that had long remained stored in the 'archives' of my own memory. In writing the book, I hope that I have added new and worthwhile scholarship to the history of education and rural schooling in Ireland, and to the social history of Co. Monaghan and Ulster.

Gerard Fealy

INTRODUCTION

This book presents a history of the national school system in Ireland, partly told through the history of rural national schools in south Co. Monaghan. It incorporates a study of the historical development of Coolfore national school, a rural school in the parish of Magheross in the western part of the Barony of Farney. The story of Coolfore is set against the background of the development of the national school system and the significant political and social changes that occurred over a period of more than a century and a half.

Established in 1831, the national school system was introduced in the wake of the Act of Union of 1801, when Ireland came under the direct control of the parliament at Westminster. The system was founded on the explicit ideal of bringing together children of all religious denominations under a single unified system, one that would gain the support of all classes. Such a unified system would reduce sectarian discord among Catholics and Protestants and would also reduce the growing influence of individual religious denominations in education. Hence, the system was to operate on the basis of separate secular and religious instruction.

Key milestones in the development of the national school system included a series of parliamentary reports, which at the time of their publication, described the way that the national schools were operating. Along with the annual reports of the Commissioners of National Education in Ireland, these reports are a window into the history of the national schools, including the rural schools of south Co. Monaghan, their pupils, teachers and the school curriculum.

The Commissioners prescribed the rules for the establishment, governance and management of the national schools; however, local powerbrokers influenced the establishment of many schools and the experiences of pupils and their teachers. In the development of Coolfore and other schools in west Farney, these powerbrokers included the successive Shirley landlords and their agents, the local Catholic clergy and the schools' district inspectors.

Like the Central Board of Health (1820) and the Irish Poor Law (1838), the national school system was an early example of state intervention in the lives of the people. As a state-sponsored, national system of mass elementary education, it challenged the power and influence of the local landlords and their agents, and it also challenged the power and influence of the denominational churches. Despite these challenges, the landlords and especially the churches wielded influence through school patronage and school management, ultimately rendering the system distinctly denominational.

The national school system was introduced at a time when the Anglo-Irish ascendency remained the dominant power in politics and land ownership. However, following the repeal of the last of the penal laws in 1829, a more confident Catholic Church and nationalist political movements were emerging influences in politics and public life. By the century's end, the power of the landlords was declining in the face of successive land reform acts. Although gradual and taking place over the late nineteenth and early twentieth centuries, the balance of power and influence transitioned from the landed class to a predominantly Catholic-nationalist class. This gradual change was the context in which the national school system developed in the years before and after Irish Independence and gave rise to the experiences of teachers and their pupils at Coolfore national school and the other rural schools in the western part of the Barony of Farney in south Monaghan.

ACKNOWLEDGEMENTS

I am grateful to the many individuals and agencies who supported and encouraged me in researching and writing this book.

I am deeply indebted to the thirteen former pupils and to the former school principal, Mr Fergus Lane, who took part in oral history interviews, generously sharing their memories of their time at Coolfore national school.

I am also deeply indebted to the many individuals who supported me in researching and planning this book, including those who are actively involved in preserving the local heritage of the Carrickmacross and Corduff districts. I am especially grateful to Mary Frances Kerley and Bernie Ruth, who provided me with valuable information and access to primary sources, offered helpful comments on the manuscript, and wrote the Foreword to the book. I am also grateful to Joseph Callan, whose knowledge of local history has been invaluable in guiding me to additional sources. Kevin Gartlan and Larry McDermott also provided valuable advice during the early days of planning the book. I also gratefully acknowledge the guidance of the University College Dublin (UCD) Office of Research Ethics and Catherine McElroy for their support in planning the oral history interviews. I am very grateful to Debbie Emerson, who transcribed the digital recordings of the oral history interviews so professionally and expertly. I am indebted to historians Dr Marion Rogan and Dr Lorraine O'Reilly, whose respective PhD theses on aspects of the history of the Shirley estate have provided me with important source material. Kevin Mulligan and Enda O'Flaherty also gave helpful information on the architecture of national schools.

I visited several libraries and archives when researching the book and I therefore wish to acknowledge the support, guidance and professionalism of all who assisted me during my research. I am especially grateful to the following who provided me with access to important documentary primary sources, and who showed great interest in my research: Theresa Loftus, Exhibitions and Research Officer, Monaghan County Museum; Jonathan Smyth, Cavan Library Services; and Dr Gary Carville, Clogher Diocesan Archives. I made several visits to the Reading Room at the National Archives of Ireland, where I consulted a range of sources on education, and I wish to acknowledge the guidance and support of the archivists and staff who were always most helpful and courteous. I also consulted the Shirley Papers at the Public Records Office of Northern Ireland (PRONI), and I am grateful to the staff at PRONI, who were most helpful in guiding me to relevant documentary materials and artefacts. I am also very grateful to the staff at UCD Library Special Collections, who provided me with access to the annual reports of the Commissioners of National Education in Ireland, and to librarian Jane Nolan and staff at UCD Maps and GIS Collections for providing me with access to historic Ordnance Survey maps. I am especially grateful to all the staff at Carrickmacross Library, who were always welcoming and supportive and showed a great interest in the project.

I acknowledge with gratitude all those individuals who kindly provided me with access to historic photographs and other artefacts, and who gave their permission to reproduce the images contained in the book. These include Liam Bradley, Monaghan County Museum; Rebecca Geddes, PRONI; Jeremy Hayes, University of Southampton; Hazel Menton, National Archives of Ireland; Dan O'Connell, Ordnance Survey Ireland; Karen Patton, St Louis Convent, Carrickmacross; and those former pupils of Coolfore who kindly provided historic photos. I also gratefully acknowledge Gerry and Rosie Callan, who provided me with access to the personal papers of Miss Rushe.

I extend my gratitude to colleagues at UCD who have supported me over several years in researching and writing on the history of education. I reserve my deepest gratitude for my wife Deirdre and our sons Mervyn and Jonathan and their respective families for their unfailing love and support.

LIST OF ILLUSTRATIONS

1. 'Barony of Farney landowners 1846', showing the Shirley estate to the west and the Bath estate to the east
2. Lough Fea House, Carrickmacross
3. Main Street, Carrickmacross, late nineteenth century
4. Former hedge school of John Cassidy at Aghalile
5. Former hedge school of Owen Sheridan at Cargaghoge
6. Section of map of Coolfore townland (undated) showing a hedge school at south-east corner
7. Site of the former thatched house at Coolfore, which served as the schoolhouse, 1845–1852
8. Section of Coolfore townland showing location of hedge school
9. Section of Coolfore townland showing Coolfore national school
10. Coolfore schoolhouse, constructed in 1871
11. Original stone plaque dated 1871 placed above the front door of Coolfore schoolhouse
12. Former Sreenty national school, Magheross parish on the Shirley estate
13. Former Ballynagearn national school, Magheracloone parish on the Shirley estate
14. Former Corduff national school, Magheross parish on the Shirley estate
15. Corcreagh (Raferagh) national school
16. Former Corvally schoolhouse and Presbyterian church, Shanco, Co. Monaghan
17. Former Drumlusty national school, Donaghmoyne parish on the former Bath estate, Co. Monaghan
18. Carrickmacross workhouse, site of the former workhouse national school, established in 1843
19. Monaghan model school, constructed in 1860 to an OPW design
20. OPW architectural drawing for a national school
21. Former Moys national school, Clontibret parish, Co. Monaghan, constructed in 1875 to an OPW design
22. St Patrick's teacher training college for males, Drumcondra, Co. Dublin
23. Female teacher training college of Our Lady of Mercy, Carysfort Park, Blackrock, Co. Dublin
24. Master Patrick Marron and wife Annie, 1899
25. Coolfore girls 1911
26. Coolfore boys 1911

LIST OF TABLES

1
'The thirst for education':
Hedge schools and elementary education,
c. 1800–1830

Before the removal of the restrictions on Catholic education in the eighteenth century, the Catholic poor of Ireland had a strong desire to have their children educated. Despite their meagre means, Catholic parents were willing to pay a local schoolmaster to conduct their children's schooling. This informal way of providing elementary education was common throughout the eighteenth century, and the schools established for this purpose were known as 'pay schools', or more commonly, 'hedge schools'. Even after the restrictions on Catholic education were removed following the Roman Catholic Relief Act of 1791, the hedge schools continued to be the main system of elementary education for the majority of children, since no system of state education existed until 1831.

In the early nineteenth century, in addition to the hedge schools, a small number of Catholic religious congregations, such as the Presentation Sisters and the Christian Brothers, were also providing elementary schooling for some Catholic children. A number of voluntary education societies also existed to support the education of the children of Protestant and Presbyterian families. These included the Society for Promoting the Education of the Poor of Ireland, the London Hibernian Society and the Association Incorporated for Discountenancing of Vice and Promoting the Knowledge and Practice of the Christian Religion.[1] These societies supported schools through grants for buildings, teaching materials and teachers' salaries. In addition, the Incorporated Society for Promoting English Protestant Schools in Ireland established private charter schools in the early eighteenth century for the purpose of promoting the Protestant religion.

Published in 1826, the *Second Report of the Commissioners of Irish Education Inquiry* recorded a total of 11,823 schools in Ireland, in which there were

12,530 schoolmasters and schoolmistresses.[2] A total of 560,549 children attended the schools. Roman Catholics accounted for the majority of the pupils (408,285), with the remainder comprising Protestants (93,452) and Presbyterians (45,304).[3] The vast majority of the Presbyterian children were in Ulster, with fewer than a thousand in the other three provinces combined. This reflected the heritage of Scottish settlers in Ulster from the late seventeenth century, where they outnumbered the children of the Church of Ireland at that time. Eighty per cent (9,532) of all the schools were categorised as pay or hedge schools.

'His little boy's education': The hedge schools

Richard Twiss, a traveller from England, wrote one of the earliest descriptions of a hedge school in Ireland in his *A Tour in Ireland in 1775*.[4] Writing with apparent disdain for the Irish, Twiss described what he saw at Dunleer in Co. Louth:

> I observed about a dozen bare-legged boys sitting by the side of the road scrawling on scraps of paper placed on their knees; these lads it seems found the smoke in their school or cabbin [*sic*] insufferable. It might perhaps be better that the lowest class of people throughout Europe were neither taught to read nor write, excepting those few who discover evident marks of genius; those acquisitions only creating new wants, and exciting new desires, which they will seldom be able to gratify, and consequently rendering them less happy than otherwise they might be.[5]

Despite Twiss' observations, its seems that the 'lowest class of people' in Ireland were intent on having their children educated, even when there was no suitable schoolhouse in which to conduct lessons. In the early nineteenth century, hedge schools were numerous throughout Ireland and were the dominant form of elementary schooling at the time; in Co. Monaghan alone, there were approximately 270 hedge schools.[6] This high number reflected the rapid growth in the population, especially in the first two decades of the nineteenth century.[7] Established by individual teachers and reliant on the financial support of parents, the hedge schools were essentially private proprietary schools and were so numerous that they competed with each other for pupils.[8]

In 1826 the Commissioners of Irish Education Inquiry commented on the hedge schools as follows: 'They arise, from time to time, as circumstances create a demand for them.'[9] This implied that they were established to meet a local need. In these schools, lessons took place in informal locations, such as a shed or barn, a mud hut constructed by the local people, the schoolmaster's own

2

house, and in the open air during good weather. In Lungs townland near Clogher village in Co. Tyrone, Mrs Dumont, the schoolmistress, conducted lessons in 'a loft over the cowhouse and stable'.[10]

Although informal and unregulated, the hedge schools were an essential system of elementary schooling for parents who were determined to see that their children received a basic education.[11] Writing in 1807, Rowson commented on the number of hedge schools and the resolve of parents to have their children schooled:

All over the county are numbers of schools, where the lower orders have their children instructed in writing, arithmetic and reading; scarcely a peasant who can muster a crown after tithe and priest's dues but is emulous to expend it on his little boy's education.[12]

In the following year, Lord Palmerston likewise commented on the desire for education and on the number of hedge schools among the Irish-speaking tenants on his Co. Sligo estate:

The thirst for education is so great that there are now three or four schools upon the estate. The people join in engaging some itinerant master; they run him up a miserable mud hut on the roadside, and the boys pay him half-a-crown, or some five shillings a quarter. They are taught reading, writing and arithmetic, and what, from the appearance of the establishment, no one would imagine, Latin and even Greek.[13]

Catholic schoolmasters organised the largest proportion of the hedge schools, and the fact that they catered for well over 400,000 children in 1824 reflected the easing of the penal laws.[14] Boys greatly outnumbered girls in the hedge schools, and this is borne out in evidence from the Commissioners' Report of 1826. For example, in the five hedge schools run by Catholic schoolmasters in the parish of Donaghmoyne in south Co. Monaghan, there were 174 boys and just thirty-three girls.[15] The relatively small number of girls participating in education reflected the low level of female participation in occupations that depended on the ability to read and write.[16] In the nearby town of Carrickmacross in 1824, in addition to the fifteen publicans and two inn keepers, among the town's trades people were six grocers, four bakers, two painters and glaziers and four tallow chandlers and soap boilers, all trades occupied by men.[17] Girls' lower participation in schooling also reflected their role in supporting childrearing and other family duties in the home.

The hedge schoolmaster and the schoolhouse

Hedge schools were run mainly by male teachers who were self-educated or had themselves been educated by a hedge schoolmaster. They charged a fee per subject, per quarter, and payment could be made in kind.[18] The schoolmaster's annual salary was based on the number of scholars attending and the ability of parents to pay, and his accommodation also depended on the support of the local parents. His income from teaching was generally small, with payment made each quarter term according to the subjects taught; the fee was 1s. 8d. for spelling, 2s. for reading, from 2s. 2d. to 3s. 3d. for writing, and up to 7s. for arithmetic.[19] The schoolmaster had sole authority over the school, and in many cases, owned the schoolhouse.[20] He was held in high esteem within the parish, and in the ranks of society, was second only to the lord of the manor and the clergyman or the priest.[21]

In his autobiography, William Carleton, the nineteenth-century novelist and a former hedge schoolmaster, described the hedge schoolhouse at which he himself was educated. Located in the townland of Skelgy in Co. Tyrone, it was built for Pat Frayne, Carlton's former schoolmaster:

> A schoolhouse was built for him – a sad house scooped out of the bank on the roadside – and in the course of a month it was filled with upwards of a hundred scholars, most of them males, but a good number of them females [...] Every winter's day, each [scholar] brought two sods of turf for the fire, which was kept burning in the centre of the school: there was a hole in the roof that discharged the functions of a chimney. Around this fire, especially during cold and severe weather, the boys were entitled to sit in a circle by turns [...] The seats about the fire were round stones.[22]

Another noted hedge schoolmaster was Peter Ursin, a native of Carrickmacross, who ran a hedge school at Drum in north Co. Monaghan in the 1820s. Ursin was a schoolmaster for upwards of eighty years, and it was said of him that 'during all that time, he stuck with unwearied diligence to his noble but troublesome calling, moving here and there as he could find a hut or a barn or a cowshed unoccupied'.[23] At Drum he conducted his school in a stable and his annual salary was about £6. 10s.[24] A Roman Catholic, he was described as 'a small man and a great teacher'.[25] His former pupils are said to have remembered 'with kindly feeling his snowy head and pleasant face as he gently led them forth on the path to knowledge'.[26] One pupil, Henry Walsh of Dunsrim, said of him:

> The last hedge-schoolmaster I mind was Peter Ursin of Cavany. He

taught in a thatched mud-wall cabin just inside Mac Kiernan's Lane. The site was immediately below the road and in wet weather was often flooded. From ten to twelve scholars used to attend it, and I was one of them. We read out of the universal books and many a time I was sent out to the hedge to cut a pointer. Most of us brought a 'creepy' stool to sit on, but others just sat on a stone with a bag on it. Peter himself was a small little man, inclined to drink too much, and very often went to Cootehill fair.[27]

Ursin never possessed a home, and instead, 'he went day after day with whatever scholar might invite him for the night'.[28] He lived to be a centenarian and his obituary in the *Northern Standard* on 2 September 1882 read: 'The last of an extinct race, he is now gone [...] where noisy boys and hard questions can no more disturb his rest.'[29]

As the accounts show, while the conditions for teaching were primitive, the hedge school was a place of learning and the teaching could be conducted in a positive, lively and good-humoured atmosphere.[30] Writing in 1836 and following the introduction of the state national school system, William Carleton commented that the hedge schoolmasters were 'as superior in literary knowledge and educational requirements [and] in moral and religious character' as the school teachers employed in the new state system.[31] If he praised their moral character, he also wrote of moral failings, which for some was the result of 'addiction to good whiskey'.[32] Carleton recalled another of his teachers, Charles McGoldrick, a priest who ran a school at Tulnavert in Co. Tyrone. A dwarf and a hunchback with a 'caustic temper', McGoldrick was 'given to bouts of lunacy':

[McGoldrick] had a head the size of a mess pot, and a neck like a bull, while his arms were powerful and of immense length. His instrument of punishment was a cudgel, with which he belaboured the boys when deficient in their lessons, so inhumanly that he often knocked them down, and not infrequently cut them to the skull.[33]

While a pupil at Coolfore national school in the late 1930s, James Murtagh of Legghimore wrote an essay on the topic 'Old schools', which described the hedge school, which his great grandfather conducted, and which was situated 'where our own byre is now'. The essay was one of several contributed to the Schools' Collection of the Irish Folklore Commission and is preserved in the Dúchas online archive.[34] In his essay James wrote:

My great grandfather taught in it. His name was James Murtagh. This school was held indoors. Those who had turf used to take some when they needed a fire in the Winter. The teacher did not lodge in any other house, but he was living in his own house. The families that attended these schools paid the school master according to their means. The subjects that were taught in the hedge schools were taught all in Irish. Very little English was taught. The books that were used were mostly all Irish books. The writing that was done was all done on slates with slate pencils. The children were arranged standing around the walls because there were no seats. There was no blackboard in the school for there was no chalk to write on it. The teacher remained all his life teaching in the district.[35]

The hedge school curriculum

The hedge school curriculum included reading, writing and arithmetic, and depending on the qualifications of the schoolmaster, could also include lessons in history, geography, book-keeping, surveying and navigation, as well as Latin and Greek.[36] While the lessons taught reflected the teacher's knowledge in the subjects, they also reflected the subjects that the parents considered important. In addition to the teacher's fee, parents also supplied the reading books and were entitled to have three periods of individual instruction daily for their children.[37] The parents placed great importance on arithmetic and on the skill of the teacher in teaching it, and 'the ordinary people of Ireland would set no store by a school in which arithmetic would not figure prominently'.[38] In his essay on the history of the hedge schools of counties Monaghan and Tyrone, John Johnston suggests that it is probable that skills were also taught in some schools to prepare the children for work in the local economy; in the case of Co. Monaghan, where linen was a local industry in parts of the county, weaving was taught.[39]

The Roman Catechism was also taught in the hedge schools, both before and after the repeal of the penal laws in the late eighteenth century, and Roman Catholic clergy examined the children in Christian doctrine.[40] The teaching of the Catholic religion was viewed with disdain by some in the Established Church, who claimed that children were being taught lessons in hatred of the Protestant religion and 'ridicule of the Word of God'.[41] Religious instruction in schools would remain a source of distrust and dispute among the main denominational Churches throughout the nineteenth century.

The lessons taught also included the classical languages of Latin and Greek, which were an important part of the hedge school curriculum and often considered necessary if a child wished to later enter Church ministry or a trade.[42] However, some politicians and writers were scornful of the idea that poor Irish children should study the classics and be educated 'above their station in life'.[43]

The government at Westminster and other commentators were likewise opposed to the teaching of Irish history, on the grounds that it would inculcate
'a foolish hankering' for freedom and promote disloyalty to the state.[44]

In his detailed history of the hedge schools, Patrick Dowling writes that
'the poorest and humblest of the schools' gave instruction in Latin and Greek.[45]
Instruction in the classics was strong in the hedge schools in Co. Monaghan,
where some of the schoolmasters were themselves instructed in Latin and
Greek, some of them by Presbyterian clergymen.[46] The hedge schools welcomed 'every scholar brought to their door' and Protestant parents frequently
sent their children to the hedge schools, where their religion was never inter-
fered with. On this fact, Dowling comments: 'The old Hedge Schools did
more to bring about friendly relations between Catholics and Protestants in
Ireland than any schools or systems of education have done since.'[47]

In 1826, the Commissioners of Irish Education Inquiry remarked that some
hedge schools admitted children of all persuasions and the schoolmaster gave
religious instruction according to the religion that parents wished their children
to learn.[48] The Commissioners commented on the fact that in these schools
'there appeared to be perfect Harmony amongst children of all Persuasions'.[49]
However, while the Commissioners did not approve of the same schoolmaster
teaching 'different and conflicting religious Doctrines', they conceded that it
was possible for children of all persuasions to be educated together.

Criticism of the hedge schools

While the historical evidence indicates that there were numerous hedge
schools in every district, questions arise as to whether they offered a stable and
reliable form of education for the poor children of Ireland. Since the hedge
schools were not regulated, it is probable that standards differed greatly in the
quality of the school accommodation and the quality of teaching. In his Parochial Survey of Ireland, William Shaw Mason described the hedge schools of
Maghera in Co. Derry in 1814:

> Schoolhouses are in general wretched huts, built of sods in the high-
> way ditches, from which circumstances they are designated hedge
> schools. They have neither door, window, nor chimney; a large hole in
> the roof serving to admit light and let out smoke. A low narrow wall
> of mud, hard baked serves as a seat. A hole cut in the mud wall on the
> South side affords ingress and egress to its inhabitants. These schools
> are fully attended in Summer, half empty in Spring and harvest time;
> and from the cold and damp, utterly deserted in Winter; so that the
> children, who periodically resort to them for instruction, usually for-
> get in one part of the year what they have learned in the other.[50]

Other writers in the early nineteenth century also criticised the hedge schools for the lack of parental commitment to their children's schooling: 'When children are able to perform any sort of work, such as herding of cattle, they are then taken from school.'[51] The Commissioners of Irish Education Inquiry also expressed concern at the lack of supervision of the hedge schools and the fact that some teachers were not properly qualified to teach: 'These Schools cannot be considered as being under any particular superintendence [...] and are frequently undertaken by persons very ill qualified to discharge the duties of Schoolmasters.'[52]

Nevertheless, the hedge schools provided an essential system of education for the poor of Ireland when no state system existed. While there is evidence of a broad range of subjects taught, the range and quality of instruction is likely to have varied considerably among the schools. For many children, education could be little more than instruction in reading, writing and arithmetic.[53] While a national education system was established in 1831 and while a number of Catholic religious orders were providing schooling for Catholic children at that time, hedge schools continued to operate up to the 1840s, the decade of the Famine. There is evidence that a significant number of the hedge schools were quasi-parochial schools that received support from the local Catholic clergy.[54]

Roman Catholic schools

With the gradual relaxing of the penal laws, a number of Catholic religious orders were established and began to provide elementary schooling for Catholic children. These schools were distinct from the hedge schools and would go on to play a prominent role in the education of Catholic children to the present day. The *Second Report of the Commissioners of Irish Education Inquiry* identified three classes of Catholic schools operating at that time: 'the Schools of the Brothers of Christian Doctrine [the Christian Brothers], the Schools of the Nuns for the Instruction of Females, and the Day Schools'.[55] Over 5,000 pupils attended these various schools in 1825.

The Christian Brothers congregation was founded in 1802 and operated its first school in Waterford. The Commissioners listed twenty-four schools connected with the Christian Brothers and 'sundry' Catholic religious orders, including the order of Carmelites and the order of St Dominick. The schools were located across eleven counties, with nine of the schools in Dublin. No Christian Brothers' school was established in Co. Monaghan at that time. Many of the schools were built of stone and lime and some schools were located in a chapel.

The Commissioners also listed forty-six 'female schools attached to nunneries', attended by 7,575 pupils. The majority of these convent schools were in Munster and Leinster, with most in Dublin and Cork, and none were in any of the nine counties of Ulster at that time. Most were non-pay schools and most of the schoolmistresses, who were religious sisters, were not paid a salary. Among the Catholic sisterhoods running schools at that time were the Presentation Sisters, who ran twenty of the schools listed in the Commissioners' Report, and the other female schools were under the patronage of various congregations, including the congregations of St Mary, St Theresa, St Ursula, St Clare and the Carmelite order. In a very small number of cases, such as Clonegal in Co. Wexford and Tullow in Co. Carlow, a few Protestant children attended these Catholic schools. In the schools of the Presentation Sisters, there was a strong emphasis on instruction in the principles of religion and Christian piety. The lessons included catechism, reading, writing and arithmetic, and girls were also instructed in knitting, needlework and spinning.[56]

In addition to the schools attached to nunneries, there were 352 Roman Catholic day schools in the country, with over 33,000 pupils. The majority of the day schools were located in Leinster and Munster, with just nineteen such schools in Ulster, including three in Co. Monaghan, at Clones, Latturken, and Tydavnet. The school buildings of the day schools were variously described as 'a good, slated house', a 'rented house', a 'poor man's kitchen' and 'an old chapel'. The schoolhouse at Tydavnet was 'a good, slated house built at the expense of the titular Bishop and the Roman Catholic inhabitants'. The school at Latturken in the parish of Monaghan was held in a chapel and had 103 pupils. At Clones, ninety-four pupils attended the day school, which was located in 'a good warm room on the first floor of a house'.[57] The Roman Catholic Bible was read in all three of the Catholic pay schools in Co. Monaghan.

While the hedge schools remained the predominant system of elementary education in 1825, the Christian Brothers' schools, convent schools and the Catholic day schools were growing in numbers. In the majority of the Catholic schools, the education was free. When compared with the other provinces, there were fewer Catholic schools in Ulster in 1825, reflecting the fact that Presbyterians and Protestants were the majority population of Ulster at the time. Although Protestant children were not excluded from these schools, very few attended them.

Protestant education societies

Aside from the hedge schools and the schools run by Catholic congregations, other schemes for the provision of elementary education for the poorer classes were available; these included the schools supported by voluntary Protestant education societies. Among these were the London Hibernian Society and the Association Incorporated for Discountenancing Vice and Promoting the

Knowledge and Practice of the Christian Religion. Along with the Bible Societies, these societies were closely aligned with the Established Church and scripture reading was 'the predominant and almost sole object of instruction'.[58]

The Protestant education societies established free schools, and because they were free, they attracted some pupils from Catholic hedge schools, meaning that they could have a proselytising purpose.[59] The societies were founded in response to the proliferation of the hedge schools, which served mostly the children of poorer Catholic families. Commenting on the hedge schools in 1811, John Leslie Foster, the MP for the Dublin University constituency, complained that the poorer classes were 'taking education into their own hands' and he called on the state to do something.[60] The state response was to give some monies in the form of a parliamentary grant to the Protestant education societies; however, these societies relied mainly on charitable donations, and not the state, to support children's education in the Protestant community.[61]

The state gave a substantial annual parliamentary grant to the Society for Promoting the Education of the Poor of Ireland, which was located at Kildare Place in Dublin, and was known as the Kildare Place Society. Founded in 1811 by a group of philanthropists, the Society was established as a non-denominational education society whose aim was to 'diffuse a well-ordered system of Education of the Poor, which shall combine economy of time and money, and bestow due attention on cleanliness and discipline'.[62] The Society's 'leading principle' was to 'afford the same facilities for Education, to all classes of professing Christians, without any attempt to interfere with the peculiar religious opinions of any'.[63]

The Kildare Place Society established schools 'wherein the poor might be instructed in reading, writing and arithmetic' and in which 'the *Scriptures without note or comment*' should be used.[64] It also established the Kildare Place Training Institution for the training of primary school teachers. By 1821, the Society was providing grants to 272 schools in Ireland for the purposes of fitting out school rooms and supplying books, training schoolmasters and schoolmistresses and appointing school inspectors. In 1824 the total number of schools solely connected with the Society was 583.[65] In that same year, it supported four Protestant charity schools in Co. Monaghan at Drum, Castleblaney, Legnacraw and Tossey.[66] In the following year, twenty-six schools in the county received support from the Society, seven of which were also supported by the London Hibernian Society.[67] Apart from a Protestant school run by Dyas O'Neil at Magheracloone, the majority of the schools which the Society supported were in the north of the county.

Despite its stated aim to be non-denominational and its support for some Catholic schools like the Presentation convent in Kilkenny, the Society's reference to scripture reading 'without note or comment' tacitly promoted the Protestant belief in the authority of the scriptures.[68] Moreover, like much of the charitable work in Ireland in the nineteenth century, the Society was founded and administered by members of the Protestant Church. For example, the original committee of the Society included Arthur Guinness of the Dublin brewing family and Samuel Bewley of the famous Dublin Quaker family. Several of its vice-presidents were members of the House of Lords.

Due to its connections with the Established Church and the Ascendency and because of its emphasis on reading the scriptures, the Kildare Place Society lost the support of Catholics, including the prominent Catholic politician Daniel O'Connell, who was hostile to the Society.[69] Catholic clergy complained to the Commissioners of Irish Education Inquiry in 1826 that the Society and the other Protestant education societies, in particular the London Hibernian Society and the Baptist Societies, were attempting to 'effect the Conversion of the Roman Catholics to the Protestant Faith'.[70] These societies were apparently active in preaching among Catholics at that time, when it was reported that they employed itinerant preachers to distribute Bibles and tracts and 'promote the Gospel in Ireland'.[71]

When the state national school system was introduced in 1831, the Kildare Place Society no longer received the parliamentary grant. However, it went on to function as the Church of Ireland College of Education for the purpose of training teachers for Anglican church schools until 2015, when it became part of the Institute of Education at Dublin City University.[72]

In 1733, the nobility, clergy and gentry of Ireland petitioned King Charles II to grant charters for the establishment of schools for the education, 'conversion and civilizing [of] Irish natives'.[73] The declared aim of the charter schools was to promote 'the salvation of souls, by rescuing the children of the poor natives from that ignorance, superstition and idolatry to which they were devoted from their infancy, and to train them up [...] in the pure Protestant faith'.[74] In 1824 there were thirty such charter schools throughout Ireland, and they offered free education to both Catholic and Protestant children.[75] However, since they were established as boarding schools to give religious instruction in the Protestant faith, they had a clear proselytising mission; Catholic children were only admitted on condition that they be educated in the Protestant faith. The charter schools fell into disrepute following a royal commission report in 1825, which found abuses, including severe corporal punishments, poor living conditions and limited instruction.[76] Following this, they no longer engaged in proselytising among Catholics, and instead, became providers of secondary education for Protestant children only.[77]

11

A system of united and general education

Having inquired into the various schemes and arrangements for educating children in Ireland, including the pay/hedge schools, the Catholic free schools and the schools supported by the various Protestant education societies, the Commissioners of Irish Education Inquiry concluded:

> None of them provide a System of general Education suited to the peculiar Situation and Circumstances of Ireland [and] ... none of them have ever been placed on such a Footing as to obtain the cordial and general Support of all Classes.[78]

The Commissioners believed that since the schools operated by Catholic religious orders provided 'a strictly Roman Catholic Education', they excluded Protestants. They were concerned that any new national system of education that provided separate Catholic and Protestant schooling would result in Catholics withdrawing from 'every opportunity of being associated with Protestants; and after a short time, two Systems would be established in the Country, in which the Children of the Two persuasions would be educated as to be more than ever estranged from each other'.[79]

The Commissioners also believed that the prospect of a future system in which Catholic and Protestant children would be educated separately was most undesirable, and that the 'evils' of separating children by religious persuasion would result in suspicion, distrust, and jealousy between them. Educating children together would, they argued, banish suspicion and effectively remove the causes of distrust and jealousy and form 'congenial Habits, [and] would tend rapidly to diminish instead of increasing the Distinctiveness of Feeling which is now but too prevalent'.[80] Having concluded that none of the existing schooling arrangements were suitable to the needs of all the children of Ireland, the Commissioners concluded:

> In a country in which such marked Divisions exist between different Classes of People, as we found in Ireland, it appears to us that Schools should be established for the Purpose of giving to Children of all religious Persuasions such useful Instruction as they may severally and desirous of receiving [sic], without having any Grounds to apprehend an Interference with their respective religious Principles.[81]

Based on this conclusion, the Commissioners called for a new national system of 'united and general Education'.

2

'Send your children to my schools': Hedge schools and scriptural schools in west Farney, *c.* 1825–1834

Unlike neighbouring counties in Ulster, Co. Monaghan was not successfully planted by the Scots and the English; the county retained a strong Gaelic character and had one of the best developed collection of hedge schools among the Northern counties, with 169 Catholic schools in 1825.[1] The *Second Report of the Commissioners of Irish Education Inquiry* of 1826 listed 281 schools in Co. Monaghan, and all but ten of these were hedge schools.[2] The Commissioners' returns showed that there were 11,011 pupils attending the schools in the county, of whom, 6,798 were boys and 4,213 were girls.[3] The religious denomination of the schoolmasters and schoolmistresses was listed as follows: 169 Catholic, eighty-seven Established Church and thirty-eight Presbyterian.

Hedge schools in west Farney

In their report, the Commissioners of Irish Education Inquiry listed forty-eight schools in the Barony of Farney in south Co. Monaghan. In the parish of Magheross, a large parish in the western part of the barony, there were twenty-three schools, attended by 603 boys and 196 girls.[4] In twelve of these schools in the parish, including the schools at Cornasassonagh, Greaghdrum-neesk, Shanco and Coolfore, the lessons were conducted in a thatched house. At Corduff Mountain the schoolhouse was described as 'a room attached to the chapel', while the schoolhouses at Corcreeghagh and Carrickadooey were each located in a barn.[5] The schoolhouses at Carrickmaclim and Corduff Kelly were each held in the schoolmaster's own home, which in both cases, was a thatched house.

Seven of the schools in the parish were located in the town of Carrick-macross. At one of these schools, the schoolmistress Bridget Lynden conducted the school in her own house. At a Protestant school in the town, the lessons were conducted in 'a good house', which the Marquis of Bath had built and whose estate was located in the eastern part of the Barony of Farney. Mr Evelyn John (E.J.) Shirley, the landlord of the Shirley estate in the western part of Farney, gave £5 per annum to six of the schools in the parish; these were the schools at Greaghdrumneesk, Cargaghmore, Aghalile, Corduff Mountain, Corcreeghagh and Drumberagh. According to historian Lorcán Ó Mearáin, this meant that these schools could not be strictly classified as pay schools.[6]

In twenty-one of the schools in Magheross parish, the religion of the schoolmaster or schoolmistress was listed as Roman Catholic. One schoolmaster, John Bell at Mullaghcroghery school, was a Presbyterian and the other, the Rev. W.T. Palmer at Carrickmacross, was a Protestant clergyman. In several of the schools in the parish, both Catholic and Protestant children attended together. For example, at the Rev. Palmer's Protestant school in Carrickmacross, attended only by boys, sixteen were Protestant and four were Catholic. At Carrickmaclim school, forty-six of the children were Catholic and eighteen were Protestant.[7] At the Presbyterian school in the nearby townland of Mullaghcroghery, all twenty-two of the children were Presbyterian. The school served the growing population of Presbyterian families in the townlands to the north-west of Carrickmacross, including Corvally, Carrickmaclim, Mullaghcroghery and neighbouring townlands.[8]

When making their returns to the Commissioners on the details of the schools in the parish, both the Catholic and Protestant clergy gave figures for the religion of the children in each school. These figures did not always correspond. For example, the Catholic returns for Corcreeghagh school listed fifty Catholic children, while the Protestant returns for the same school listed forty-eight Catholic and two Protestant children. At most of the schools, the Authorized or Protestant Version of the Bible was used. This included some schools that were under the control of Catholic clergy; however, in some schools both the Authorized Version and the Douai or Catholic Version of the Bible were read (Appendix 2).[9]

In addition to the hedge schools and those supported by E.J. Shirley, the Weymouth grammar school was also located in Carrickmacross town. Founded in 1711 by Viscount Weymouth, the Marquis of the Bath, it was described as a 'public classical school' and reported to be 'extremely well situated in every respect, there being no great public school within twenty miles of Carrickmacross'.[10] The founding statutes decreed that 'the master is to be a University graduate, well skilled in Humanity, Grammar Learning and Practical Mathematicks, who shall [...] conform to the [...] Church of Ireland'.[11]

14

The schoolmaster in 1808 was Rev. Dr Shields, a classicist who 'devoted himself sedulously to the discharge of his duties'. At that time, he was helped by three assistants who also taught the classics. The school had accommodation for fifty boarders, and it had a large classroom and a playground, along with eight acres of land. In 1809 it had forty-seven boarders and eleven day-scholars and most of the day-scholars were Catholic. Later in 1825 William Twiss Palmer was the schoolmaster, and at that time the school had just twenty scholars and the number of scholars was reported to be falling.[12]

Coolfore hedge school
Several hedge schools in Magheross parish were located in the hinterland to the north-west of Carrickmacross, including schools at Lurgans, Aghalile, Coolfore and Greaghdrumneesk, and a little further north at Corduff Mountain. The school at Coolfore had forty-eight children, forty males and eight females, all Catholic.[13] Patrick McMahon, a Roman Catholic, was the schoolmaster and his total annual income was about £25.[14] The lessons were conducted in a thatched house and the 'probable cost' of renting it was about £10.[15]

Dated 1834, the Ordnance Survey (OS) map of Coolfore indicates that the schoolhouse was located at the extreme southernmost end of the townland.[16] It was situated at a sharp bend in the road, where a small river, also turning at the bend in the road, ran alongside. The thatched schoolhouse sat between the road and the river that drains the nearby hills at the north-western part of Coolfore townland and which empties into Lough Aphouca near Carrickmacross.[17]

During the 1930s, the Irish Folklore Commission enlisted national school pupils to write short essays on local folklore. With the aim of preserving stories in the oral tradition, the essays were based on interviews with parents, grandparents and neighbours, and under the guidance of their teachers, pupils at Coolfore national school contributed fifty-four essays to the Commission that are now part of the Dúchas Schools' Collection.[18] Among the pupils to contribute an essay was Laurence McMahon of Coolfore, who wrote about the former hedge school at Coolfore, which was conducted by his great grandfather. Laurence wrote:

> Long ago there was a school in our lane in an old house across the road from the present school and the name of the teacher who taught in the school was a man called Patrick McMahon. He was my great grandfather. This man was not a stranger but a local and he lodged in his own house. The scholars brought a lump of turf once a week to the school for the fire. The subjects that were taught in these schools were Irish and mental arithmetic. The children attending the school

paid the master. The writing was done on slates with a slate pencil, and it was also done with a quill pen and ink.[19]

While the hedge school at Coolfore was located on the Shirley estate, it was not supported financially by E.J. Shirley or by any other benefactor. Instead, the scholars' parents made contributions to the schoolmaster's salary. The parochial returns to the Commissioners of Irish Education Inquiry noted that scriptures were not read at the school.

The Irish Society, evangelism, and scriptural schools on the Shirley estate
Published in the *Leamington Spa Courier* on 10 January 1857, E.J. Shirley's obituary recorded that when he inherited his Co. Monaghan estate in 1810, he 'found an ignorant and debased population'.[20] Such derogatory statements on the Irish were not uncommon in the period and reflected a colonial belief that the Irish, especially the rural peasantry, were a primitive people who, it was presumed, needed to be raised up from their ignorance by their betters through education and moral and religious instruction in the Word of God.

In the early decades of the nineteenth century, a spirited Protestant evangelical movement also held this view, believing that the welfare of the poor Irish could be achieved through conversion to Protestantism.[21] The movement was conducted by conservative Anglicans in Ireland and England and was aimed at converting Catholics to the Protestant faith.[22] Referred to as the 'Second Reformation', it played an important role in the way that education was conducted in some of the schools on the Shirley estate in the early nineteenth century.

In her study of the Irish Society in Farney and Kingscourt, Marion Rogan writes that in this period, evangelical Protestants embarked on a deliberate strategy to teach the scriptures to the population of illiterate Irish-speaking Roman Catholics. This proselytising strategy was devised and operated through the Irish Society for Promoting the Education of the Native Irish through the Medium of their Own Language.[23] Founded in 1818, it was generally known as the Irish Society and it had a strong presence at nearby Kingscourt in Co. Cavan and in the Barony of Farney, through E.J. Shirley's participation. The Rev. Robert Winning, the Presbyterian minister of Carrickmaclim (1812–32) and Ervey (near Kingscourt) (1812–42) and supervisor of the Kingscourt District, established the Farney branch of the Irish Society as a branch of the Kingscourt District in 1840; the Kingscourt District was itself the largest branch of the Society in Ireland.[24]

To achieve its aims, the Society established and supported rural schools in districts where Irish was the spoken language of Catholic peasants, and in these schools, it taught adults and children to read the scriptures in their native Irish language. In the decade 1811 to 1821, three-quarters of the population of Farney spoke Irish.[25] The majority of the teachers in the hedge schools on the Shirley estate and in the schools supported by Shirley were Roman Catholic.

The Greaghnarogue Resolutions
In late December 1825, the Kingscourt District of the Irish Society convened a meeting at Greaghnarogue, a townland three miles to the north-west of Carrickmacross, attended by 113 Irish Society teachers and 262 of their adult scholars.[26] While some of the teachers, like Thomas McKittrick, were local and Catholic, many of those attending were from Kingscourt and from Nobber and Moynalty in north Co. Meath. Under the direction of Rev. Winning, the meeting adopted five resolutions concerning 'the reading of the Scriptures in our venerated beloved [Irish] tongue'.[27] The resolutions declared the sacred scriptures to be 'the source of all spiritual knowledge, and the proper basis of all moral instruction' and resolved that the native Irish were 'most *anxious* and *solicitous* for both moral and religious instruction'.[28] The meeting also resolved that 'the reading of the holy scriptures is our right as man, our duty as Christians, and our privilege as Roman Catholics'.[29]

Signed by 'upwards of 490 Roman Catholic teachers and scholars' and later published in the *Dublin Evening Post* on 16 March 1826, the document caused great controversy and opposition from the Catholic hierarchy, notably from Bishop Patrick Curtis of Armagh, Rev. John Halpin, the Catholic parish priest of Nobber, and from Daniel O'Connell's Catholic Association.[30] Much of the controversy concerned the authenticity of the Greaghnarogue Resolutions, in particular the question of whether all the Catholic teachers present at the meeting at Greaghnarogue had voluntarily signed the document and whether the declared number actually attended the meeting.

The Greaghnarogue Resolutions was a significant expression of the Protestant evangelical movement at the time and was a noteworthy event in the Second Reformation. The controversy which arose in the wake of the gathering was also of note, particularly for the notoriety resulting from the proselytising efforts of the Irish Society in the schools that Shirley supported on his west Farney estate.

Shirley's schools
Known for his evangelical zeal, E.J. Shirley was part of the group known as the 'Bible gentry' and was the vice-president of the Irish Society from 1843; he also supported several Society schools in south Co. Monaghan.[31] Of the

forty-five schools in the Barony of Farney in 1826, about half were located in the parish of Magheross, and many were conducted in the teachers' own homes. Shirley supported eight of the schools that were located on his estate, through an annual grant of £5; however, the scriptures were read in just three of the schools (Table 2.1).[32] It is unclear if all of the children attending the Shirley-supported schools at that time were Irish speaking.

In addition to the eight schools supported by Shirley, there were several 'scriptural schools' elsewhere in Farney, including Patrick Meehan's school at Peaste and John McArdle's school in Lisirril, near Ballytrain, and the evidence indicates that the Catholic teachers in these schools taught the scriptures through Irish.[33] McArdle was also a scripture reader, specially chosen by the Irish Society to teach and examine the scriptures and act as a spiritual instructor in his district. There were several schools in Farney where the scriptures were taught by mainly Catholic teachers, and where in the period 1837 to 1839, the Irish Society inspectors examined the teachers and scholars in their knowledge of the scriptures.[34] The schools were at Shanco (Michael Cooney), Drumgossat (Francis Markey), Drumgurra (Bryan McKittrick), Rakeeragh (Ross McCabe), Carrickmaclim (Peter Ward), Drumgowna (Frances Connelly), Carrickmacross (Patt Kiernachann), Raferagh (Pat Jones), Carghogue (Patt Murray), Carrickartagh (Michael Cooney), Greaghnaroog (Francis Connolly), Lisirril (Terence McArdle and Bernard Rock), Peaste (Pat Meehan) and Ballytrain (unnamed teacher).

Table 2.1 Hedge (pay) schools supported by Mr E.J. Shirley, 1826–27[35]

School	Teacher	Teacher's religion	Pupils' religion (number)	Aided by§	Scriptures read
Carghamore*	Owen Sheridan	RC	RC (42)	Mr Shirley	Read
Greaghadromnisk*	James Meighan	RC	RC (52); Pres (2)	Mr Shirley	Not read
Aghalile*	John Cassidy	RC	RC (48)	Mr Shirley	Not read
Corduff Mountain*	Owen Rush	RC	RC (61); Pres (1)	Mr Shirley	Not read
Corcreagh*	Bernard Larkin	RC	RC (50); EC (2)	Mr Shirley	Not read
Drumberagh**	Michael Callan	RC	RC (33)	Mr Shirley	Read
Clontrane***	James Callan	RC	RC (46); Pres (2); EC (2)	Mr Shirley	Read
Corlay***	Sylvester Courtney	RC	RC (50)	Mr Shirley	Not stated
§ 'Mr Shirley, the Landlord, gives 5l. per annum'.*Magheross parish; **Donamoine (Donaghmoyne) parish; ***Magheracluny (Magheracloone) parish					

When the state-run national school system was introduced in 1831, one of its founding principles was that religious and secular instruction should be separate, so as to enable children of all denominations to learn together. For this reason, the Established Church was initially strongly opposed to the new system, which operated under strict rules set down by the Commissioners of National Education in Ireland. Addressing a gathering of his tenants at Lough Fea House in November 1837, E.J. Shirley demonstrated his disdain for the Commissioners' rules, when he asked rhetorically: 'Can you object because the sacred Word of God is daily ready [at school]?' Stating his position on the importance of Bible reading at the schools on his estate, he declared that 'all the evils of this and every country arise from a want of that very knowledge which alone can save their souls'.[36] Shirley then entreated his tenants, who were mostly Roman Catholic, to:

Send your children, without fear of man, to my schools, where the Bible (even your own Douay Version) is daily read, and trust to the merciful and kind Providence, that a proper and lasting effect may be produced on their youthful minds, by continual reading of the Divine Word of God.[37]

Referring to those Roman Catholic clergy who prohibited the reading of the Bible in schools as 'really illiberal', Shirley advised his tenantry on how they should act:

If the Bible should ever be prohibited by any of the Roman Catholic clergy of Farney (which God forbid) I trust you all would exert yourselves legally against such an evil, and in that extreme case, I would recommend your selecting a Priest for yourselves, who would allow of the Bible being read by all, both in and out of School, and I am confident that a Pastor would find ample support on the Shirley Estate.[38]

The Shirley archives at the Public Records Office in Belfast contain a large poster entitled *Proofs from the Holy Scriptures selected and arranged by C.B. – 1837 for Schools, and as a Reference in Cottages*.[39] The poster was published 'for the benefit of the Ladies Irish Island Association, Auxiliary to the Missions for Achill and other islands'. It contained extensive lists of psalms and references to chapters in the various books of the Old and New Testaments. It is probable that the poster was displayed in Shirley's scriptural schools, as a way of ensuring that the scriptures were a part of the school curriculum.[40]

To support the evangelical mission on his estate, in 1839 Shirley also appointed Captain Richard Bowden as the estate's 'moral agent'. Bowden was responsible for enforcing Shirley's directives concerning moral and religious matters; this included the teaching of the Word of God in the scriptural schools, which Shirley supported financially.[41] Bowden was also the school inspector for the Irish Society in the Farney scriptural schools, and he examined the Roman Catholic teachers and scholars in their knowledge of the scriptures.

A most tyrannical agent

Located at the extreme north-west end of the Shirley estate and supported by Shirley with an annual grant of £5, Corduff Mountain school was attended mainly by Catholic children. Although not appointed as a 'moral agent', Alexander (Sandy) Mitchell, who was Shirley's agent from 1826 to 1843, took upon himself the responsibility for moral and religious matters on the estate, as evidenced by his role in the Corduff Mountain school affair, which occurred sometime in the late 1830s.[42] Recounted some quarter of a century after Mitchell's death, most probably by Rev. T. Smollen, the parish priest of Donaghmoyne, the affair concerned Mitchell's insistence that Catholic children at Corduff Mountain should read the Authorized Version of the Bible.[43]

Described by Smollen as 'a man [who] seems to have proposed to himself to trample on the rights, liberty, religion, and consciences of the Catholics of Farney', Mitchell came into conflict with the Catholic bishops and local clergy as a result of his proselytising action at Corduff.[44] The Bishop of Clogher, Edward Kernan, who was residing in Carrickmacross at the time, could not agree to the reading of the Authorized Version in Catholic schools and withdrew the Catholic children from the schools, including the school at Corduff Mountain. In response, Mitchell instructed Owen (Ogy) Rushe, the clerk of Corduff Catholic chapel, to conduct lessons in the sacristy of the chapel. When the bishop's representative, Fr Felix Keown, failed to get legal redress to have Rushe removed from the sacristy, the local people took the law into their own hands, and in Fr Smollen's words: 'came at night in a body and levelled the sacristy to its foundations, tearing and scattering to the winds on the top of Corduff mountain all the bible and proselytizing tracts there accumulated'.[45]

The affair did not end when Rushe left the district. The local children of Corduff had no schoolhouse, and to provide a place for their schooling, Fr Keown secured a grant from the Commissioners of National Education towards the building of a schoolhouse on the grounds of Corduff chapel. Mitchell's response was both vengeful and mean spirited; he decreed that no stone, sand, or lime should be supplied from any part of the Shirley estate for the building at Corduff.

Determined to build the schoolhouse, Fr Keown sought the help of parishioners from the churches in Donaghmoyne parish, which were on the Marquis of Bath estate. The response from the Donaghmoyne parishioners was quick and a convoy of horses and carts from Donaghmoyne brought all the materials that were needed to build the schoolhouse. Perhaps with a degree of hyperbole, local lore spoke of a convoy of carts stretching the four miles from Carrickmacross to Corduff. The schoolhouse at Corduff was completed in 1840 and was approved as a national school in connection with the Board of National Education in that same year.[46]

It is possible that Smollen's account was informed by the local folklore accumulated over many years and by his own personal encounters with Mitchell, or by second-hand reports from his fellow priests.[47] The fact that he used the pseudonym 'A Farney Man' when writing about Mitchell gave him the freedom to describe Mitchell and 'agency realities' in the way that he did.

The conflict at Corduff occurred around 1840 and historian Peadar Livingstone suggests that E.J. Shirley, a semi-absentee landlord, was unaware of Mitchell's actions in actively enforcing scripture reading in the schools.[48] Following the incident at Corduff chapel, Mitchell built a schoolhouse and residence for Rushe in the neighbouring townland of Greaghlane and insisted that the tenants on the estate should send their children to that school.[49] Whether the school attracted local children is unclear; however, given the existence of the new school at Corduff Mountain, it is also unlikely that the school at Greaghlane was a success. In any event, Rushe's school was established to give religious instruction in the scriptures, a practice contrary to the fundamental principles on which the national schools were established. The annual reports of the Commissioners of National Education contain no mention of a school at Greaghlane, and had it succeeded in attracting children, Shirley would not have sought support from the Board of National Education, given his opposition to the Board's fundamental principle regarding religious instruction.

Opposition to scriptural schools

In practice, the evangelic mission of the Irish Society involved conversions to the Protestant faith, through teaching the Holy Scriptures and actively renouncing key tenets of Roman Catholic doctrine, such as the sacrifice of the Mass, purgatory, the practice of praying to the Virgin Mary and the angels and saints.[50] The practice of reading and examining the scriptures in Catholic schools inevitably resulted in strong opposition to Protestant evangelism from both Catholic clergy and laity. Referred to as the 'Bible War', this opposition had become an endemic sectarian struggle and it was fought in debates and articles in the local newspapers and in the conduct of parliamentary elections, especially during the 1830s.[51] Irish Catholics mobilised against the evangelical movement, and through prominent national Catholic leaders like Daniel O'Connell and James Doyle, the Bishop of Kildare and Leighlin, faced down the movement, and in the process, achieved greater Catholic freedoms through the repeal of the last remaining penal laws. The Bible War ultimately gave rise to a more assertive Catholic clergy and community and a growing Catholic identity.

Meanwhile, in west Farney the tensions and conflicts between the Catholic teachers in the Irish Society scriptural schools and the local Catholic clergy and local Catholics raged on into the early 1840s. The clergy condemned the teachers for allegedly reading the scriptures, and in response, the teachers complained of being persecuted from the altar. At Carrickmacross, Fr Keown condemned several Catholic teachers on the Shirley estate for allegedly reading the scriptures, and from the pulpit, he named the teachers as Patrick Sheridan (Corraghy), Owen Sheridan (Cargaghmore), Mary O'Neill (Corduff Kelly), Bernard Hand (Cornasassonagh), Peter Ward (Carrickmaclim) and Owen (Ogy) Rushe (Greaghlane).[52] While some Catholic schoolmasters converted to Protestantism, many others did not, but continued to practice the reading of scriptures in their schools.

Following public condemnation by Catholic clerics, some teachers were threatened and attacked; John McArdle of Lisirril, who had apparently converted to Protestantism, was badly beaten and Owen Sheridan of Cargaghmore was also severely beaten.[53] Five Irish Society teachers were subsequently murdered, including Thomas McKittrick, who was closely associated with the Greaghnarogue Resolutions. In her study of these events, historian Marion Rogan cautions that, in the absence of corroborating evidence from unbiased sources, not all of the teachers' murders can be attributed definitively to their working as Irish Society teachers.[54] Many of the teachers who were persecuted moved from Farney or emigrated; for example, Peter Ward of Carrickmaclim emigrated with his family to America under the post-Famine assisted emigration scheme, which Shirley's agent William Steuart Trench promoted at Shirley's behest.[55] By the mid-1840s, the number of scriptural schools in Farney had declined. A major factor in their decline was the establishment of the state-run national school system in 1831, in which English was the sole language of instruction.

If the Irish Society's evangelising strategy was to teach the scriptures through the native Irish language, then it was doomed to failure on that basis alone, since the language was in decline in south Monaghan in the years after 1830. While just over half of the population of Farney spoke Irish in the period 1821 to 1831, within three decades (1851–61), this number had fallen to fewer than a quarter.[56] In common with most of the eastern part of the country, the language was in retreat in Farney and was rarely spoken in the later years of the nineteenth century.

Clontrain school

Aside from the tensions and conflicts associated with Shirley's scriptural schools, the religious tensions and denominational self-interests associated with elementary education came to the fore when the new state system of national education was established in 1831. The system enabled schools to be operated in connection with the Board of National Education. The Board's administrative arm, the Commissioners of National Education in Ireland, was the body responsible for approving applications for grants to establish national schools under the Board. The Established Church and E.J. Shirley were opposed to the new state system, essentially on the grounds that religious instruction was not permitted during normal school hours. Thus, some local schools on the Shirley estate, which sought support from the Board, could become the focus of Shirley's opposition. Having applied for support from the Commissioners through Catholic patronage in 1834, Clontrain school was one such school.[57]

Founded in 1822, Clontrain school was located at the southernmost end of the Shirley estate in the parish of Magheracloone. It was conducted as a hedge school in a thatched house, which was in good repair. The school was three miles south of Carrickmacross, where a new schoolhouse was being built at that time. Elsewhere in the district, according to the Commissioners, there were 'four or five miserable schools got up by the masters for their own pupils and under no patronage or direction'.[58] The schoolmaster at Clontrain was James Callan, a Catholic. In the records of the Commissioners, Callan was described as: 'Qualified to teach reading, writing, arithmetic, English grammar, Bookkeeping, mensuration, and algebra, and is willing to be examined by any inspector [...] he is besides a sober moral well-conducted man, and much esteemed in this neighbourhood.'[59]

Like several other schools on his estate, Shirley contributed an annual grant of £5 to Clontrain school and the scholars' parents contributed the balance of the schoolmaster's salary, which came to £20. The *Second Report of the Commissioners of Irish Education Inquiry* of 1826 noted that the Authorized Version of the Bible was read at the school.[60]

In January 1834, when Rev. Daniel Boylan, parish priest of Magheracloone, applied to have Clontrain school connected with the Board of National Education, he sought a grant towards the teacher's salary and a stock of schoolbooks and other school requisites. In the initial application to the Commissioners, Fr Boylan was the named school manager and the application noted that, while there were very few Protestants in the parish, they had previously signed their names in favour of the school. Fr Boylan set out the case for state assistance, which included reference to E.J. Shirley's position:

> Fifteen or even ten pounds given annually would be of infinite service in a very poor and populous district, where many children stay from school for want of means to pay the master, and where too, every obstacle is thrown in the way of your system of education by the Landlord, Mr Shirley, who refuses to let any schoolhouse in connection with the Board of National Education, be built on his property [...]

> The school may be said to be fully under the direction of the master [and] it is visited occasionally by the parish Priest and has been visited by Mr Shirley's agent Mr Mitchell and his clerk, a fellow of the name of Smyth, but as they failed in compelling the children to read their books, it is hoped they will not further interfere with it.[61]

It appears that Mitchell and Smyth were, in Fr Boylan's words, 'endeavouring to compel the Catholic children to read the Protestant Testament, and in consequence, the school is deserted by most of the children'.[62] Nevertheless, he 'hoped this persecution will shortly cease', so that the children could return to the school. Fr Boylan assured the Commissioners that since Mr Shirley's agent had given up interfering with the school and since religious instruction would take place on Saturdays only, the school was 'at liberty to adopt the Regulations of your Board'. As the named applicant to the Board for grant support, Fr Boylan was effectively seeking to conduct the school under Catholic patronage and under the management of the local Catholic clergy and free from Shirley's influence.

The application was approved and Clontrain became a national school connected with the Board of National Education on 24 April 1834. In December, the district inspector appointed by the Commissioners conducted an inspection of the school, after which he reported that 'this School is aided by Mr Shirley, who is opposed to the National Board [of Education]'. Shirley had, by then, withdrawn his support for the school, and based on Shirley's opposition, the Commissioners concluded that it was 'not deemed expedient to accept the Board's annuity', and accordingly, withdrew the grant to Clontrain in July 1835.[63]

Shirley's intervention meant, in effect, that the school at Clontrain could not operate as a national school under the new state-supported system. His intervention was consistent with the early opposition to the new state national school system from the Established Church and with his own proselytising efforts on his estate. The case of Clontrain school showed how the landed class could wield power and influence over a state body like the Board of National Education, through maintaining a prerogative in supporting or not supporting a local school. Shirley would later exercise this same prerogative in relation to Coolfore national school.

The evangelism and overt proselytising in Catholic hedge schools like Clontrain reflected the wider power struggles between members of the Established Church and the Catholic hierarchy. When Catholic parents withdrew their children from proselytising schools, the precise impact on the children themselves is uncertain, although it is probable that their education suffered. In any event, schooling had become a key battleground in a class and religious conflict; only in a unified system of elementary secular education, free from the threat of proselytising, could such conflict be avoided.

3

'Education for the poorer classes': Stanley's letter and the national school system

As early as 1812, the Commissioners of Education in Ireland had recommended the appointment of a Board of National Education to oversee a system of education that would admit children of all religious denominations and would not interfere with the particular religious beliefs of any one denomination.[1] Later in 1825, the Commissioners of Irish Education Inquiry, having examined the state of education in Ireland, concluded that a new 'united and general' national education system was needed. The Commissioners believed that no one system of schooling was suited to the education of all the classes and all the denominations. Each system had limitations and none of them provided a general education suited to 'the peculiar situation and circumstances of Ireland' and none had 'the cordial and general support of all Classes'.[2]

The idea of a national system of education was to bring together children of all religious denominations under a unified arrangement that would, it was believed, promote religious tolerance and harmony between Catholics and Protestants. However, what lay behind the idea were concerns to improve basic literacy and numeracy that would, in turn, reduce poverty and improve the position of future generations, bringing the Irish closer to the empire and its values.[3] Education was also seen as a way of improving the moral qualities of the peasantry.

Lord Stanley's plan

The precise plan to unite all children in a common state-supported national school system was set down by Lord Stanley, who was the Chief Secretary for Ireland during 1830 and 1831.[4] As Chief Secretary, he introduced the Irish Education Act into Parliament, which was based on the recommendations of the 1812 report of the Commissioners of Education. In a letter to the Duke of Leinster in October 1831, Stanley set out the arrangements for administering the new national education system.[5] He wrote that 'a Board for the superintendence of a system of National Education in Ireland' was to be established and he invited Leinster to be the president of the new Board. He then set out the government's motives in establishing the Board and the Board's powers.

Lord Stanley wrote that the schooling arrangements at the time were contrary to the ideal of an education system that admitted children of all religious persuasions.[6] His plan was for a system that offered 'a combined literary, and a separate religious education'. To achieve this, the Board of Education 'should be composed of men of high personal character, including individuals of exalted station in the Church [… and] it should consist of persons professing different religious opinions'. The Board should have 'complete control over the various schools which may be erected under its auspices'. It should require 'that the schools be kept open […] on four or five days of the week […] for moral and literary education only', and that the remaining day be given over to religious education, conducted separately, according to the religious denomination of the children. Lord Stanley's plan was essentially 'to unite in one system children of different creeds'. As a system of 'national education for the poorer classes of the community', it should be free.

Lord Stanley also set out the Board's authority to make regulations for administering the national education system. This included the authority to grant aid for the erection of schools, recommend teacher appointments and establish school inspectors to visit and report on schools. Each school approved by the Board should have a local school manager with responsibility for recruiting and dismissing teachers, monitoring the school and supporting the school ethos.[7]

The Commissioners of National Education in Ireland

Following Stanley's letter, the Commissioners of National Education was the body established in 1831 to administer state funds to establish and support national schools. Acting as the administrative arm of the Board of National Education, the Commissioners soon began to receive applications for grants to support teachers' salaries and to build national schools, and by January 1832, the Commissioners had approved grants to the first schools under the new system.[8] A school supported by a grant was required to 'put up conspicuously on the School-house [the inscription] "National School", *and no other*' and the rules stated that 'when a School-house is built partly by aid from them (the Commissioners), a stone is to be introduced into the wall having that inscription upon it'.[9]

The Commissioners made a distinction between 'vested' and 'non-vested' schools. The former were those schools over which the Board of National Education had legal ownership or control and were therefore bound by the Board's rules; the vested schools were built with the support of the Board, which provided two-thirds of the construction costs, with the balance provided by local subscriptions. Non-vested schools were those constructed entirely from local subscriptions and vested in diocesan trustees; these were bound by the rules only so long as they received support from the Board.[10] This meant that the Commissioners, in effect, accepted the existence of faith schools, such as those run by Presbyterian and Catholic religious congregations.

The Commissioners provided funding for the construction of national schools, and the Commissioners' own architectural department provided the architectural designs for the first national schools. However, after 1856 responsibility for the design of national schools was transferred to the Office of Public Works (OPW), and after that time, national schools were constructed according to a standard architectural plan, which the OPW produced.[11] There were a number of plans, each based on a maximum number of children. For example, the Type I school plan was a design for the smallest schoolhouse, suitable for schools of up to 35 children, while Type V was a plan for a five-room single storey schoolhouse designed to accommodate up to 220 children. The OPW's school architectural plans also included standard templates for fireplaces and suitable schoolroom furniture.[12]

The Commissioners approved national schoolbooks, including reading books and books on arithmetic, book-keeping and a selection of books on scriptures that contained non-contentious religious content for use in 'secular and moral instruction'.[13] They also provided funding towards desks, books and teachers' salaries, which was a great relief for poor Catholic families who experienced difficulties in meeting the fees and other expenses to maintain their local hedge school.[14]

In their *Second Report* for the year 1834–35, the Commissioners reported that 1,106 national schools were operating, attended by 145,521 children, and in that year, they had made grants for the building and fitting out of 119 schoolhouses.[15] In Co. Monaghan, forty-five national schools were operating under the Board of National Education, with a total of 5,656 children enrolled and forty-six teachers, all but one of whom were male.

While there was considerable distress and a fall in school attendances in 1847, the worst year of the Famine, in 1849 the Commissioners' reported that national schools were operating across the country with large attendances. In that year there were 4,109 national schools, with over half a million pupils attending.[16] The schools in the poor law union workhouses also came under the supervision of the Commissioners and there were 107 such schools at that time. Among the four provinces, Ulster had the highest number of schools, 1,674, and there were 114 national schools in Co. Monaghan, with over 13,000 pupils. There were ninety-seven male teachers and twenty-one female teachers in the county at that time.

Religious tensions and the national school system

The national school system was established at a time when relationships between the Catholic Church and the Established Church were not good. In the years after full Catholic Emancipation was finally granted in 1829, the Catholic Church had become more self-confident and more influential in Irish social life.[17] However, this new-found influence did not bode well for the new national schools system, which was established on the principle of bringing children of all denominations together in a unified system, albeit one that mandated separate secular and religious instruction.

In 1835, the Commissioners of National Education reported that combined applications for grants had come from both Catholic and Protestant clergymen and laymen, and that the new system of education had 'proved generally beneficial and acceptable to Protestants and Roman Catholics, according to their respective wants'.[18] The Commissioners wrote that 'all the parties are daily manifesting more and more their approval of it'. However, this belied the reality that there was strong opposition to the new system, particularly from the Established Church. In 1832, seventeen Anglican bishops declared in a joint letter that the new system would 'tend rather to embitter existing animosities by marking more distinctly the difference of creed in the public school'.[19] The Anglican bishops' opposition to the new system was partly on the grounds that religious classes, specifically Bible lessons, were separated from secular classes in the school curriculum.[20]

Despite this general opposition from the Anglican hierarchy, in Co. Monaghan there was some initial support from Protestants, as demonstrated by the fact that several national schools, such as those at Magheracloone, Unshenagh and Liseenan, were attended by both Protestant and Catholic children.[21] However, in the period 1834–35, fifty applications to the Commissioners for support had come from the Roman Catholic clergy, one from the Protestant clergy and four from the Presbyterian clergy. These applications were made separately by each denomination and not jointly, as Lord Stanley had intended.

Opposition from the Established Church in Co. Monaghan was evident when the Rev. William Pratt, the local rector at Glaslough, refused an invitation from the local Catholic priest, Fr Patrick Moynagh, to support a joint application to establish a school at Knocknagrave. The Rev. Pratt's refusal was on the grounds that his bishop had issued instructions prohibiting his clergy in the Clogher diocese 'from signing any document pertaining to the new Board of Education'.[22] Similar to E.J. Shirley in the Barony of Farney, the Protestant landlords of the Barony of Truagh in north Co. Monaghan also expressed their opposition to the new Board by distributing posters that declared their disapproval and advising their tenants that they would not be encouraged to attend the schools supported by the Board.[23]

Separate denominational schools
Mutual distrust between the Churches in the 1830s meant that the ideal of shared schooling among all denominations would not be achieved. While the Board of National Education was made up of Protestant, Presbyterian and Roman Catholic commissioners, it faced opposition from groups like the Presbyterian Synod of Ulster.[24] Compromises resulted in minor changes to the Board's rules concerning the timing of religious instruction, and in 1839, Correen Presbyterian school in Co. Antrim was granted aid and was permitted to run the school according to its own rules.[25] Wishing to maintain control over schooling in the Protestant community, the Established Church founded the Church Education Society in 1839, creating a separate and rival education system. However, the Society struggled financially, and ultimately, was unable to offer an alternative national school system.

By the end of the first decade after 1831, many national schools were governed by trustees of a single denomination. As the nineteenth century progressed, more and more schools became vested in Catholic-only patrons or Protestant-only patrons, and by the middle of the century, the national school system had become essentially denominational in character. While schools approved under the Board of National Education were obliged to have a local management committee, in practice, in the Catholic schools the committee was typically the local parish priest, an arrangement which strengthened Catholic control over the national schools attended by Catholic children.[26]

The establishment of the national school system in 1831 did not mean that the hedge schools ceased to exist. Several continued to operate; however, through applications for financial support from the Commissioners of National Education, many simply changed from being pay schools to become national schools connected with the Board of National Education, and many of these were already under the patronage of the diocese or the local landlord.[27] While schools came under the control of one single denomination, the Commissioners continued to insist on the separation of religious and secular instruction, and national schools were obliged to display a notice in the classroom that read 'Secular Instruction'; this notice had to be displayed at all times, except when religious instruction was taking place.[28] Instruction in the various subjects was exclusively through the English language and the approved reading books used in the new national schools contained little reference to the distinctiveness of the Irish language, culture, or tradition.[29]

'Of calm temper and discretion': Teachers and their training
Under Lord Stanley's instruction, the Commissioners of National Education were charged with 'establishing and maintaining a model school in Dublin, and training teachers for country schools'. To that end, in 1835 the Commissioners had plans to set up teacher training establishments, which they believed, would 'completely remove' incompetent teachers who were still practising at that time. They wrote:

> If we are furnished with adequate means by the State […] we have no doubt whatever that a new class of Schoolmasters may be trained, whose conduct and influence may be highly beneficial in promoting morality, harmony and good order, in the country parts of Ireland.[30]

In that year, the Commissioners purchased Tyrone House in Marlborough St in Dublin, where they established a national teacher training college and two model schools, one for boys and one for girls.[31] By 1867, the Commissioners had established twenty-six interdenominational district model schools. The model schools were established with three purposes: to promote the united education of Protestants and Catholics in common schools; to exhibit the best examples of national education; and to give preparatory training to young apprentice teachers.[32] Apprentice teachers spent six months in the model schools, followed by two years of practical teaching at a schoolhouse.[33]

A model school opened in Monaghan town in 1861. While Catholic Church authorities disapproved of Catholic children attending the model schools, a small number generally did attend.[34] For example, at the Monaghan model school in 1871, among the 383 children enrolled, 216 were Protestant, 141 were Presbyterian and seventeen were Catholic.[35]

Teacher training at Tyrone House involved instruction in subjects like education, history, geography, literature, natural philosophy (science), mathematics, mastery of the Board's approved reading books and teaching practice in a model school.[36] In addition to learning the skills of teaching, the Commissioners wished to develop teachers who were on the same social level as their local community and who were:

> Living in friendly habits with the people, not greatly elevated above them, but so provided for as to be able to maintain a respectable station, trained to good habits, identified in interest with the State, and therefore anxious to promote a spirit of obedience to lawful authority.[37]

While school patrons were responsible for appointing their own schoolteachers, the Commissioners needed to be satisfied as to the character and general qualification of teachers:

> He should be a person of Christian sentiment, of calm temper, and discretion; he should be imbued with a spirit of peace, of obedience to the law, and of loyalty to his Sovereign; he should not only possess the art of communicating knowledge, but be capable of moulding the mind of youth, and of giving to the power which education confers, useful direction. These are the qualities [...] which the Commissioners are anxious to find, to encourage, and to reward.[38]

In 1849, the Commissioners also published twelve 'practical rules' for national teachers, which placed much emphasis on the teacher's moral conduct. The rules advised teachers on the ways to manage the school, such as keeping a school register and a roll of pupils, teaching according to the 'improved method' and managing school finances. The practical rules advised teachers about their own personal behaviour, directing them to 'avoid fairs, markets, and [...] above all, POLITICAL meetings of every kind [... and] set an example of cleanliness and neatness in their own person'. In their dealings with the children, they should:

> Impress upon the minds of their Pupils, the great rule of regularity and order [...] omit no opportunity of inculcating the principles of TRUTH and HONESTY [...] treat them with kindness, combined with firmness, [...] aim at governing them by their affections and reason, rather than by harshness and severity.[39]

Teachers were expected to be 'well qualified persons', of 'considerable skill and intelligence [...] character and ability' and be able to teach a 'system of instruction' that was very different to the teaching used in the hedge schools.[40] For example, in teaching arithmetic, it was not sufficient to merely teach by unexplained rules but rather to 'convey elements of mathematical knowledge and training the mind to accuracy of thinking and reasoning'. Thinking and reasoning were also to be introduced into the teaching of reading and writing:

Children are found to be more easily taught to read when, while they are learning to pronounce and combine syllables and words into sentences, they are receiving information. Their writing proceeds better, when, while they are learning the mechanical art, they are learning the use of it.[41]

By prescribing precise methods of instruction in school subjects and through the system of apprenticeship teacher training, the Commissioners wished to show that the new regulated national school system, with its skilled teachers fully trained in the art of teaching, was different to the unregulated hedge schools.

The training college at Tyrone House and the district model schools were set up according to the united education principle, as envisaged by Stanley. The apprentice teachers acted as 'monitors' while undergoing training.[42] The Commissioners believed that recruiting paid monitors was the most suitable means for 'improving the best pupils in our schools, and thereby preparing them to become efficient teachers'.[43] Monitors were paid a small annual salary of between £4 and £7.

The Commissioners looked to recruit future teachers from the ranks of 'deserving pupils or paid monitors', and in a circular to district school inspectors in January 1856, they informed them of a plan to increase the number of male teachers. They requested the inspectors to 'furnish the names of deserving lads from time to time as they come under your notice', writing:

The lads recommended [are] to be at least 17 years of age, of good moral character; of sound constitution; of respectable appearance; pleasing manners and address; of good literary attainments and possessed of a good aptitude for teaching. Such young persons in short as would after a course of training for one or two years be likely to prove efficient and skilful Schoolmasters.[44]

The Commissioners stipulated that the district inspectors should submit names of 'young lads' from several religious denominations.[45]

Opposition to model schools
By December 1848, a total of 2,311 teachers had been trained in the training college and the district model schools. The Catholic bishops lacked control in the management of the district model schools, and in the 1850s they began to express opposition to the schools, viewing them as the state encroaching on education.[46] The bishops also opposed mixed gender in the model schools, and in 1863 they banned Catholics from attending model schools. The

bishops' opposition was a major cause of delay in establishing district model schools and this meant that the overall number of teachers who were fully trained was low. For example, by 1870, about one third of teachers in all the national schools were formally trained and the proportion trained in the Catholic schools was little more than a quarter.[47]

The Catholic hierarchy also opposed teacher training institutions established under the Commissioners of National Education, and in 1884 the Commissioners agreed to support denominational training colleges, which was a significant concession to the hierarchy.[48] As a result, a number of Catholic teacher training colleges were established. These included Our Lady of Mercy Training College for women at Baggot Street in Dublin, which later moved to Carysfort in south Co. Dublin; St Patrick's Training College for men at Drumcondra in north Co. Dublin; Mary Immaculate College in Limerick City; St Mary's College in Belfast; and De La Salle College in Waterford.[49] These colleges trained teachers to teach in Catholic-only national schools, which were the majority of schools in Ireland.

Despite the establishment of separate men's and women's teacher training colleges, by the end of the nineteenth century, fewer than half of all national schoolteachers were trained. The majority of the teachers who attended the training colleges had commenced training under the monitor or apprenticeship system, meaning that they had attained a primary education only and were therefore from less well-off families, since secondary education was not free.[50] In terms of their ability to teach, many teachers were not well regarded. Most were past pupils of the schools in which they were teaching, and many were from a farming background, with some continuing to farm in their spare time.[51]

Gender differences
The operation of the national schools reflected prevailing social attitudes about the role of women in the nineteenth century. Teachers' salaries were based on a ranking system of three levels or 'classes' and on whether the teacher was male or female. The class ranking was based on the teacher's qualifications and proven capacity and efficiency to run a school; for example, in 1839 a first-class male teacher, the highest class, received an annual salary of £20, while his female counterpart received £15.[52] Pay disparities according to gender also applied to the second and third classes of teachers. A mistress 'employed to teach needlework' held the lowest rank in the schools and received the lowest salary at just £6 per annum.

Male teachers greatly outnumbered females. For example, in 1834 three-quarters of all teachers (888) were male, and one-quarter (307) were female.[53]

In Ulster the gender difference was even more marked, with 391 male teachers and just fifty-four females in the entire province. In Co. Monaghan there were forty males and just six females in that year. The situation had changed little in over a decade or more, with female teachers accounting for fewer than a fifth of all schoolteachers in both Ulster as a whole and in Co. Monaghan.[54] Furthermore, the majority of female teachers were at the lower grade of assistant teachers and monitors, and it was not until the expansion of convent national schools in the late nineteenth century that many more females were trained and found employment as teachers.[55]

For much of the nineteenth century, women were not permitted to enter the learned professions like medicine and law, and there was also an economic bias in favour of men when it came to employment opportunities. Having a state job with a salary was seen as an important financial opportunity for men at a time of considerable economic hardship, when farm holdings could not support all the adults in a family.

Gender differences were also reflected in the teaching of subjects; the schoolmaster generally taught subjects like arithmetic and took the more senior classes, while the schoolmistress took the junior classes and taught subjects like reading, writing and sewing.[56] In the training of female teachers, the Commissioners wrote that needlework formed 'an important element in the classification of female teachers', and at teacher training examinations, the female pupil teachers and monitors were required to 'exhibit hemming, stitching, tucking, and working a button-hole' and to complete 'some specimens of knitting'.[57]

District inspectors

The national schools were answerable to the state, and this meant that each school and its teachers were subject to inspections from district inspectors appointed by the Commissioners of National Education.[58] Six regional head inspectors oversaw the work of the district inspectors. The district inspectors submitted reports of their inspections to their head inspector, who in turn, reported to the Commissioners. School inspectors had considerable power, and following a school inspection, the inspector's report could determine whether a teacher got promoted or received a salary bonus. The district inspector could arrive at a school unannounced under the rule that he was 'not to give previous notice to the conductors of any schools of the time of his visit, but rather endeavour to arrive with each when he is unexpected'.[59]

In 1838 the Commissioners divided the country into twenty-five inspectoral districts; Co. Monaghan and parts of counties Cavan, north Meath and west Louth were in District 24. Each district inspector was responsible for visiting all the schools in his district once every year. Following each visit, he communicated with the patron or manager 'information concerning the general state of the school, and pointing out such violations of rules, or defects, if any, as he may have observed, and he is to make such suggestions as he may deem necessary'.[60]

The duties of the district inspector were wide ranging. He examined the visitors' book, the daily report book and inspected the schoolbooks to check that they complied with the books that were sanctioned by the Board of National Education. During his inspection visit he should:

Use every means to obtain accurate information as to the discipline, management, and methods of instruction pursued in the School.

Examine all the classes in succession, in their different branches of study, so as to enable him to ascertain the degree of efficiency of the instruction imparted.

Examine the class Rolls, Register, and Daily Report Book; and to report with accuracy what is the actual number of Children receiving instruction at the School, and what is the daily average attendance.±

The district inspector was advised as to the precise way that he should submit his reports, including how to report on the pupils' attainments in reading, writing, grammar and arithmetic. Consistent with the principles on which the national schools were established, the district inspector should 'avoid all discussions of a religious or political nature'. During his visits he should 'exhibit a courteous and conciliatory demeanour […] and pursue such a line of conduct as will uphold the just influence and authority both of [School] Managers and Teachers'.

The Commissioners' rules gave the district inspector clear instructions to guide him in his work. For example, he was advised on how to be tactful and sensitive when communicating findings of an inspection visit to the schoolteachers:

In all his intercourse with the teachers, he will treat them with the most perfect kindness and respect, apprizing them privately of what he may see defective, and noting it to be reported to the Board [of National Education], but by no means addressing them authoritatively or animadverting upon their conduct in the hearing of their scholars.[62]

After 1846, 'with the view to encouraging improved habits amongst our teachers', the Commissioners allocated a sum of £10 to each of the twenty-five national school districts.[63] This sum was to be distributed as 'a premium' among the masters and mistresses who were 'most distinguished by the order, neatness and cleanliness observed in themselves, their pupils and school-houses'. In the following year, Patrick Maginness, a schoolmaster at Carrick-macross, was among five teachers in Co. Monaghan to receive a premium; he received £1.19s.[64] Inspectors themselves were also offered a financial incentive for efficiency when, in 1855, the Commissioners introduced new improved pay scales for two new classes of inspector, 'with the view of rendering the work of the inspection of their school more efficient by holding out [...] the promise of promotion and the hope of reward as motives of encouragement to the energetic discharge of its duties'.[65] District inspectors were warned that salary increases would be withheld where deficiencies were found in 'the amount of work done in the business of inspection' and 'want of punctuality' in submitting reports.

Reports
While district inspectors' reports could be critical of a teacher's performance, district and head inspectors could also praise teachers. Mr M. Fitzgerald, the head inspector for the Dublin region, commented on two teachers in the West Dublin model school, one newly qualified and one retiring:

> Miss Adams is a promising young teacher, well qualified, and most at-tentive to her duty. She has given every satisfaction since her appoint-ment. In Mrs. Tickell, the Commissioners lost a most valuable servant; a patient and painstaking teacher and a person who had the regard of everyone connected with the school by her gentle disposition and quiet unobtrusive manner.[66]

When submitting their reports, district inspectors could report teachers for misconduct, poor record-keeping or falsifying school attendance figures; however, where a head inspector found no evidence of misconduct, he could defend a teacher. For example, J.G. Fleming, the head inspector in east Ulster, accused a district inspector of bringing 'a charge of wilful falsification of ac-counts' against a teacher in his district. In his annual report to the Commis-sioners, Fleming wrote that there was no foundation for the district inspector's charge against the teacher, which was 'a misconception of facts', and he had the 'utmost confidence' in the teacher's school records.[67] When two members of a Royal Commission on Primary Education were visiting schools in 1868, they reported that the teacher in one school in Ulster had falsified the record of attendance. Having reviewed the school records, Mr A. O'Callaghan, the head inspector in west Ulster, found the records to be 'perfectly correct' and he accused the two gentlemen of making a charge 'of the gravest character', writing that 'no such condition of things, as that reported by these gentlemen, could exist'. He accused the two gentlemen of 'inexcusable negligence'.[68]

Based on reports from head inspectors, the Commissioners frequently reprimanded teachers for transgressions of their rules, such as not maintaining the required school hours or not making provision for religious instruction at the recommended time of day. Other common reasons for teachers being reprimanded included pupils' poor proficiency, falsifying school attendance records and being absent without permission. For example, in 1861 the teacher at Shantonagh male school in south Co. Monaghan was 'severely admonished' for a number of transgressions, including:

> For sending a boy out when the Inspector approached [...] for the purpose of securing a fictious attendance, for neglect of promotion, [for] non occupation of pupils and also for absenting himself on 25 and 26 April without the Manager's permission.[69]

In 1863, the teacher at Lisdoonan national school in Donaghmoyne parish was admonished for closing the school before the appointed time, and later that same year, was again criticised for the 'backward state of the school'.[70] In the same year, the female teacher at the Carrickmacross Female Industrial School was directed 'to exert herself in advancing the proficiency of her classes'.[71]

'Know her place': Girls' education in the national schools

From the earliest years, schooling was a gendered process, and the schoolhouse was a place where gendered practices were developed and expressed. School attendance and enrolment reflected social attitudes towards girls' education, particularly among poorer families. For example, school attendance among girls in Magheross parish and elsewhere in Co. Monaghan was low, relative to boys. This was also replicated more widely in Ireland and reflected parents' attitudes to their daughters' education and the fact that many girls were kept at home to support the domestic economy and assist with childrearing in large families.[72]

The disparity between boys and girls was also reflected in pupil enrolments. For example, in Co. Monaghan in 1834, there were 3,476 boys and 2,180 girls enrolled, while in neighbouring Co. Tyrone, twice as many boys as girls were enrolled.[73] These differences did not reflect the distribution of girls in the wider population, suggesting that many girls of school-going age were not attending school. However, these disparities were not evident across all counties at that time, or across schools more generally in the later decades of the nineteenth century.[74] The growth of convent schools in the mid-nineteenth century was an important factor in increasing girls' participation in education.[75]

The type of opportunities available to the majority of girls in the mid-nineteenth century included working in the home, domestic service, or work in cottage industries like lacemaking or weaving flax into linen. Girls' education was considered less important than that of boys and school lessons included teaching the skills that were needed for the home and for local industries. To teach these skills, schools with a single male teacher employed a workmistress to teach needlework, cookery, dressmaking, and later, domestic organisation, poultry and dairy management.[76] Reporting on girls' improved proficiency in needlework in 1872, Mr Simpson, the district inspector for District 24, observed:

An important change for the better is observable here. The teaching of plain sewing is becoming more real. Not only are the children taught hemming and stitching on scraps, but garments are being much more frequently made and repaired in the schools. At a recent inspection in a country school, 34 of the boys wore shirts made by the female pupils, the breasts of which – elaborately stitched – necks and cuffs, were composed of the strips issued from the department, intrinsically not worth much, but invaluable from the skill and dexterity acquired in the work. Plain knitting is also well taught.[77]

Needlework was an essential part of girls' schooling experience, and while it resulted in the production of wearable garments, the fact that girls sewed shirts for boys seems to reinforce the ascribed role of girls in the family and their place in society.

The subject matter of the reading books, which the Commissioners for National Education approved, also reflected the prevailing views on the role of women and girls in the mid-nineteenth century. School books were selected to convey 'knowledge of a variety of subjects' and teachers should 'not merely be able to teach their pupils to read and write […] but they be able to aid in forming the minds of children'.[78] Among the approved books was *Reading Book for the use in Female Schools*.[79] Published by the Commissioners in 1839, the lessons in the book were designed to 'convey information which will be found more generally useful to girls'. The lessons were presented as short articles and poems that conveyed subtle, and at times, not-so-subtle messages about virtuous womanhood and the woman's place. Titles of articles included: 'On cleanliness', 'On tidiness', 'On beauty and good sense', 'Duties of a housekeeper', 'The sick chamber' and 'The manufacture of pins and needles'. An article entitled 'On Female Acquirements' contained the following passage:

> She should bear in mind that knowledge is not to elevate her above her station [...] It is to correct vanity and repress pretension. It is to teach her to know her place and her functions; to make her content with the one, and willing to fulfil the other. It is to render her more useful, more humble, and more happy. Such a woman will be, of all others, the best satisfied with her lot. She will not seek distinction, and therefore, will not meet with disappointment [...] She will be happy in her own home, and by her own hearth, in the fulfilment of religious and domestic duty, and in the profitable employment of her time.[80]

In an article entitled 'Good management', the girl reader learned that 'order, neatness and cleanliness should be practiced by the mother of a family, if it were for no other reason than by example to form her children to habits which will be so essentially useful to them in later life'. Many of the articles and poems promoted morality and Christian doctrine, including 'Integrity', 'A good conscience', and 'Influence of Christianity on the female character'. The message conveyed in these articles was that the social role of girls and women was divinely ordained.[81]

The prevailing ideas on girls' education and their ascribed role in society came to dominate educational and wider social policy discourses throughout the nineteenth century and for much of the twentieth century. These discourses led to inequities in both educational advancement and career opportunities for women in many areas of public life.

4

'Anxious for improvement': Schools and schooling in Farney, 1835–1853

By the 1840s the hedge schools were being gradually replaced by state-supported national schools connected with the Board of National Education. The children of the majority Catholic population attended the national schools, while the schools supported by Protestant education societies operated under the patronage of the Church Education Society from 1839 to 1869.[1] The model schools also became important places for the schooling of Protestant and Presbyterian children.

Catholic and Presbyterian communities in Co. Monaghan welcomed the new national school system, which they saw as a way of imposing some order on the then unregulated and haphazard teaching arrangements in the hedge schools.[2] They saw the advantages of the new system, in terms of providing for teacher training and oversight of schools by school inspectors, as well as providing standard textbooks and funds to improve the quality of school buildings. Despite the opposition of Protestants to the Board of National Education and the more general desire of Catholic and Protestant clergy to conduct their own separate schooling, there are examples of Protestant support for the national school system in Co. Monaghan. For example, the Church of Ireland rector of Magheracloone parish supported the proposal to establish the former Catholic parish hedge school as a national school connected with the Board of National Education. There are other examples of Protestant support for national schools in the county, resulting in several national schools being attended by children of mixed denominations.[3]

Despite these examples of inter-denominational cooperation, from the earliest days after 1831, Church leaders were intent on remaining independent in the education and religious formation of the children of their respective denominations. Applications for grant aid to the Commissioners of National

Education reflected this, with few applications for support coming from joint Catholic and Protestant patrons. The growth of Catholic male and female religious teaching orders, like the Presentation Sisters and the Christian Brothers, further ensured that the new national school system would be denominational in character. When the Commissioners consented to the establishment of Catholic training colleges like St Patrick's in 1884, the education of children in separate Catholic and Protestant national schools was by then the norm.

Applications to the Commissioners

In 1841 the total population of Ireland had exceeded eight million and the number of national schools connected with the Board of National Education had increased to reflect this growth in the population. In that year there were 2,337 national schools with 281,849 pupils enrolled.[4]

Applications to the Commissioners of National Education for grant aid to erect a schoolhouse, or to fund a teacher's salary and schoolbooks in an existing school, were made by the school patron or manager. In those schools in which the children were mainly Catholic, the school manager and named applicant was typically the local parish priest. Each application was accompanied by a report prepared by the district inspector, who visited the school. The inspector's report included detailed information about the school, its location and facilities and the schoolteacher's qualifications and teaching ability. Inspectors also added comments on the merits or otherwise of each application for grant aid, and these could include comments about the district in which the school was located and the people of that district. Inspectors' reports that accompanied applications from schools in Co. Monaghan frequently included comments on the conditions of poverty and the 'wretched state of the people'.[5] In one such report, a district inspector remarked unfavourably on the people of Lisdoonan in the parish of Donaghmoyne:

> There is hardly in any part of Ireland so turbulent or violent a class of people as the inhabitants of Lisdoonan. The adults, I consider irredeemable and unless a good education be afforded them, the rising generation will be like their fathers – violent and turbulent to an extent bordering on barbarism.[6]

Such disparaging comments about the poorer population by state officials reflected a readiness to attribute the circumstances of poverty to the supposed poor moral character of the people. In 1835, some few years after the national school system was established, the surveyor Lieutenant Robert Boteler wrote about the schools in Magheross parish and remarked: 'Schools by their introduction have led to a slight improvement in the moral habits of the people [of Magheross], who seem anxious for improvement.'[7] Once the Commissioners approved an application for grant aid for a school, that school became a national school connected with the Board of National Education. The level of financial support granted was normally two-thirds of the amount applied for, with the local community expected to raise the remaining one-third.[8] Grants were approved on the condition that the applying schools agreed to comply with the Board's rules and regulations for approval as a national school. To reflect the fundamental principle of a unified education system with separate secular and religious instruction, the rules included the requirement that a new schoolhouse building should not be erected on 'ground connected with a place of worship'.[9]

School attendance
Although the national schools were established as a system of free education for the poorer classes, it is unlikely that the very poor were in a position to benefit from the new system, since school attendance records show that it was mainly the children of the medium and larger sized farmers, tradesmen and shopkeepers who benefitted most.[10] Average school attendance was generally much lower than the numbers enrolled in the schools; for example, at Coolfore national school in Co. Monaghan in 1845, the year that the school first applied for state grant aid, 131 pupils were on the school rolls in the six months to the application, but the average daily attendance was just seventy, of which number, forty-one were males and twenty-nine were females.[11]

Attendance rates remained low in the decades after 1831; as late as 1870, just 36 per cent of school-going children attended school regularly; this was due to the difficult economic circumstances prevailing at the time.[12] In rural districts, the demands of farming, particularly during the busy harvest seasons, were also a major factor in irregular school attendance. In general, children did not remain in school beyond the fourth grade; for example, at Carrick-macross boys' school in 1862, where there were 114 pupils, just four boys were enrolled in the fourth and higher classes.[13]

Schools in Carrickmacross
In his OS returns for Magheross in 1835, Lieutenant Boteler listed several schools in the parish, including four in Carrickmacross and five in the surrounding townlands.[14] In Carrickmacross, there were three national schools and a Sunday school. One of the schools was newly erected in 1834 at a cost of £280, paid in one-third part by the Board of National Education and in two-thirds' part by local subscription. The school patron was the Catholic

Bishop of Clogher, and the school manager was the parish priest at Carrick-macross. The schoolhouse was a two-storey building, measuring fifty feet by twenty feet.[15] The schoolmaster was Mr. J. McGinn, who trained at the Kildare Place Training Institution. A Catholic, he was paid a salary of £27 per annum, £15 of which was covered by the Board of National Education.[16]

In the male department of the new school there were 214 boys, all but one of whom were Catholic. In the female department all 200 of the pupils were Catholic and the schoolmistress was Miss Catherine Harte, also a Catholic.[17] However, in 1836 Miss Harte was dismissed as incompetent and was succeeded by Miss Gleeson, who was described as 'active, loquacious, and competent'.[18] However, she too was later dismissed in 1841, but she refused to hand over the keys to her successor, and as a result, the female pupils were accommodated in the boys' school until May 1848, when the Bishop of Clogher, Dr Keenan, obtained a court order for re-possession of the female department.[19] In that year, 233 boys and 104 girls were enrolled at the school.[20] Later in 1852, a paid monitor, Philip Conlan, was also employed.

According to Lieutenant Boteler's survey, the other three schools in Carrickmacross had been established before 1831. One, a Protestant Sunday school established in 1825, was supported by private subscription and the proceeds of an annual charity sermon; it had 130 Protestant pupils and one Catholic pupil. The second Protestant school was established in 1828 and it too was supported by subscriptions; it had fifty-four Protestant and two Catholic pupils and both boys and girls were enrolled. Also established in 1828, the second Catholic school in the town had 100 pupils, forty-five boys and fifty-five girls.[21]

In 1835, the Weymouth grammar school was closed and was scheduled to undergo repairs. In the previous year, the schoolmaster, Mr Palmer, had abandoned the school and rented it to soldiers who were quartered in the town. On hearing of this, the Marquis of Bath gave a donation to re-establish the school and the military men were removed.[22] By 1839 the Commissioners of National Education reported that the Weymouth grammar school had been rebuilt and was 'flourishing and improving in consequence of the high character of the master', the Rev. Maurice McKay.[23]

Carrickmacross workhouse school
Each poor law union workhouse had a school connected with it and the Carrickmacross workhouse was no exception. The workhouse school was established in 1843, the year after the workhouse opened, and was one of 109 schools in poor law union workhouses in that year. The school was under the management of the local clerk of the Carrickmacross Union. The male and

female schoolrooms in the workhouse were of a standard size, measuring twenty-eight feet by twenty-seven feet, with one male and one female teacher to each room; the female teacher was Mary McGinniss.[24] A school annex was added to the main building in 1851.

The Commissioners of National Education records for September 1848 show that there were 200 boys and 148 girls enrolled in the school. This large number is unsurprising, since the Famine of the previous three years had left many families destitute. Some few years later in 1852, the numbers on the rolls were even greater, with 632 children, all but seven of whom were Catholic.[25] However, in September of that same year, the number enrolled had fallen considerably to 414, suggesting improved circumstances for the local population, but also likely the result of emigration under an assisted emigration scheme instituted on the Shirley and Bath estates in the years during and after the Famine.[26]

George Nicholls, the Poor Law Commissioner for Ireland, saw the workhouse school as a place where the children should be educated for their station in life, and in his view, that station was limited to domestic service for girls and labouring or apprenticeships for boys.[27] For that reason, schooling in the workhouse was to be limited to three to four hours per day, where the children were to be taught reading, writing and the principles of the Christian religion.[28] The Commissioners of National Education supplied the workhouse schools with books and other materials and district inspectors visited them.

In their annual reports, the Commissioners commented on the level of compliance with the 'fundamental principle' of separate religious instruction in the workhouses, writing: 'the duty of giving religious instruction to those of each creed belongs to a chaplain, of their own communion [...] therefore, we see the national school system is carried into complete effect'.[29] However, the Commissioners were otherwise critical of the quality of education in the workhouses, reporting on untrained teachers, poor teaching, overcrowded schoolrooms and inadequate furniture and schoolbooks.[30] In 1853, James Kavanagh, the head inspector for the workhouse schools, commented that they were 'schools only in name', given the poor conditions and the fact that teaching was 'altogether a secondary duty', since the teachers were required to conduct other duties in the workhouse.[31] Kavanagh wrote:

The class of children most neglected in the Workhouse are the poor infants, from three to four up to seven years. The common practice in the more crowded houses is to huddle them together in a corner of the School, or into an adjoining room, there to sit silent, listless, and stupid for hours under the terror of a wardswoman, an adult pauper, or a monitress […] Not a ray of childhood's mirth beams from their eyes, the hum of no song gladdens their ear.[32]

In the early 1850s, the Commissioners introduced agricultural instruction in the workhouse schools. In 1852, there were twenty-three workhouses with agricultural departments attached, and the Commissioners' report of that year included an appraisal from Dr Kirkpatrick, who wrote of the 'satisfactory and encouraging' progress in developing workhouse agricultural departments and of 'the efficient training of pauper children in a knowledge of agricultural pursuits'.[33]

Central Female Industrial National School and its branch schools

The Marquis of Bath estate in the eastern part of the Barony of Farney comprised 15,000 acres and a population of 13,000. When Tristram Kennedy became agent to the Bath estate in 1846, he identified a great need for industry and education among the poor tenants:

[Mr Kennedy] found a mass of population miserably ignorant, and without any adequate educational provision. Hardly one in four of the population could read and write, and the standard of agriculture was the lowest. There was no other industry of course. Mr. Kennedy became speedily convinced that the first and most necessary step was to provide ample means of literary and industrial education for all the children.[34]

Soon after the pressures of the Famine had lessened and with the support of E.J. Shirley, Mr Kennedy established the Carrickmacross Central Female Industrial National School, along with seven branch schools on the Bath estate, and an agricultural school with model farm buildings at Broomfield.[35] The Central school was located in a rented house in the town, paid for by the Bath and Shirley estates, and along with the branch and agricultural schools, was connected with the Board of National Education. When first established in 1849, the Central school had 138 female pupils who learned knitting, sewing and quilting, while a class of fifteen pupils were trained in 'fancy and lace-work'.[36] Mr Kennedy later reported to the Commissioners of National Education on the method and purpose of instruction at the school:

The pupils are taught in a progressive course, commencing with the plainest and simplest, and advancing to the most delicate and difficult operations of needlework and the kindred arts, so as to enable them to administer to the wants of all classes, from the humblest cottager to

46

the most liberal encourager of industry. After spending a period of twelve months in this training, it is no uncommon thing for them to be able to earn from 3s. to 5s. per week, each according to their artistic skill; very expert hands, of whom there are not a few, often gain even more.[37]

According to Mr Conwell, the district inspector, beyond the material benefits that the new industry was providing, the Central school and its branches were also having the effect of 'implanting sound moral and religious feelings and creating and fostering a spirit of industry and independence'.[38] He explained enthusiastically:

The system thus carried out has already been attended with the best results. Through a wide portion of the barony of Farney the casual looker-on cannot fail to observe the neat appearance and gentler manner of the younger females, and in their looks an expression of self-reliance and content. To those who had known them ill-fed and ill-clad, careless of cleanliness, and dejected, if not morose, the transition is at once extraordinary and most cheering. Assuredly, the project is most judicious, and no less humane, which, by a remunerative employment of its younger members, seeks to ameliorate the condition and raise the tone of an entire population.[39]

In 1852, 135 girls were enrolled in the Central school; all were Roman Catholic. In that year, the school was under the management of Charles Townsend Esq. and William Steuart Trench, who succeeded Mr Kennedy as the agent to the Bath estate. The staff of the school consisted of one teacher, Harriet Smyth. Alice McCabe and Alice Hogan were employed as the paid monitresses and one workmistress was also employed. At the time, the district inspector, Mr Conwell, presented a 'special report' to the Commissioners on the Central school and its seven branch schools.[40] In a detailed report, he wrote:

The School is exclusively attended by females, and presided over by an excellent and energetic teacher, Miss Smyth, assisted by a Workmistress in the industrial department, and a paid Monitress in the literary department. The literary instruction given in the school is necessarily of an elementary character, such as reading, writing, the rudiments of arithmetic, geography, and grammar [...] From four to five hours every day are regularly employed by the pupils in industrial training.

At a former period, various descriptions of needlework were carried on; but lacework (guipure and appliqué) having been found the most remunerative, is now the only kind of work executed in the Central or Branch schools. The articles manufactured at the Schools vary with the changes of fashion, and include every variety of lace good suitable for ladies' dress; robes, trains, trimmages, collars, lappets, skirts, squares, flounces, half-shawls, mantillas, sleeves, scarfs, veils, caps, head-dresses, pocket handkerchiefs, &c.[41]

What marked out the Central school from the other schools in the district was the fact that adult women were enrolled as pupils. While the number of pupils enrolled was 147, the average daily attendance at the Central school was just thirty-two and Conwell explained this variance:

Perhaps more adults attend the Central [school], than any other School on the [Bath] estate. Many of these being mothers of families, find it in their interest to make good use of every moment; and wisely conclude that the time spent walking to and from the School might be better employed sitting at their work, at home, during the hours their husbands are at work, and their children, if old enough, are at School. They are however, considered as belonging to the School, for the Teacher must provide them with well-drawn patterns, good material, and be satisfied that they are in good working order.[42]

Established to serve the wider district, the branch schools were essentially rural national schools for both boys and girls, and were located on the Bath estate at Drumlusty, Ballymackney, Blackstaff, Kidnaminsha, Broomfield, Aughnafarcon and Ashburton. The schoolhouse in each of the branch schools was described as follows:

Each of the Branch Schools consists of a neat stone and lime cottage, slated, ceiled, and boarded, containing one room, lofty, well lighted and ventilated, with a sufficient supply of school furniture and apparatus, besides a vestibule in front, provided with rows of pins for caps, bonnets and cloaks; and surmounted by a handsome cut-stone belfry, with a well-toned bell, which is rung every morning, one hour before the school business commences.[43]

The Central school and its seven branch schools provided a structure around which an important local cottage industry developed. Conwell reported that 'a skilled and diligent worker' could earn from 7s. to 9s. per week, while the 'ordinary workers' could earn an average of 5s. each week. The earning capacity of all eight schools was demonstrated in a report, which Tristram Kennedy compiled in 1854.[44] Mr Kennedy, then the MP for Co. Louth, reported that there was a combined total of 598 pupils enrolled at the Carrickmacross Central school and the seven branch national schools, with the highest number of pupils, 149, enrolled at Carrickmacross. The total combined earnings of all eight schools in the five-year period 1849–53 was £3,218. 18s. 6d., with a little over half the amount earned from sales by the Carrickmacross school.

The teachers at the Central school and its branches were trained in the craft of lacemaking and became expert in Italian lacemaking under the patronage of Miss Reed of Culloville in south Co. Armagh, and subsequently, under Mrs Tottenham, wife of the rector of Donaghmoyne.[45] The fine Italian lace technique was originally introduced into the area in 1820 by Mrs Grey Porter, the wife of Rev. John G. Porter, rector of Carrickmacross.[46] The lace schools supported by Bath and Shirley provided much needed employment and income from a ready market for the schools' produce, where the lace was exported to high-class fashion shops in London.[47]

In the decades after it was first established, the Central school remained connected with the Board of National Education, and in 1872, Mr Simpson, the district inspector, wrote of the school's importance to the local economy and its growing reputation: 'The one industrial school in this district, "Bath and Shirley" (Carrickmacross), continues to maintain its high prestige, and to afford the means of support to a large number of poor girls.'[48] By the 1880s, the lace-making skills and the lace produced by the pupils of the school had gained a good reputation, as shown in the Commissioners' annual report for the year 1883. In his report, Mr H. Worsley, the district inspector, wrote:

> In the Carrickmacross Industrial National School, twenty-five girls are at present learning appliqué lace-making, and with very fair success. A large number, after leaving this school, earn a livelihood by making the two kinds of the famous Carrickmacross lace—guipure and appliqué.[49]

While lacemaking had declined somewhat at the Bath and Shirley schools, in 1888 the sisters at St Louis Convent in the town revived the craft, where they taught lacemaking skills to the secondary school pupils. The traditional craft of lacemaking in the town was preserved, and today Carrickmacross Lace is made under the auspices of the Carrickmacross Lace Co-operative.

Rural schools in Magheross parish in west Farney
Lieutenant Boteler's OS returns for November 1835 listed five rural schools in Magheross parish; these were at Carrickmaclim, Mullaghcrogery, Cornasas-

singah, Cargaghmore and Corduff Mountain.[50] With the exception of the school at Corduff, which was under the management of the Catholic clergy of the parish, these rural schools were supported by an annual donation from E.J. Shirley and by subscriptions from the pupils. Like the school for boys and girls at Carrickmacross, the school at Cargaghmore was newly founded in 1834.[51] Lieutenant Boteler's records provide details of the numbers of pupils and their religion in the five rural schools; the total number of pupils enrolled in the schools was 306, of whom 186 were boys and 128 were girls (Table 4.1).[52]

Table 4.1 Rural schools in Magheross parish, 1835[53]

School	Date established	Number of Catholics	Number of Protestants	Number of males	Number of females	Total number
Carrickmaclim*	1818	45	25	52	18	70
Mullaghcrogery*	1825	14	38	32	20	52
Cornasassinagh*	1824	50	0	30	20	50
Cargaghmore*	1834	60	10	30	40	70
Corduff**	1808	60	4	42	30	64
Total		229	77	186	128	306
*Supported by E.J. Shirley and the scholars; **Supported by the scholars						

With the exception of the school at Cornasassinagh, both Catholic and Protestant children attended the rural schools in the parish, with the schools at Carrickmaclim and Mullaghcrogery having the highest number of Protestant pupils. The OS records also show that the number of boys enrolled was approximately twice that of girls.

In addition to the schools listed in the OS returns of 1835, Lieutenant Boteler also mentioned 'a small school held in a man's cabin in the townland of Derrylavin' near the town. This was a hedge school, where the schoolmaster, a Catholic, received 1d. per week from each pupil. Fifty-five boys and twenty girls were enrolled at the school and most of the pupils were Catholic, with just seven Protestant children enrolled. Later in 1837, in addition to the five rural schools listed in the OS returns, there was a school in the townland of Coraghery and one at Corduff Kelly, both of which Shirley supported.[54]

George Sudden's reports
During the mid- to late 1840s E.J. Shirley commissioned his clerk of works, the architect George Sudden, to conduct a review of 'the state of the schools on the Shirley Estate'.[55] Sudden prepared six one-page reports, two for each

of the years 1846, 1847 and 1848. Each short report was based on visits he made to the schools and contained the names of the schools, the teachers' names, the number of pupils enrolled in each school, along with brief comments. In the reports for 1846 and 1847, eight schools were listed, as follows: Lossets (Boys and Girls), Corvally, Carrickmaclim, Carrickmacross, Corduff Kelly, Lisdoonan, Cargamore and Corduff.[56] The school at Carrickmacross was the Protestant school supported by Shirley and by the Church Education Society and was not connected with the Board of National Education.[57] In his report for 1848, Sudden also listed a school at Terrygarvan, near Carrickmacross.[58]

Shirley did not support all of the schools on his estate. With the exception of the schools at Corduff and Lisdoonan, none of the schools listed in Sudden's reports were included in the Annual Report of the Commissioners of National Education for the year 1848.[59] The Commissioners' report for that year also included the rural national schools at Sreenty, Coolfore and Corcrin, all of which were on the Shirley estate, but none of which Shirley supported at the time and none were listed in Sudden's reports. This indicates that the schools at Lossets (Boys and Girls), Corvally, Carrickmaclim, Corduff Kelly, Cargaghmore and Terrygarvin were hedge schools, and the remainder of the schools on the estate were national schools connected with the Board of National Education (Table 4.2). Hence, almost two decades after the establishment of the national school system, over half of the schools on the Shirley estate were not connected with the Board of National Education.

School	Date established	Pay/hedge school	National school
Lossets*	Unknown	✓	
Corvally*	c. 1850	✓	
Carrickmaclim*	1818	✓	
Corduff Kelly*	1824	✓	
Cargaghmore*	1834	✓	
Terrygarvan*	1848	✓	
Lisdoonan*§	1832		✓
Corduff	1844		✓
Coolfore	1845		✓
Sreenty	1846		✓
Corcrin	Unknown		✓
* Supported by E.J. Shirley; § parish of Donaghmoyne			

Table 4.2 Rural schools on the Shirley estate, 1846–48

George Sudden's reports provided figures for the numbers of pupils enrolled at the schools in 1847. The highest number reported at a single school in that year was ninety-five pupils at Corduff national school. In the remaining schools, the total number of pupils enrolled and 'paid for by Mr Shirley' was 338.

In his reports, Sudden briefly commented on school attendance and on the children's progress in learning. For example, at Carrickmacross school the children were reported to be doing 'remarkably well', while at Lisdoonan the attendance was 'generally bad'. In 1847 he wrote that 'everything seemed regular and the Schools [were] well attended, with the exception of Lossets Male School'. Sudden wrote of his particular concerns regarding the male and female schools at Lossets: 'The Master and Mistress seem to be attentive to the Schools, but nothing can yet be said of their efficiency' and he wrote: 'I fear Mr Crilly [the schoolmaster] will never have a great attendance'. Sudden elaborated on this concern:

> I fear much that the Master is not well adapted to the situation, he seems to want energy & application very much, & makes very little effort to bring on the children or increase the number.[60]

Sudden also commented briefly on the health of Mrs Crilly, the schoolmistress at Lossets. Having been unwell in 1846, in the following year she was 'improving in health but still delicate'.[61] In 1847 Mrs Howel, the schoolmistress at Carrickmacross, was reported to have 'gone to the Salt Water on leave' and Mr Sheridan, the schoolmaster at Cargamore, had also gone on leave to the Salt Water.[62]

George Sudden's reports to Shirley highlighted a number of facts about the circumstances of the children at the schools on the estate. He made his reports during and immediately after the Famine years, and aside from hunger, fevers were common among the children. In 1847, he reported that the children at Carrickmaclim school were 'generally very small', and he noted that they were also small at Corduff Kelly school. Additionally, many of the children were absent from Cargamore and Lisdoonan schools due to fever. The evidence in Sudden's reports indicates that the general health of the children on the estate was not good, most likely the result of the effects of malnutrition.

E.J. Shirley's motives

George Sudden's reports identified eight schools supported by E.J. Shirley, which were not connected with the Board of National Education, and this demonstrated that hedge schools persisted for many years after the establishment of the state-supported national school system. Shirley's support for the schools showed his disregard for the Board and the power and influence which he wielded locally. By commissioning Sudden to report on the state of the schools over a three-year period, Shirley demonstrated an interest in a significant aspect of everyday life on his estate. However, as a semi-absentee landlord, this interest may have been less about concern for the education of his tenants' children and more about monitoring and controlling education at a time when schools were in the frontline of a longstanding religious conflict that was heightened by the establishment of the national school system. E.J. Shirley was an ultra-conservative evangelical Christian who was said to be 'opposed to every species of radical innovation and change' and who had a history of promoting proselytising practices in the schools which he supported.[63]

Notwithstanding his evangelical motives and his opposition to the national school system, some years before he had commissioned George Sudden's reports, Shirley sought to reduce religious tensions around schooling on his estate, when in 1841 he granted the grounds of Corduff chapel to the Board of National Education, where the local people had recently constructed a schoolhouse.[64] Shirley also granted the chapel grounds at the nearby townland of Corcreeghagh.[65] An article published in *The Northern Standard* on 16 October 1841 suggests that Shirley was more tolerant than his then agent Sandy Mitchell, who was in constant conflict with the local Catholic clergy and the people of Corduff over his proselytising and his generally hostile demeanour. The article reported on Shirley's action in giving grounds for schools and churches in the three main parishes on his estate:

> Mr Shirley having taken into consideration the wishes of his tenantry, and the wretched state of Corduff and Corcreeghagh chapels, has offered an acre of ground for a chapel and burial ground, in the centre of the parish of Magheross, on the following conditions: - 1st – To grant a lease in perpetuity to trustees at 1s. per annum, to be used for no other purpose than for a chapel and burial ground, which is to be free to the tenants. 2nd – The present chapel ground of Corduff mountain (on which a National School has lately been built) and the chapel ground of Corcreeghagh to be given up, and regranted to the Board of Education Ireland. The chapels of Lisdoonan and Magheracloone to take out similar leases as Magheross. Mr Shirley's schools still to continue for the use of those tenants who will take advantage of them; but every Roman Catholic tenant is to use his own discretion as to where he will send his children to be educated.[66]

The new male and female schools at Corduff were connected with the Board of National Education in the previous year, and a few years later in 1845, a second rural school in Magheross parish was connected with the Board. This was the school at Coolfore townland.[67]

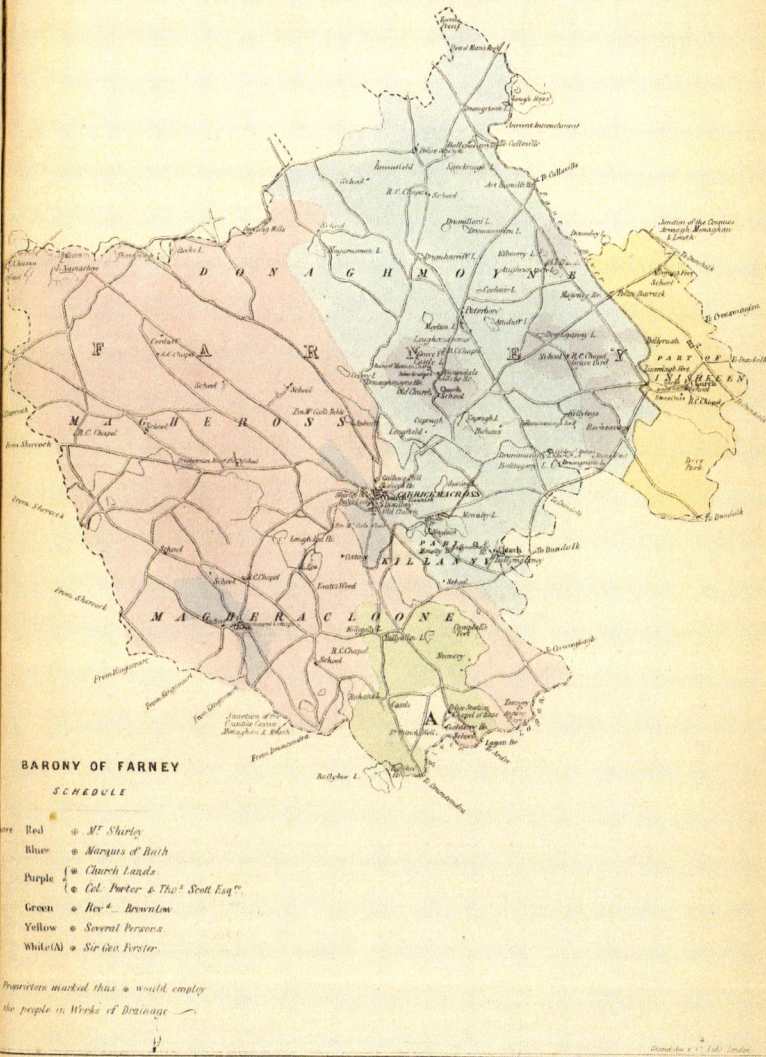

1—'Barony of Farney landowners 1846', showing the Shirley estate to the west and the Bath estate to the east (Courtesy University of Southampton)

2—Lough Fea House, Carrickmacross (Courtesy Monaghan County Museum)

McMahon Street, Carrickmacross.

195/8

3—Main Street, Carrickmacross, late nineteenth century (Courtesy Monaghan County Museum)

4—*Former hedge school of John Cassidy at Aghalile (Courtesy Corduff Raferagh Heritage)*

5—*Former hedge school of Owen Sheridan at Cargaghoge (Courtesy Corduff Raferagh Heritage)*

6—*Section of map of Coolfore townland (undated) showing a hedge school at south-east corner (Courtesy Deputy Keeper of the Records, Public Record Office of Northern Ireland and the Shirley Estate, ref. PRONI/D3531/S/56/27)*

7—*Site of the former thatched house at Coolfore, which served as the schoolhouse, 1845–1852 with stream in mid-ground (Image © the author)*

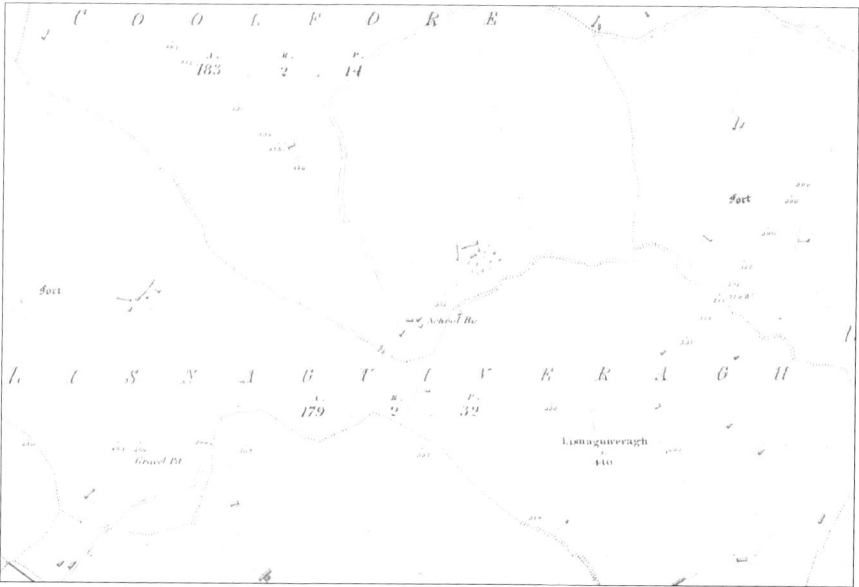

8—Section of Coolfore townland showing location of hedge school [Tiff File Extract]. Scale: 6 inches to 1 mile (1834), Monaghan 028, UCD Library Dublin (accessed 6 December 2022) (Courtesy Ordnance Survey Ireland)

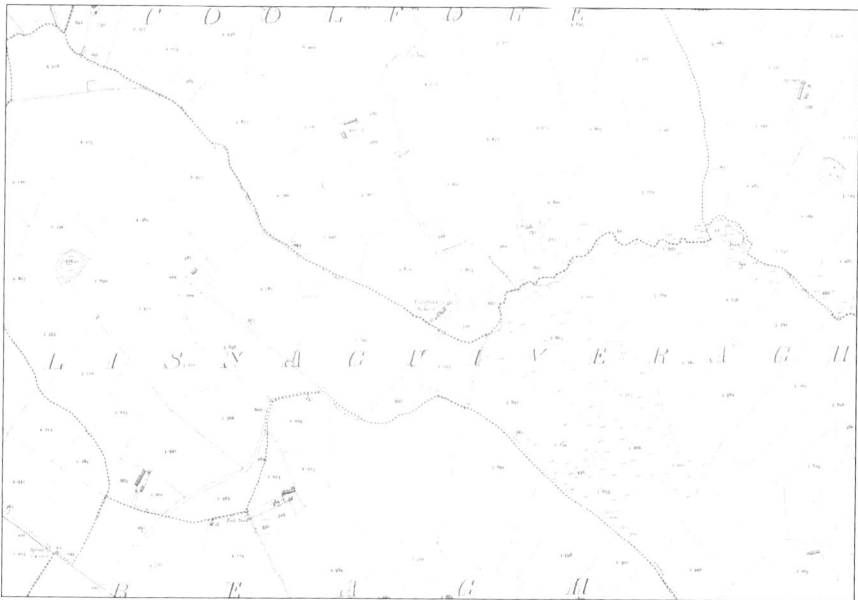

9—Section of Coolfore townland showing Coolfore national school [Tiff File Extract]. Scale: 25 inches to 1 mile (1908), Monaghan 028-13, UCD Library Dublin (accessed 6 December 2022) (Courtesy Ordnance Survey Ireland)

10—*Coolfore schoolhouse, constructed in 1871 (Courtesy Mr M. Ward)*

11—*Original stone plaque dated 1871 placed above the front door of Coolfore schoolhouse (Courtesy Mr M. Ward)*

*12—Former Sreenty national school, Magheross parish on the Shirley estate
(Courtesy 'Corduff Calling' 1983)*

*13—Former Ballynagearn national school, Magheracloone parish on the Shirley
estate (Courtesy Mary Duffy McBrearty and Máirín Duffy, USA)*

14—*Former Corduff national school, Magheross parish on the Shirley estate (Courtesy Corduff Raferagh Heritage)*

15—*Corcreagh (Raferagh) national school (Image © the author)*

16—*Former Corvally schoolhouse and Presbyterian church, Shanco, Co. Monaghan (Image © the author)*

17—*Former Drumlusty national school, Donaghmoyne parish on the former Bath estate, Co. Monaghan (Image © the author)*

18—Carrickmacross workhouse, site of the former workhouse national school (Image © the author)

19—Monaghan model school, constructed in 1860 to an OPW design (Image © the author)

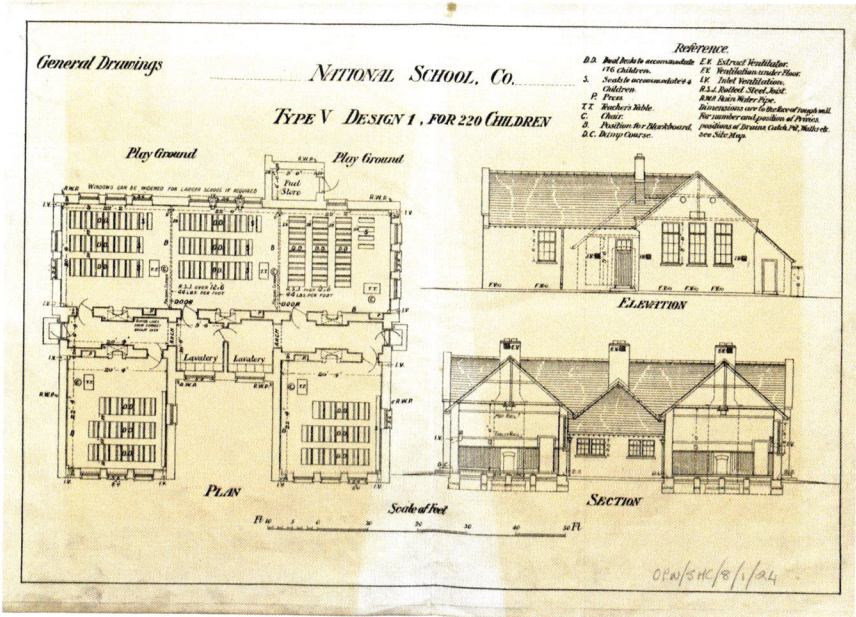

20—OPW architectural drawing for a national school (Courtesy the National Archives of Ireland, ref. NAI/OPW/5/HC/8/1/24)

21—Former Moys national school, Clontibret parish, Co. Monaghan, constructed in 1875 to an OPW design (Image © the author)

22—St Patrick's teacher training college for males, Drumcondra, Co. Dublin (Courtesy Irish Historic Picture Company)

23—Female teacher training college of Our Lady of Mercy, Carysfort Park, Blackrock, Co. Dublin (Courtesy Irish Historic Picture Company)

5

'Good grounds': Coolfore national school, 1845–1852

Within a decade after the new national school system was introduced, over a quarter of a million pupils were enrolled in schools supported by the Board of National Education.[1] While evidence for the levels of school attendance was not officially collected on a national basis until the 1861 census, the returns from the district inspectors of national schools provide some evidence that school attendance was irregular. Nevertheless, indirect evidence of the impact of the national school system may be gleaned from the fact that the levels of illiteracy among the population had fallen and numeracy was improving in the decades after 1840.[2]

During the 1830s and 1840s the available funds for national schools were low and grants were given mainly for books and school furniture, for upgrading existing schoolhouses and for supplementing the pupils' contributions to the teachers' fees.[3] In 1848 there were 114 national schools in Co. Monaghan connected with the Board, in which 18,811 pupils were enrolled.[4] In Magheross parish nine national schools were connected with the Board, including four schools in the town of Carrickmacross; these were the male and female schools, the workhouse school and the Central Female Industrial National School. Also located in the parish and close to the town was a school at Corcrin, which was under the patronage of Charles Townsend Esq. of the Bath estate. Located at the extreme north-eastern part of the Shirley estate, but in the neighbouring parish of Donaghmoyne, the national school at Lisdoonan was connected with the Board in 1832; it was under Roman Catholic patronage and the school manager was Rev. J. Duffy.

The other rural national schools connected with the Board and in the parish of Magheross and on the Shirley estate were at Sreenty, Corduff and

Coolfore, all located to the north-west of Carrickmacross. The case of Coolfore national school is particularly noteworthy. The school was connected with the Board under Roman Catholic patronage in 1845. Although it was successfully operated as a national school for a number of years, its location and circumstance brought it the attention and disfavour of E.J. Shirley.

Coolfore national school, 1845

While Patrick McMahon conducted a hedge school in a thatched house at Coolfore as early as 1826, a national school at Coolfore was first connected with the Board of National Education in August 1845, following an application 'for aid towards payment of teacher's salary and for supply of books &c.' The initial application to the Commissioners of National Education was received on 20 June 1845.[5] The applicant and the named school patron was Fr James Mulligan, Catholic curate at Carrickmacross, who was also the school manager of the national schools at Sreenty, Corduff and Carrickmacross at the time. The following information was recorded in the initial application:

> Nearest post town – Carrickmacross, North
> Description of the [schoolhouse] – 33 feet by 13
> Schoolrooms – 1
> Furniture – 8 desks & 10 forms
> Teacher – Patrick Murtagh, age 24.
> Average daily attendance – 60
> School hours from 10 until 4
> Time of religious instruction – Saturday
> The books used have not been of the [National] Board
> All facility will be made for visitors
> The school shall be managed by a Committee
> Correspondence Rev. James Mulligan.[6]

On foot of the initial application from Fr Mulligan, the district inspector, Mr Michael Coyle, inspected the school and prepared a report, which he submitted to the Commissioners for their consideration. The report was dated 1 August 1845 and contained details about the schoolhouse and its location, its teacher and the average daily attendance of pupils. According to Mr Coyle's report, the school was first established in July 1844 and was located three miles to the north of Carrickmacross and three miles' distant from the school at Corduff. The report stated:

There are several hedge schools in the neighbourhood, some ½ m., 1 m., and 1½ m. distant between Applicant School & Carrickmacross. They are generally held in private dwelling houses and called by the names of the respective teachers.

In approving grant aid to schools, the Commissioners' rules advised that school buildings should be erected on ground not connected with a place of worship, such as a church, chapel, or meeting house. The district inspector's report confirmed that the school was not connected to any society and that it was not attached to or erected on any church, chapel, or meeting-house ground, and was not connected with any religious establishment.

The schoolhouse and the schoolmaster
The schoolhouse at Coolfore was built of stone and had a thatched roof and was 'in good repair'. The OS map of Coolfore townland for the years 1829 to 1841 shows the hedge schoolhouse that was mentioned in the *Second Report of the Commissioners of Irish Education Inquiry* of 1826. That hedge school was also described as a thatched house and it is probable that the same thatched house was used for the school then seeking grant aid from the Commissioners in 1845.[7] Its dimensions were thirty-three feet broad, sixteen feet long and seven-and-a-half feet in height, while its internal dimensions were thirty feet by twelve feet. The house was rented from the owner, Owen McMahon, at a cost of £1 per annum and secured to the schoolteacher under a written contract for the purpose of education, and it was used solely as a schoolhouse. McMahon, a local farmer, owned two other houses at Coolfore.[8] The furniture in the schoolhouse consisted of six desks, six forms and two boards placed along the wall. The schoolroom was capable of seating about eighty children, and it was well ventilated.

The teacher was Patrick Murtagh, then aged twenty-four years. He had received no instruction in a model school and was never previously employed as a teacher, except at Coolfore school. Mr Murtagh produced no testimonials in respect of the application to the Commissioners. However, in his report that accompanied the application, Mr Coyle wrote that Murtagh's character was excellent, and as to his 'literary acquirements', he wrote:

[Mr Murtagh] reads pretty well and writes a good hand. He understands Arithmetic, Mensuration, Euclid, and Algebra tolerably. He knows the rules of Grammar well but has read scarcely any English authors. His method of teaching is bad, but in this respect & with regard to literary acquirements, he is a good subject for improvement, and I would like to encourage him.[9]

At the time of applying for grant aid, the school was in receipt of no annual funds for either the teacher's salary or for the upkeep of the schoolhouse. However, the scholars paid the schoolmaster's salary at a rate of between 1s. 6d. and 7s. 6d. The amount payable by each pupil was regulated by the teacher, meaning that the school was essentially a pay or hedge school at the time of the application to the Commissioners. Should the application succeed, the rates payable by pupils would be reduced. At the time, about thirty pupils on the school register were unable to pay; nevertheless, Mr Murtagh admitted them to the school.

Pupils
If approved for aid, the school and its patron undertook to comply with all the conditions for approval as a national school as set down in the Commissioners' rules; this included displaying 'National School' over the schoolhouse door, keeping a school register and using only the books supplied by the Commissioners. In the application, the school patron also undertook to comply with the requirement to give religious instruction in accordance with the Commissioners' rules and regulations and be open to all religious denominations.

In 1845, the population of Magheross parish was approximately 5,000. The school at Coolfore was located in a very 'populous neighbourhood', in which the inhabitants were reported to be 'generally very poor and ignorant and unable to provide for themselves', and education was therefore seen as being necessary 'to improve their condition'.[10] Mr Coyle's report to the Commissioners gave details of the number of pupils enrolled. There were 111 pupils present at the time of his inspection, sixty-nine males and forty-two females.[11] In the previous six months, 131 pupils had been enrolled at the school, seventy-eight males and fifty-three females. However, the average daily attendance in that period was just seventy pupils, or approximately half of the pupils on the school register. In his report, Mr Coyle remarked that he did not expect any increase in the average daily attendance at the school.

Regarding the lessons taught at the time, the children were engaged in 'the ordinary branches of secular education' every day from 9 a.m. to 4 p.m. during the summer and every day from 10 a.m. to 3 p.m. during the winter. Lessons were also conducted at the school until 1 p.m. every Saturday.

'Good grounds'
Coolfore school was not under the direction of any committee at the time of the application for aid. While preparing his report to the Commissioners, Mr Coyle communicated with the local Protestant clergyman, Rev. W.

Thompson, seeking his view on the application for aid. Rev. Thompson responded that, as he was committed to the local Church Education Society, he did not wish to express an opinion in reference to the application from the school at Coolfore. Mr Coyle also sought the views of the local Presbyterian clergyman on the application but received no response. As the prospective patrons, the local Catholic clergy of Magheross parish approved the application.

In his report to the Commissioners, Mr Coyle wrote that the information gained from his inspection was satisfactory and that therefore the application rested on 'good grounds'. He wrote that, should the Commissioners favourably entertain the application for aid, the school might 'do much to remedy the forlorn state of the wretched people', and on that basis, he recommended the application 'to the favourable consideration of the Board [of National Education]'. The application for grant aid was referred to a sub-committee of the Board, and on 28 August 1845, it approved the application. The school at Coolfore was afterwards a national school connected with the Board, with the assigned roll number 4537. A grant of £1 5s. was made for books for 150 children and a contribution to Mr Murtagh's salary was also provided. Over the following two years a total of £6 5s. was granted.

In the returns for September 1848 for all the schools in the parish of Magheross, approximately 1,167 pupils were enrolled, with Coolfore national school having 149 boys and sixty-seven girls. The schoolmaster's salary was £14 at the time. In 1850, Fr Mulligan moved from Magheross parish and Fr Thomas MacNally replaced him as the school manager.

Coolfore national school was non-vested at the time, meaning that as long as it was in receipt of annual grants from the Board of National Education, it was bound by the rules of the Board.[12] As a non-vested school, the school patron or local manager could determine what religious instruction could be given. Coolfore school was, in effect, a denominational school under the patronage of the Catholic diocese, and with the local parish priest acting as its school manager. As the landlord of Coolfore and its surrounding townlands, E.J. Shirley owned the land on which the schoolhouse was built.

Religious denomination of scholars

In March 1852, there were 140 national schools connected with the Board of National Education in Co. Monaghan, in which just over 13,000 children were enrolled.[13] The majority of the children in the schools were Roman Catholic (79 per cent) and the remainder were Presbyterian (11 per cent) and Protestant (9 per cent). At that time, nineteen national schools in the entire Barony of Farney were connected with the Board, including seven schools in the parish of Magheross.[14] This included the rural schools at Corduff and Coolfore, but not the school at Sreenty, which had burned down in the previous year.

While the population of Farney was predominantly Roman Catholic, there were substantial numbers of Protestant and Presbyterian families in the hinterland to the north-west of Carrickmacross.[15] In the district served by Coolfore national school, 80 per cent of the population were Roman Catholic, and the remainder were Protestant (12.5 per cent) and Presbyterian (7.5 per cent). The district served by Corduff male and female schools had a somewhat similar distribution of Catholics, Protestants and Presbyterians to that of Coolfore district, although Presbyterians comprised just 5 per cent of the population in that district. In contrast, there were relatively few Protestants and Presbyterians in the town of Carrickmacross.

Of the 121 pupils enrolled at Coolfore national school in 1852, just two were Protestant and none were Presbyterian. At Corduff male and female schools, the rolls contained the names of 232 Catholics, three Protestants and just one Presbyterian. It therefore appears that while a substantial number of Protestant and Presbyterian families lived in the districts served by Coolfore and Corduff schools, this was not reflected in the proportion of children of their respective congregations enrolled in either school.

Since E.J. Shirley and the Established Church were opposed to the national school system, it is not surprising that most Protestant children did not attend Coolfore or Corduff schools, but instead attended one of the schools supported by Shirley, such as the rural schools at Carrickmaclim and at Corvally, in the townland of Shanco, or the Protestant school in Carrickmacross. In August 1848, the schools supported by Shirley had a combined total of 342 children enrolled and several Shirley-sponsored schools were still operating on the estate in the early 1850s.[16] Although the Presbyterian Church supported the Board of National Education, the Presbyterian families of the district had an alternative school at Carrickmaclim.[17]

District inspectors' reports

In 1852, the district inspectors of national schools were asked to report to the Commissioners of National Education on 'the religious denominations of the pupils attending national schools in their respective districts' and on the extent to which the principle of a 'united education' had been carried out in their district.[18] In his returns for schools in parts of Co. Donegal, the sub-inspector Mr R. Robinson, reported that the attendance of different denominations was 'mixed in proportion to the population'.[19] He gave evidence of a sample of twelve schools with mixed denominations of mainly Roman

Catholic and Presbyterian children; however, the exception was at the Letterkenny male and female schools, where the scholars, teachers and the school manager were reported to 'profess the Roman Catholic religion'. Commenting on the returns which he submitted, Mr Robinson remarked:

> In my opinion, that it arises, not from any opposition given by the [Established] Church clergyman, but because it happens here that the persons belonging to the Established Church form the more respectable class, and, therefore, are unwilling to allow their children to mix with the children attending these Schools.[20]

This somewhat derogatory remark betrayed a prejudice towards the Roman Catholic population, which Robinson conceded was 'for the most part throughout the county very poor'. Mr R. Nesbit, the district inspector for parts of counties Derry and Donegal commented that the factor preventing Protestants from sending their children to national schools of mixed denominations was the Board's rule prohibiting the celebration of public worship in schoolhouses.[21] W.A. Hunter, the district inspector for District 14, which included parts of counties Monaghan and Armagh, reported that the objects of the Board in respect of mixed denominations had been 'fully attained'; however, he noted that there was some opposition to mixed denominational schooling in the district. District 15 then included parts of counties Cavan and Monaghan, including all the schools in the parish of Magheross in west Farney, and the district inspector was Eugene A. Conwell. Based on information supplied by 117 of the schools in his district, Conwell reported that, in 108 of the national schools, 'the children of different religious denominations attend and fully in proportion to the percentages of persons of various creeds in the vicinity of each school'. He reported that there was no mixed attendance in just nine of the schools.

Conwell's report on the religious denominations attending the schools in his district was based on returns he received from the school managers, who were asked to state if there were any circumstances 'which may have conduced to or prevented the attendance of children of different religious denominations'. The manager of Coolfore national school submitted the following response:

> The erection and opening of an endowed school in the neighbourhood of this school I believe to be the principal, if not the only cause why children of different religious denominations from Roman Catholics have not attended.[22]

The name of the 'school in the neighbourhood' was not indicated, although it is probable that the reference was to the school at Corvally, which was endowed by Shirley and newly erected in about 1850. Although located beside the Corvally Presbyterian church, Corvally school served the Protestant families that worshipped at the nearby Ardragh church, which Shirley also endowed.

In the case of Corduff school, the response somewhat confirmed this, with the school manager reporting: 'I believe the erection of a school at the Ardragh Presbyterian Meeting-house to be the only cause of the non-attendance of more pupils of the Established Church, Presbyterians, and other Protestant Dissenters'.[23] At Carrickmacross, the school manager reported that 'the establishment of a *free* school in the town, in connection with the Established Church, has, I believe, prevented the children from that church, Presbyterians and other Protestant Dissenters, from attending the National School'.[24]

Based on the text of the responses received, it is probable that all three responses were written by Fr Thomas MacNally, the Catholic curate of Magheross parish and the school manager of all three of the schools. What is noteworthy in the responses is the fact that many of the national schools in the parish had become almost exclusively Catholic within twenty years of the national school system being established. The preponderance of Catholic schools in Magheross parish reflected the distribution of Catholics in the wider population of south Co. Monaghan. In the neighbouring parish of Magheracloone, for example, the school manager of Coolderry national school reported that 'there are no Protestants in the neighbourhood of this school'.[25]

Elsewhere in Co. Monaghan, Mr Conwell reported on the religious denominations of the children in thirteen national schools in the Barony of Dartry in the north-west of the county. The school managers who reported on the circumstances of their schools presented a generally harmonious picture, with most reporting that children of mixed denominations attended the schools and that there was no interference with the religious convictions of pupils. The manager at Granshaw national school in north Co. Monaghan remarked optimistically:

> The choice of parents about the Teacher, and his care and abilities in advancing the children, are the only causes of attendance [...] They are and have been of different religions at each School, and [are] at peace about religion.[26]

'Permanently closed'

The Commissioners of National Education had the authority to strike a national school off the Roll of National Schools. For example, in 1845, the year in which Coolfore national school was first connected with the Board of National Education, sixty-four national schools were struck off.[27] The majority of these (forty-two) were in Ulster. The reasons for striking off varied, and in many instances, the Commissioners' decision to strike off a school was related to that school's failure to comply with the Commissioners' rules. The most common reason recorded was that the school was 'withdrawn' or 'closed by manager'; however, the Commissioners' annual report for 1845 gave no additional information. Another common reason was the unsuitability of the schoolhouse or the failure of the school manager to procure a lease on the schoolhouse. In many cases, the reason indicated for striking off was the teacher's incompetence.

Several schools in Munster and Connaught were closed on account of the pupils being transferred to a new schoolhouse built with a grant from the Commissioners. In Ulster, five schools were struck off on the grounds that they were in 'violation of the rule [as] regards religious instruction' and a further two were struck off 'in consequence of local opposition', suggesting a religious-sectarian reason. At Fahy in Co. Galway, the national school was struck off because the schoolroom was found to be used 'as a place of public worship'.[28]

In 1849, Patrick Murtagh left Coolfore national school and was replaced by two teachers, James McCabe and Patrick McCaffrey. Mr McCabe was first appointed as a schoolteacher at Rakeeragh school in 1836.[29] Soon after the new teachers were appointed, difficulties arose in relation to the management of Coolfore school, when in March 1850, Mr Butler, the district inspector, ordered Fr MacNally to withdraw the salary of James McCabe, on account of him 'being reported incompetent'. Mr Butler instructed Fr MacNally to appoint a competent teacher instead and to withhold McCabe's salary 'until he gave up possession of the [school]house, free stock &c'.[30] Subsequently, Mr Butler reported to the Commissioners that the school manager had acted upon and carried out the orders. The school was temporarily closed in April 1850 and the schoolhouse was re-possessed from James McCabe. On 1 June 1850, Mr Peter Nowlan was appointed as the schoolteacher to replace McCabe.

Coolfore national school continued to operate under Mr McCaffrey and Mr Nowlan during 1850, 1851 and most of 1852; however, in November 1852 the district inspector advised the Commissioners that the school was closed permanently 'by order of Evelyn J. Shirley (Esq.)'. The schoolhouse, which was rented from Owen McMahon at that time, was a property on Mr Shirley's estate, and the reason given for ordering the school to be closed was that 'the children in the locality were attending it in considerable numbers in preference to two schools built and endowed by Mr Shirley in the same neighbourhood'. On 23 December 1852, the school was struck off the Roll of National Schools, all grants were cancelled, and all stock returned to the Education Office in Dublin, and the Commissioners' report for that year recorded that the school at Coolfore was 'permanently closed'.[31]

E.J. Shirley's claim that other schools in the district that he endowed were losing pupils to Coolfore national school was a remarkable justification for seeking the closure of the school. The fact that a local landlord like Shirley could demand the closure of a state-approved national school demonstrates the power and influence of the landed class at the time. The fact that the Commissioners complied with Shirley's demand is equally remarkable.

Shirley's opposition to the school at Coolfore is unsurprising, since it was consistent with his opposition to the Board of National Education and the national school system, an opposition which he shared with other Protestant landlords and with Protestant clergy in Co. Monaghan.[32] Having previously prohibited the school at Clontrain on his estate from becoming connected with the Board under Catholic patronage in 1834, Shirley's action in having Coolfore school removed from the Roll of National Schools in 1852 was not unprecedented.

Alternative schools
In early 1852 when Coolfore national school was still connected with the Board of National Education, the number of children on the school rolls for the six months up to 31 March was 120; of this number, seventy-nine were boys and forty-one were girls and all were Roman Catholic.[33] After the school was struck off, these children were left without a school and the parents of the district were obliged to seek alternative arrangements for their children's education. Since Shirley ordered that Coolfore school should close permanently, it is unlikely that the teachers continued to conduct lessons at McMahon's thatched house.

The two schools 'built and endowed by Mr Shirley in the same neighbourhood' were not named in the Commissioners' report for 1852' however, it is probable that they were those at Corvally and Carrickmaclim. Neither school was connected with the Board of National Education at that time, and it was only later in the century that they became connected, by which time E.J. Shirley's son Evelyn Philip had succeeded him.

At the time when Coolfore school was struck off, there were just two rural national schools in Magheross parish connected with the Board; located some three miles' distance to the north of Coolfore; these were the Corduff boys' and girls' national schools. Another nearby rural school was at Lisdoonan in the neighbouring parish of Donaghmoyne. Located in Carrickmacross, a distance of up to three miles from Coolfore, were the town's boys' and girls' national schools. All of these nearest schools were connected with the Board and were under Catholic diocesan patronage.

In 1845, when Coolfore school first sought grant aid from the Commissioners of National Education, there were 'several hedge schools in the neighbourhood', and these were generally held in private dwelling houses. Earlier in 1826, the Commissioners of Irish Education Inquiry listed a hedge school in the neighbouring townland of Greaghadromnisk and one at nearby Aghalile townland and they also listed several hedge schools named after their respective schoolmasters.[34] Additionally, the OS map completed between 1829 and 1841 indicates a schoolhouse in the neighbouring townland of Greagh- naroog at approximately one and a half miles from the schoolhouse at Cool- fore. Since none of these schools were listed in George Sudden's reports to Shirley in the late 1840s, it is unlikely that they were operating in 1852. Nevertheless, it may be that some local hedge schools were revived in response to the closure of Coolfore national school, thereby providing an alternative place for lessons for some of the children.

Aside from a school at Tiragarvan near Carrickmacross, which was located at approximately two miles from Coolfore, most of the schools listed in Sudden's reports were located between four and six miles from Coolfore. It is therefore unlikely that these schools offered a viable alternative for the children of Coolfore and the neighbouring townlands. Since the Bishop of Clogher had earlier withdrawn children from schools in which the Protestant version of the Bible was read, it is also unlikely that the Protestant schools at Magheross or at Corvally were viable alternatives for most of the pupils. Hence, the national schools at Carrickmacross, Corduff and Lisdoonan were the likely alternative schools for many of the children of the district around Coolfore. In any event, it would be another twenty years before the Com- missioners of National Education would again consider an application for grant support for a national school at Coolfore.

6

'Satisfactory progress':
Schools, teachers and pupils, 1870

Afundamental principle of the national school system was to provide combined secular and moral education to children 'of all persuasions, as far as possible' in the same school. However, by the second half of the nineteenth century there was a growing denominational divide in establishing and managing the national schools.[1] The divide reflected divergent views on the purpose of elementary education, in particular, on the role of schooling and the place of religious instruction in the school curriculum. In 1852, out of the total of 4,795 schools, just 175 were under the joint management of two denominations.[2]

Despite the growing trend towards separate denominational patronage of schools, a remarkably high number of national schools were still attended by children of mixed denominations. For example, in Co. Monaghan in 1870, out of the 141 national schools, ninety-three were under Catholic teachers, and while no Protestant children attended these schools, a small number of Presbyterian children attended. In forty-six schools under Protestant teachers in the county, Protestant, Catholic and Presbyterian children attended in approximately equal numbers.[3]

At local parish level, some Protestant clergymen placed their schools under the Board of National Education.[4] Additionally, some Catholic children attended national schools supported by the Church Education Society. For example, of the 70,000 children on the rolls of the Society's schools in 1868, 6,000 were Catholic.[5] Given the relatively high numbers that were then attending mixed denominational schools, the Commissioners of National Education commented that there was 'a remarkable degree of readiness on the part of the people to frequent mixed schools'.[6]

In 1870, the national school system had been operating for almost forty years, and patterns and trends in the way the system functioned had become well established. In that year, a Royal Commission of Inquiry reported on the operation and effectiveness of the system, including 'whether the children profit by the opportunities offered to them, and to what extent'.[7] The Royal Commission's report, together with the annual report of the Commissioners of National Education for that year, provide a window into the state of national schools at that time.

The patrons and managers of the national schools

In 1870, just a quarter of the national schools were vested in the Board of National Education, with the majority vested in local patrons, such as Catholic diocesan trustees or a local landlord. Catholic clergy made up the vast majority of Catholic school patrons, with 1,150 clerical patrons, as compared to just 203 lay patrons. In the Presbyterian schools the majority of patrons were also clerical, while in the Protestant schools the majority were lay patrons (Table 6.1). The denomination of the school patron also mirrored the denomination of the school manager and that of the majority of pupils enrolled.

Table 6.1 School patrons by denomination

Religious denomination	Clerical patrons	Lay patrons	Total of patrons	Total of schools
Roman Catholic	1,150 (85%)	203 (15%)	1353	4,487
Protestant	152 (34%)	294 (66%)	446	828
Presbyterian	318 (62%)	193 (38%)	511	805

At that time, the Catholic Church had become dominant in the lives of the majority Catholic population, aligning itself with local and national causes like tenants' rights and land reform. As the managers of national schools, Catholic clergy had the power to recruit their own teachers, and in this way, controlled and influenced the lives of the children and their parents through schooling.[8] As a rule, Catholic school managers did not appoint Protestant teachers and the Church Education Society similarly recruited only Protestant teachers in their schools. Hence, with some exceptions, especially in Ulster, the national school system had become increasingly parochially organised, denominationally segregated and clerically managed.[9]

Published in 1870, the Royal Commission of Inquiry into Primary Education in Ireland (known as the Powis Commission) listed 8,618 schools in Ireland for the year 1868.[10] Of this number, 6,520 were national schools connected with the Board of National Education; this included 133 convent schools, eighty monastery schools and 690 private schools.[11] The Church

Education Society supported 1,266 schools that were not connected with the Board. The average attendance in all the Society's schools was just twenty-seven, while that of the state national schools was approximately sixty.[12] Reflecting their growing presence in the national school system, the convent and monastery schools had the highest average pupil attendance figures; in the convent schools it was 243.5 and in the monastery schools it was 240.

The Commissioners of National Education reported that almost one million children were on the rolls of the national schools in 1870.[13] The majority of national schools connected with the Board had between fifty and 100 pupils on their rolls. Roman Catholics made up 81 per cent of all the pupils enrolled in the schools, while approximately 7 per cent were Protestant and 11 per cent were Presbyterian and mainly in Ulster.

The Church Education Society
As the Established Church, the Church of Ireland had long held a privileged position, since Church law was state law in areas like marriage, and it was also influential in drafting legislation in areas like education.[14] However, this position was diminished when the Church opposed the state-supported national school system, and instead, established the Church Education Society to endow its own parochial schools. Its position and influence were further diminished when it was separated from the Church of England in 1869 and disestablished as the official state Church in Ireland in 1871.

After 1871, the future viability of Church Education Society schools was becoming precarious when the Powis Commission showed that pupil attainments in the Society's schools were, in most respects, inferior to those of the state national schools.[15] A census report of 1871 also showed that illiteracy levels had declined more rapidly among Catholic and Presbyterian children than among Protestant children and that the independent Protestant schools had fallen behind the state national schools in terms of educational standards.[16] Along with worsening finances, these reports added to the vulnerability of the Society; however, it remained steadfast in not cooperating with the Board of National Education.

In 1883, the Chief Secretary for Ireland, George Trevelyan, proposed the establishment of teacher training colleges under private management to be supported by the state, and after much internal debate, in 1884 the Church of Ireland agreed to accept state funding to support its own denominational training college. The college was established at Kildare Place in Dublin and the model school associated with the college became a national school. This meant that the Church of Ireland had finally permitted its schools to be connected with the Board, a relationship it had resisted for over fifty years. The

Church Education Society disclaimed all connections with the new college at Kildare Place, and the Society's future role was confined to supporting poorer Protestant schools.[17]

Schoolhouses

The Powis Commission reported on the circumstances, condition and upkeep of schoolhouses, noting that sites on which the national schools were built were well-chosen in the majority of cases. Additionally, schoolhouses connected with the Board of National Education were of a better quality than those not connected. The majority of the schools were conducted in buildings with a slated roof, and in most schools, the roof, walls and windows were reported to be in good repair. However, in some schools that were locally-vested in church or other patrons, the state of repair of the roof was bad. Additionally, in the non-vested schools over which the Board had very little real control, up to a quarter were conducted in schoolhouses with a thatched roof, and in a great many of these schools, the roof was in bad repair.

In the schools connected with the Board, the floors of most of the school-rooms were constructed of wooden boards, although some had earthen floors, and in schools not connected with the Board, over one-fifth had an earthen floor. The Powis Commission wrote that 'such schools must be very cold in winter, and the health of children remaining for several hours, without much motion, many being bare-footed, must in the end suffer'; it added:

A cold earthen floor, very often undrained, by keeping the air of the school-room nearly always saturated with watery vapour, which absorbs the heat, exerts a very depressing effect on the teacher and children [...] This is no doubt, one of the causes which help to produce irregularity of attendance, especially of young children.[18]

While pictorial charts were 'an important means of instruction', over half of the schools had no charts on the walls of their schoolrooms and about one-tenth had no maps on display.

In the national schools the outdoor lavatories were referred to as 'out-offices', and the Powis Commission reported on the number of out-offices and their condition 'as to drainage'. Almost 90 per cent of the schools had out-offices 'of a suitable character' and over half were reported to be in a good state of repair and properly drained. However, in over a thousand non-vested schools there were no out-offices. In District 18 in north Co. Monaghan, the district inspector, Mr Eardley, wrote that 'in more than half the schools there are either no out-offices, or they are kept in such a filthy state that their removal would be less objectionable than their continuance'.[19] He also complained that many farmers were reluctant to provide a site to erect a school-house, for fear that the scholars would do 'serious injury' to crops and fences.

J.G. Fleming Esq. was the head inspector for national schools in Belfast and parts of counties Antrim, Down, Armagh and north Monaghan. He wrote of how gratifying it was to know that 'several excellent schoolhouses have been built within the past few years in places where they were much wanted', and he reported that the schoolhouses in his district were, in general, 'commodious, well lighted, and sufficiently ventilated [and] amply supplied with books, stationery, and maps'.[20] However, Fleming also remarked on the very poor condition of some schools in his district:

> Some ten or twelve of the 124 school-houses which I visited during the past twelve months were, from one cause or another, unsuitable for educational purposes. In one of these cases the manager has refused to take any steps to have the defects, so frequently brought under his notice, remedied, or even mitigated. In consequence of this neglect, the teacher who had charge of the school to which I now refer, has been obliged to resign from ill-health. And no wonder – her small, badly-ventilated school was usually so over-crowded with children, that the air which she was obliged to inhale during many hours of the day soon became, from its foulness, very oppressive and unhealthy. This, I am bound to state, is a most exceptional case.[21]

Another head inspector, Mr Patterson, remarked that school buildings were of a better class than 'the former hovels' that were in every way unfit for school purposes, and in some districts, improvements were going forward rapidly. Other inspectors also reported that unsuitable school buildings were gradually disappearing and being replaced with better schoolhouses.

Teachers

In 1870, there were 8,678 teachers in the state-supported national schools; almost three-quarters were principal teachers, and the remainder were assistants. Two-thirds of the principal teachers were male, and one-third were female. Most principal teachers were under forty years, with males generally older than females, and most of the male and female assistant teachers were aged under thirty years. About half of the principal male teachers and a third of the principal female teachers were married.

The religious denomination of the teachers and assistant teachers generally reflected the distribution of Catholics, Protestants and Presbyterians in the population of Ireland at that time; hence, the majority were Catholic.[22] However, while Protestants made up about 12 per cent of the population of Ire-

land, just 6 per cent of teachers were Protestant. The Powis Commission explained that this was likely due to the fact that, when Protestant landlords
provided a schoolhouse for their tenants, they kept the patronage in their own
hands, but frequently appointed Catholic teachers when their tenants were
Catholic. Additionally, many Protestant teachers were employed in Church
Education Society schools and their numbers were therefore not included in
the annual reports of the Commissioners of National Education.

Not adequately provided for
Mr A. Purser, the Chief Inspector, described teachers' circumstances in 1871,
as follows:

> Teachers were for the most part very poorly qualified for their posi-
> tion, and indeed it was no wonder that persons of fair education de-
> clined to enter the Board's service, considering the miserable salaries
> paid, especially those of the lower grades.[23]

In that year there were 1,332 teacher vacancies. Most of these resulted
from teachers moving from one school to another or from teachers leaving
teaching to take up another occupation or emigrate. About a tenth of vacancies were the result of teacher dismissals for incompetence, breaches of
rules or misconduct.

Teachers' salaries were based on a ranking system of three grades or 'classes'
of teacher and according to whether the teacher was male or female. In addition to the salary paid by the Board of National Education, teachers' income
was also supplemented from local sources, such as parents. The annual salary
of a fully trained male teacher was £53, and school fees from local donations
could add another £10 or £12. A female teacher's salary at the same class
was £42, and they too could earn up to £10 or more from school fees. The
annual salary of probationer teachers was £15.

Teachers' salaries could be half that of assistants in drapers and other shops,
less than one third that of the constabulary and of clerks in mills and distil-
leries, and little more than the pay of railway porters. District inspectors believed that poor pay placed teachers below the social position that they should
occupy, and they urged the Commissioners to increase teachers' salaries.

Mr P.T. Macaulay, a district inspector in Co. Donegal, wrote of the 'para-
mount importance of increasing the salaries of those meritorious public servants', so as to reflect 'the important duties they were bound to discharge'. To
emphasise his point, he wrote somewhat rhetorically:

> What energy or hearty goodwill can a poor teacher bring to the dis-

charge of his duties in a school, who leaves his wife and family in a wretched cabin, shivering with cold, and enduring, as I know them to do, the gnawing pains of hunger, and when his 'weary task is done', returns to find them worse than when he left, without fire and without food.[24]

Macaulay was no less rhetorical when describing the poor circumstances of underpaid female teachers:

Or with what vigour of mind and body will a poor female [teacher] enter her daily task, who, poorly and thinly clad, comes dripping with rain or covered with frozen snow, exhausted and footsore after a journey of miles, into a cheerless and uncomfortable school-room on a dark December morning, without a fire or dry garment, or a face to welcome her, condemned to remain for hours shivering with cold on a damp earthen floor, and doomed to bear away to her miserable home the seeds of disease, perhaps of death.[25]

While Macaulay's heart-rending descriptions of conditions were, no doubt, sincere, it is unlikely that these same conditions were experienced by all schoolteachers. Nevertheless, the high number of teacher vacancies suggests that teaching was not an attractive career, especially for young men.

In 1870, Mr A.J. Simpson was the district inspector for District 24, which included the national schools in south Co. Monaghan and parts of Cavan and Meath. He wrote of the problem of securing teachers in the rural schools in his district, writing that since there were few endowments and no school fees, the teachers' only source of income was the state salary. This meant that the schoolteachers were 'not adequately provided for in the present, nor have they generally any resources in case of sickness or old age'.[26] Simpson remarked that young men were unlikely to take up teaching when better earnings could be secured elsewhere, serving as artisans or shop helps. He wrote that a good pension was also necessary to attract men into teaching, to prevent teachers from 'drifting off to other services or emigrating' and to ensure that they had adequate provision for their retirement.[27] Some district inspectors believed that the solution to securing better pay for teachers rested with the local community, through taxation of ratepayers and landed proprietors.

J.G. Fleming, the head inspector in Belfast, also commented on the fact that many male teachers had emigrated to Australia and New Zealand, where they had successful teaching careers. He wrote of the difficulty in inducing 'smart intelligent lads' to become teachers, since they would not undertake 'the tedious, drudgery of the school-room'.[28] Fleming described the situation where school managers were obliged to appoint young men as probationary teachers, but who 'owing to their imperfect education', failed to pass their first or even second teacher examinations. Despite this, the young men who presented themselves for the teacher examinations impressed him with their good conduct, demeanour and appearance, qualities which, he believed, should be expected for 'the efficient discharge of responsible and important duties'.

Mr MacSheehy, the district inspector in Co. Wicklow, warned that schools were declining in efficiency as a result of discontent among teachers and he suggested that young men were likely to find 'little attraction' in teaching: 'It is a post too subordinate, a life too monotonous, too closely restricted and too carefully watched to be other than distasteful to the aspiring and rather restless youth of the present and coming time.'[29]

Another major impediment to men entering teaching was that their tenure was not secure, and a teacher could be dismissed without much notice or cause. A more practical concern was that, in some rural districts, teachers could find it hard to secure suitable lodgings close to their school. For example, a teacher in Co. Meath who could not find lodgings near his school at Kiltale was obliged to walk the six miles from Trim. This daily round journey of twelve miles during the winter months had such a depressing effect on him that he resigned after seven months. His replacement fared no better and resigned after just one week, having 'lost his reason'.[30]

Female teachers
There was a good supply of female teachers at that time, and securing female teachers was related to the fact that their services were cheaper, and there were other factors too, as Mr MacSheehy wrote:

> Girls are steadier for their age and are found to be more amenable to the control of school managers. Further – a point of no slight significance – if their relatives do not live near the school, they can find lodgings in the neighbourhood far more readily than men could.[31]

However, some district inspectors held biased views on the suitability of female teachers to teach boys, and many inspectors wrote of the importance of having male teachers in mixed boys' and girls' schools. Additionally, some believed that male teachers achieved better results in arithmetic than females, and one inspector attributed female teachers' supposed inability to get good results in reading to their tendency, when reading to pupils, to 'lisp, and keep their teeth closed, rendering it difficult to catch the sense or meaning of the words which they strive to utter'.[32] Such assumptions concerning women's intelligence and capabilities were common among men in nineteenth-century educational discourse. However, many inspectors considered females to be as efficient as males, with one inspector writing that 'good female teachers are more useful than bad male teachers'.

Where teacher appointments were based solely on their proximity to the school and not on the teacher's ability or experience, this could have a detrimental effect on the pupils' learning. One district inspector, Mr Roantree in Co. Cavan, complained of 'the spirit of clannishness' which existed in relation to teacher appointments, writing that the inhabitants of each parish regarded 'as parochial property' the teacher positions that became vacant in their parish schools. He described a case in which the fathers of four or five female assistant teachers, whose daughters were overlooked for a position in favour of a 'stranger' from an adjoining parish, called to the school manager, their own clergyman, and threatened to pull down the schoolhouse. Some positions remained vacant because parishioners had put forward candidates who were deemed incompetent and not appointable.[33]

Teachers' training
Reporting in 1870, the Powis Commission wrote that 'the progress of the children in the national schools of Ireland is very much less than it ought to be', due to the fact that just one-third of teachers had received formal training.[34] The Commission wrote that professional training and competence to teach were essential:

> Piety and devotion are admirable qualifications for guiding the minds of young people in the highest aspect of education, but do not make up for the want of professional training, and of technical instruction in the art of teaching [...] It is necessary that the teachers in all schools which are supported from public funds should be competent secular teachers. We recommend that all teachers, religious as well as lay, should give proof of their competence to teach before they are entitled to class salary.[35]

The Commission recommended that all teachers should have a period of twelve months' training before taking up an appointment in a national school and that trainee teachers should no longer be recognised as principal teachers. It also recommended that the state should support denominational teacher training colleges, and that the model schools should be phased out in the training of teachers. After 1883, teacher training was extended from one to two years in the state-supported denominational colleges.[36]

To ensure greater efficiency and value for money, the Commission also recommended a system of payment by results, in order to 'secure a better return for the outlay and labour in the National system', and to achieve this, it recommended that 'each teacher, besides a fixed class-salary, should receive an addition according to the number of children whom the Inspector, after individual examination, can pass as having made satisfactory progress during the year'.[37] The recommended payment-by-results scheme was introduced some years later in 1879 and remained in place until 1924.[38]

'Tolerably fair': Pupils' proficiency

In the national school system, each district inspector was responsible for inspecting the teachers' competence and the pupils' proficiency in the school subjects.[39] District inspectors visited each school in their district and dedicated one visit each year to an examination of every pupil present, in as many of the subjects as time and circumstances permitted. At other visits, an inspector could, at his discretion, select classes and subjects for examination. Inspectors also conducted incidental visits that were designed to have 'a salutary influence on the conduct of the teachers, and on the discipline of the schools'.[40]

Where senior pupils only were examined, teachers tended to focus their teaching on these pupils, meaning that the junior pupils could receive less attention or be taught by monitors, who were not qualified as teachers. Mr Eardley, the district inspector in District 18 in north Co. Monaghan, explained:

There is an inclination on the part of the teacher to confine his instructions to the more advanced scholars, leaving the young children to the paid monitor, should there be one in the school, if not, to some of the senior pupils. A first-class teacher of nearly thirty years' standing told me 'he did not like to be wasting his time with the little children'.[41]

Eardley wrote that 'this absurd notion' was generally shared by teachers, although few would admit it.

In their annual reports to the Commissioners of National Education, district inspectors reported on the scholars' proficiency and progress in the main school subjects, including reading, arithmetic, penmanship, grammar, geography, and in the 'extra branches', such as singing, drawing and sewing. When reporting on the scholars' proficiency, inspectors also reported on the teacher's ability, commenting on the quality of instruction or the time given to instruction in the various subjects.

Reading

Many teachers considered reading to be the most important subject, and it therefore tended to receive the most attention. When examining reading, inspectors looked for proficiency in the quality of expression, the way that pupils pronounced and grouped words, the pace of reading, the spelling of words and the pupils' understanding of what they were reading. Some inspectors also mentioned the peculiarities of local 'coarse' accents, which could interfere with the correct pronunciation of words.

Children themselves liked reading, especially when they were making progress, although the presence of the district inspector could make them nervous and affect their performance. One inspector wrote that a serious impediment to good reading was that some children spoke and read 'in a low and timid voice'. Another observed that the pupils did not 'speak out with sufficient fullness and freedom'. When reading aloud, children, especially the boys, also tended to read in a higher pitched voice than in normal conversation. Reporting on reading proficiency in schools in Co. Donegal, the district inspector, Mr Macauley, commented that, 'with rare exceptions, all read too fast, and in a tone which is monotonous and unintelligible'.

Not all inspectors found poor reading proficiency. In Co. Derry, Mr Duggan reported that 'the general character of the reading shows a decided improvement in clearness of articulation and in expression', which he attributed to care in teaching and excellent textbooks. Mr Bole in Coleraine also found a 'marked and gratifying improvement' in reading, where 'the monotonous drawl' had disappeared. In Co. Monaghan, Mr Eardley observed some steady improvement in reading, as did Mr Simpson in Co. Cavan where, although rough and with local mispronunciation, the reading was 'intelligible and intelligent'.

Inspectors recommended that more time be devoted to reading and to explaining the meaning of phrases, and that schools should be provided with school libraries. On the quality of the teaching of reading, one inspector observed: 'I fear that most of the teachers *listen* to their scholars while reading, few *teach* them to read.'[42]

Grammar

In grammar, inspectors examined pupils in the parts of speech and their ability to understand a sentence and its parts. Similar to reading, pupils' lack of proficiency was attributed to irregular school attendance, to 'unskilfulness' in teaching and to the time and attention given to the subject. Some inspectors suggested remedies to improve grammar, including 'continual watchfulness' by the teacher and getting the pupils to 'speak grammatically while in school'.

While some inspectors reported good results in grammar, most reported poor proficiency, one writing that many pupils leave school with 'very little useful knowledge of grammar'. Inspectors attributed poor proficiency in grammar to the pupils' use of language at home, where incorrect language in their ordinary conversations had 'a pernicious effect of undoing in the evenings and mornings, what the teacher does during the day'. Mr Wood, a district inspector in Co. Sligo, was so disheartened at the very poor results in his district, where fewer than 10 per cent of the pupils knew the basic parts of speech, that he suggested that grammar should no longer be taught:

> The policy of appropriating any portion of school-hours to instruction in grammar becomes doubtful, and the question suggests itself, would not the time wasted in vainly trying to teach a useless and unattractive subject be better devoted to increasing the amount of instruction in the essential subjects of reading, writing and arithmetic?[43]

Other inspectors shared this view, one commenting that 'the teaching of grammar was a great source of loss of time and neglect of the junior classes'.

Arithmetic
In arithmetic, pupils were examined in their proficiency in simple and compound rules and notation, and in tasks like addition, subtraction, division and proportions. Some inspectors believed that the junior classes should be instructed in the addition tables, so that they could do simple mental arithmetic, and that arithmetic should be skilfully taught, with the teacher making good use of the blackboard. Some schools taught the rules of arithmetic, while others taught practical and mental arithmetic. One inspector wrote that arithmetic was 'of great importance to farmers' children, who attend the national schools in large numbers, [and] should be able to calculate the price of corn as well as the rent of land and the price of butter'.

Mr Kennedy, the district inspector in Co. Tyrone, believed that poor and irregular attendance, particularly by the senior pupils who were seldom in school for more than three or four months of the year, resulted in poor proficiency in the more advanced rules of arithmetic. Mr Morell in Belfast North reported that the 'pernicious practices' of copying and prompting in some schools meant that it was difficult to obtain an accurate record of pupils' proficiency in arithmetic. Copying and prompting was seen in other districts too; in Co. Longford, Mr Bradford wrote: 'Copying and prompting are practiced in too many schools, to the great injury of the pupils, both in the acquisition of arithmetic and the formation of their future character.'[44]

Some inspectors reported improved proficiency in arithmetic, including in 'the more elementary rules'. Mr Nesbit in Co. Galway wrote that 'the more advanced pupils can work questions in practice and [...] explain the principles'.[45] However, most inspectors reported deficiencies in arithmetic, such as lack of knowledge of the basic rules and lack of accuracy in completing tasks. Inspectors held the teacher responsible for poor proficiency, due to not giving sufficient time to the subject. One inspector compared female teachers unfavourably to males in the teaching of arithmetic, with the following generalisation:

> The proficiency in this subject is very different in different schools; in almost all the larger schools, which are under male teachers, it is unquestionably good but in the smaller schools, and especially in such as under female teachers, it is very unsatisfactory.[46]

Penmanship
Examining pupils in penmanship involved inspecting the legibility and elegance of handwriting and the general appearance of the writing, such as the size of the letters, the spacing of the words, and the care and neatness of copybooks. Practice at writing was seen as very important since it 'educates the eye and the hand, and is, moreover, a most interesting occupation for these little ones, with whom school-time hangs so weary'. Inspectors considered that children themselves took pleasure in writing and in seeing their own improvement. Many inspectors reported satisfactory proficiency in penmanship, commenting on the care of copy-books, the neatness of the writing and on the satisfactory progress shown. However, several inspectors found good handwriting in only a few of the schools that they inspected, which resulted from 'want of careful and constant supervision'.

An adequate supply of copy-books with engraved lines, pens and good quality ink were seen as essential to the teaching of penmanship. The ink supplied by the Board of National Education was described as 'of a very inferior quality, [being] thin, watery, and of the faintest shade of black'. One inspector wrote that good handwriting should be taught by example, using the blackboard and 'actively superintending' the pupils while they copied from it.

Geography
In geography the pupils learned definitions of terms used in the subject, the location of countries on maps, and the names of seas, rivers, mountains and so forth. Like other subjects, inspectors reported mixed results, with some stating that there had been 'a marked improvement' in knowledge of the subject and others reporting 'decidedly low' proficiency. The lack of knowledge

in the subject resulted from poor teaching and the poor quality of the maps. One inspector complained that geography was 'worse than ludicrous, because it directs the pupils from useful pursuits', and there were reports that some parents saw geography as a waste of time and were opposed to their children learning the subject.

Needlework

In 1870, needlework was taught in all districts, and it was exclusively taught to the female scholars by female teachers, who were themselves examined in needlework before they could teach it. In some schools, junior assistants, monitresses and workmistresses taught needlework. Girls from the age of seven were taught stitching, hemming, button-hole work, plain sewing and knitting, and the more senior classes were taught 'fancy work', embroidery and ornamental knitting. Pupils were required to prepare samples of their needlework for inspection as to the quality and neatness of the work.

Out of economic necessity, girls also developed proficiency in sewing and other needlework at home. While inspectors generally reported good proficiency and progress in this subject, some reported unsatisfactory results. Poor school attendance, poor teaching or the lack of sewing materials were seen as the main causes of poor results. Some teachers complained that cotton material and wool yarn were too expensive.

'Other branches': Singing and agriculture

Inspectors also examined pupils in singing and drawing; however, these subjects were taught in the minority of national schools in 1870. Inspectors' reports on pupils' proficiency were generally confined to a few words and phrases like 'average', 'good', 'generally fair' and 'tolerably fair'. At the Ballymena district model school, the head inspector, Mr Fleming, was impressed with the pupils' singing, writing: 'the little ones [...] sang several appropriate airs with great taste and sweetness'. Fleming was likewise impressed with the singing at the Monaghan model school, where the children sang 'sweetly and correctly'.

In national schools where agriculture was taught, boys from third class upwards took 'simple' indoor lessons, learning a blend of simple science and practical knowledge about agriculture, including the rotation of crops, the manures to apply and the feeding of cattle and pigs. These schools used a dedicated textbook, entitled *Agricultural Class Book*, which the Board of National Education supplied. Mr T. Baldwin was the Superintendent of the Agricultural Department at the Board, and he conducted inspections of the schools where agriculture was taught. Describing the method of instruction in the ordinary national schools that gave lessons in agriculture, Baldwin wrote rather condescendingly:

It would look like mocking poor and ignorant farmers in remote districts of Ireland to begin their agricultural instruction with chemistry or botany. It is more useful to show them how to raise turnips than to give them a philosophic exposition of Liebig's theories.[47]

In addition to teaching methods, Baldwin's reports tended to focus on the management of the land and crops. Reporting on the Broomfield agricultural school on the Bath Estate in Co. Monaghan, he wrote:

Broomfield School, near Castleblaney, County Monaghan. Visited on 2nd July 1870. The turnip crop was badly sown, being in a zig-zag line on the drills. This crop as well as the potato contained too many weeds. The field of permanent grass was also weedy, and it contained several heaps of stones which ought to have been removed after they were collected.[48]

At Cormeen near Monaghan town, five boys in the agricultural class presented for examination and their answering was reported to be 'indifferent'. The school farm consisted of seven statute acres close to Lord Rossmore's demesne, and in his report, Baldwin wrote that there was no systematic crop rotation yet established but was being considered, and the management of the manure was very bad.

School attendance
In 1870, the average daily attendance for all the schools nationally was 359,199, or just over one third of the approximately one million pupils enrolled. Attendance nationally could be as low as one quarter of all pupils enrolled, with attendance in Connaught being exceptionally low.[49] School attendance was influenced by various factors, such as distance to travel to school, outbreaks of fevers, teacher absence, or more often, the demand for labour on the family farm.

Both the schoolteachers and the district inspectors believed that poor and irregular attendance were part of the reason for poor pupil proficiency in school subjects, and attendance was, in turn, related to the demands of the home economy, including the labours of spring and harvest. One district inspector, Mr Hamilton in Co. Donegal, described the irregular pattern of daily school attendance, which left little time for actual teaching:

In the majority of schools, the time devoted to instruction is nom-
inally from ten to three o'clock, but in very many schools not more
than two and a half or three hours each day are actually given to instruction. The teacher, perhaps, reaches the school after ten o'clock;
then the pupils begin to drop in. By the time they all assemble, twelve
o'clock, the hour for marking the rolls, has nearly reached; and the
calling of the rolls is often followed by a cessation of business (if business has been begun) for an interval of fifteen to thirty minutes.
Under such circumstances, how can favourable results be expected?[50]

Mr Kennedy, a district inspector in Co. Tyrone, described how, in the winter
months, the schools were full, but during the spring, autumn and summer
months, they were 'almost deserted'. He also commented that there was a
strong temptation among teachers to mark pupils present when they were
absent. Another inspector, Mr Irvine in Co. Derry, reported that many
teachers were in the habit of closing their schools for weeks at a time when
attendance was very low, so as to keep up the average attendance. This happened at potato harvest time when many schools were closed for a whole
month. Most district inspectors believed that attendance could be improved;
however, some cautioned that compulsory attendance was not the answer, as
it could be 'unjust and oppressive'.

7

'A school is very much required here': Coolfore national school, 1872–1912

On 10 February 1872, twenty years after Coolfore national school was closed on the order of Evelyn J. Shirley, the Commissioners of National Education received an application 'for aid towards payment of teacher's salary and for supply of books, &c.' in respect of a school at Coolfore.[1] At that time, Evelyn Philip (E.P.) Shirley was the landlord at Lough Fea House, having succeeded his father in 1856. John Thomas Holland Esq. of Belle Vue, Carrickmacross, who was Shirley's agent, prepared and signed the application, in which Shirley was the named school patron and Holland was the named school manager and correspondent.

In the application for aid, Mr Holland gave details of the schoolhouse, the teachers' names and ages and the average daily attendance of the pupils. He also confirmed that the school complied with the rules of the Board of National Education, which was a requirement for all schools seeking grant aid. This included a declaration that the school hours were from 9.30 a.m. to 3 p.m., that religious instruction was given separately from 2.30 p.m. to 3 p.m. and that visitors of all denominations had free access to the school.

Mr A.J. Simpson was the district inspector for District 24, which included the parish of Magheross. In line with the standard procedure, he visited the school and made a report on the application to the Commissioners.[2] In his report, Mr Simpson gave details of the school and its location, and he commented on the merits of the application. He noted that the school was established on 1 January 1872. The schoolhouse was located two and a half miles distant from Carrickmacross, and in addition to the schools in Carrickmacross, the nearest rural schools were at Corduff, Lisdoonan and Corvally, each three miles distant. There were 'at least forty houses' within a circuit of a half mile from the schoolhouse.

Having communicated in writing with the clergymen of the different denominations in the area, Mr Simpson received no objections to the application for aid for the new school. Nor were there any objections from the residents of the district. The school was not connected with any other society at the time, and in his report, Mr Simpson declared that the school was not previously connected with the Board of National Education. It is possible that, as the district inspector, Simpson was unaware that a previous school at Coolfore had been connected with the Board between 1845 and 1852. However, as Shirley's agent, it is probable that Mr Holland was aware of it. Since E.P. Shirley provided the funds to erect the new schoolhouse, which was completed in 1871, his likely intention was to distinguish the new school from the former school that was under Catholic patronage and struck off at his father's behest in 1852. Moreover, the former schoolhouse, which at the time was in a rented thatched house, was located on a different site on the opposite side of the road from the new schoolhouse.

Everything favourable

The schoolhouse at Coolfore was located on a 'by-road between the old and the new Carrick to Ballybay road', and in his report, Mr Simpson described the schoolhouse as 'quite new'.[3] Nestled in rolling drumlins, it was located at a bend in the road and beside a small river over which there was a little stone bridge. A slated stone house, it was constructed on an elevated site close to the road. The building contained a single schoolroom, which was located in the upstairs part of the schoolhouse and was described as warm and well ventilated. The interior walls of the schoolroom were plastered, the ceiling was coved, the floor was boarded, and it had a fireplace. The downstairs portion of the schoolhouse, which was not in communication with the schoolroom, was occupied by the schoolmaster.

The schoolroom consisted of a teacher's table and chair, seven desks and thirteen forms or benches. There were two sets of open shelves and a drawer for storing school materials. While there was no blackboard and no clock, there were racks to suspend the school timetables. In his application for aid, Mr Holland gave a detailed description of the schoolhouse and its circumstances:

The nearest post town is Carrickmacross in the County of Monaghan and is distant two miles from the School in a south-easterly direction. The house is of two stories and is newly built. It stands in about ½ an acre of ground, on a slight elevation above the road. It is in the clear 30 ft by 16 ft. It contains on the ground floor one sitting room 11ft 3*in* by 16*ft* & in height 8*ft* 2*in* – one kitchen, same dimension – one bed-room 11ft by 6ft and in height 8ft 2in – entrance hall 6ft by 4ft. On first floor, one schoolroom with three windows on each side – &

a covered porch (4ft 6in square) approached by stone steps on outside of gable – coal closet under steps – Two privies in one detached building in garden at side of house.

There is one schoolroom – 30*ft* in length by 16*ft* in width in the clear and 12*ft* in height – There are two open cupboards in the wall – one each side of fireplace.

The school furniture consists of seven desks with forms attached 9*ft* long (National Board pattern) – six single forms & a table and drawer & chair for master. Fixtures for maps are being made. There are cap and cloak racks in porch and school-room.[4]

The schoolbooks to be used were those supplied by the Board of National Education. Holland wrote that, while Mr Shirley had not yet fixed the amount of local aid, 'it will probably be the same as at Ballaghnagearn & Sreenty Schools (£10 a year)'.[5] Later in 1881, a dividing wall was erected in the out-offices, to create separate boys' and girls' privies.

The application to the Commissioners requested aid for the payment of salaries for two teachers, a principal teacher grade II, at £28 per annum and an assistant teacher grade III at £16 per annum. Then aged twenty-five, the principal teacher was James McBride, and he was appointed as a class II principal. The assistant teacher was Mary McBride, aged nineteen years and the sister of James. Both teachers were Roman Catholics and were appointed on 1 January 1872. Mr McBride had attended the model school at Bailieboro and was previously a junior monitor at Sreenty national school between 1863 and 1864; however, he was not a fully trained teacher.[6] In his report, Mr Simpson noted that he had known the two teachers for four years and was satisfied as to their fitness for the office. Both were previously employed at Laragh national school in the nearby parish of Aughnamullen and Mr Simpson declared they were 'well qualified [and] of good character' and their method of conducting a school was excellent.[7]

In addition to the salary requested from the Commissioners, the teachers' salaries would be supplemented by £10 per annum and an additional £15 per annum would be raised from the scholars. A number of scholars were admitted free gratis on the decision of the principal teacher. The teachers' lodgings at the schoolhouse were free.

In his report to the Commissioners, Mr Simpson confirmed that the school would follow the usual rules, such as the keeping of a register and records of attendance, and that books used would be those approved by the Board. The school was open to children of all denominations and the giving of religious instruction would not interfere with the 'secular business of the school'. Religious instruction was conducted on the last hour of each day for Roman Catholic children, and ordinary secular instruction was conducted from 10 a.m. to 2 p.m. each day and on Saturdays from 10 a.m. to 12 p.m.

Regarding the proportion of the population of the neighbourhood whose children were likely to attend the school, Mr Simpson confirmed that the local population was 'all of a class [likely] to avail themselves of a national school'. When the school first opened in January 1872, 179 pupils were enrolled, ninety-two boys and eighty-seven girls. Since the school had been opened for just two months, the average daily attendance was reported for January and February only and was 104 pupils, fifty-four boys and fifty girls. Regarding the grounds on which he should recommend the application to the Commissioners for aid, Mr Simpson concluded:

A school is very much required here. The Teachers are well qualified, the [school]house suitable and all the circumstances favourable. I have therefore to recommend that a full grant be made.[8]

Having considered the application and the district inspector's accompanying report, on 22 February, the Commissioners concluded: 'everything favourable [and] grant recommended', after which Coolfore school was officially connected with the Board of National Education in District 24. Master McBride's salary was £28, while that of Miss McBride was £16. The obligatory plaque was placed above the front door of the schoolhouse; written in old Gaelic script on a block of sandstone, it read: *Scoil Naisiúnta Cuíl Fuar Coolfore National School 1871.*[9]

In 1880, John T. Gibbings Esq. replaced Mr Holland as E.P. Shirley's agent and was the school manager of Coolfore. Two years later in 1882 when E.P. Shirley died, his son Sewallis Evelyn (S.E.) Shirley succeeded him and became the named school patron.

The schoolhouse

When Coolfore national school was connected with the Board of National Education in 1872, the national school system had become well established, and there were a dozen national schools in the parish of Magheross. The new schoolhouse at Coolfore was undoubtedly a welcome sight for the parents of the district, and their children could expect to find it no more than a mile and a half distant from their home. The school was much needed in the local area, as evidenced by the high number of pupils enrolled when it was first connected with the Board.

Bearing the inscription *Coolfore National School 1871* above the front door, the schoolhouse was a fine building in the locality. Funded by E.P. Shirley, it was a well-constructed, slated, two-storey house, with a well-proportioned façade of three bays with a centre gabled windbreak to the front and a chimney stack at each gable. Each window had cut-stone sills and sixteen panes in a casement rather than sash design, giving the schoolhouse a somewhat nuanced local expression that had echoes of the Tudor style adopted for other buildings on the Shirley estate earlier in the century.[10]

The schoolhouse was sturdily constructed with thick walls of rubble sandstone and rendered in a lime roughcast as weathering insulation. The building design and construction followed a common vernacular form, more widely used in rural dwellings but one that could easily be – and frequently was – adapted for schoolhouses.[11] External stone steps and a parapet wall were attached to one gable. These led to a separate entrance, projected in a small porch at the top of the steps, to the upstairs room, a design that enabled the separation of the classroom from the schoolmaster's downstairs' living quarters. This feature was evident in other similar two-storey schoolhouses, such as at Edgeworthstown in Co. Longford.[12]

Although there were some similar-sized farmhouse dwellings nearby at that time, when first erected in 1871, the new schoolhouse, with the underlying formality of its symmetry and proportions, must have appeared an imposing structure in the landscape, particularly as it stood on a raised site overlooking the road. In this situation, it was not unlike a modest parochial house or rectory, or a substantial farmhouse of the period.[13]

In addition to the new schoolhouse at Coolfore, E.P. Shirley also built two others on his estate, at Sreenty (1857/8) and at Ballynagearn (1862) in the parish of Magheracloone. All three schoolhouses were constructed according to the same vernacular form that was widely used for rural schoolhouses in the early years of the national school system, including several elsewhere in Co. Monaghan.[14] However, the two-storey schoolhouse design like that at Coolfore was much less common after 1856, when the OPW provided standard architectural drawings for all national school buildings that the Board funded.[15]

The new schoolhouse provided its pupils with a reasonably comfortable schoolroom in which to learn and a small playground in which to play. The school at Coolfore also provided a ready situation in which unclassed teachers and monitors could train and develop their teaching skills and prepare for their teacher examinations.

Teachers and monitors at Coolfore national school

The number of teachers, assistant teachers and monitors to be approved by the Commissioners of National Education in any school was based on the average pupil attendance at the school, as reported by the district inspector each year. Teachers and monitors were appointed by the school manager and the appointment was approved by the district inspector. An assistant teacher was only permitted when the average attendance was seventy pupils or more, and fifty was the minimum average pupil attendance before a monitor could be appointed. Where the average attendance fell, a school could lose an assistant teacher or workmistress.

After October 1872, a new grading system for teachers and monitors was introduced.[16] The three categories of schoolteacher were principal, assistant and junior assistant, and the salary was based on a teacher's grade or 'class' and whether employed as either first or second division in their class.[17] The annual salary for males ranged from £24 for assistant teacher to £50 for first class, first division, while for females it ranged from £20 for assistant to £42 for first class, first division. Previously known as 'probationers', teachers who had not yet been examined and duly qualified were 'unclassed teachers'.

Paid monitors were also categorised according to different classes, and their salaries reflected their class as well, ranging from £4 to £20. With satisfactory progress, a monitor could rise from a junior to a more senior rank and could progress to be a junior assistant or assistant teacher. Monitors were generally first appointed while in their teens and were selected from the most able and promising scholars in the district. On the recommendation of the district inspector, a monitor could go forward for examination as an assistant teacher. Female monitors were generally referred to as monitresses.

When Coolfore was first approved as a national school in 1872, the Commissioners approved two teachers' salaries, those of Master McBride, principal teacher, and Miss McBride, assistant teacher. Two years later, the Commissioners also approved the appointments of two paid monitors, Patrick Marron, aged sixteen, and Bridget Mee, aged fourteen.

With the exception of the small single-teacher Protestant school at Magheross in the town of Carrickmacross, none of the nine schools in the parish of Magheross received local aid, and hence, all of the teachers' salaries were made up exclusively from the state grant from the Board. However, teachers could receive additional payments in the form of gratuities for good results and for instructing monitors. For example, in 1876 Coolfore national school received £13 17s. 6d. in gratuities for results. In that same year Master McBride was paid a gratuity of £1 10s. for instructing Patrick Marron and Bridget Mee, and in 1878 he received a gratuity of £1 for instructing the monitress Mary Keenan. When traveling to examination centres, teachers and monitors were also paid a travel allowance at a rate of 2½d. per mile and a lodging allowance. For example, when Patrick Marron was a monitor in

1879, he was paid 10s. 5d. for traveling to Bailieboro for the teachers' examination.

James and Mary McBride
James and Mary McBride, the first teachers to be appointed to Coolfore in 1872, continued to teach there for about ten years. While they were reported to be 'well qualified', they had not completed the full teacher training course, and on that basis, Master McBride was a teacher second class, first division, and Miss McBride was assistant teacher second class, second division. In 1877, the McBrides were called to take the Board's examinations for teachers; however, both absented themselves from the examination, advising the district inspector that they were 'not prepared'. Despite this, in 1879 Master McBride was promoted to first class, division one, the highest grade.

Later, in January 1882 the Commissioners ordered that Miss McBride's salary be withdrawn, effective from 31 December 1881, since the average attendance was 'insufficient to warrant its continuance'. A year later in January 1883, Mr Gibbings, the school manager, advised the Commissioners that James McBride had left for America on the previous day. While his resignation was dated 31 December 1882, Master McBride had taught up until 27 January 1883, just two days before his departure.[18]

From his address in Braddock, Pennsylvania, McBride wrote to both Mr Gibbings and the Commissioners requesting payment of outstanding salary due to him for the month of January. However, Mr Gibbings was unsympathetic and advised the Commissioners that Mr McBride 'went away suddenly to suit his own convenience'. Mr McBride wrote on a number of occasions seeking payment; however, the matter was concluded when, in May 1883, the Commissioners advised him that, since the school manager declined to certify him as teacher beyond 31 December 1882, they too could not recognise him beyond that date. Mr Gibbings' refusal to support McBride's request for payment of outstanding salary seems vindictive and arbitrary. The reason for Mr McBride's decision to leave Coolfore school so abruptly and emigrate is not clear. While the district inspector's reports recorded his character and that of the school as satisfactory, the loss of the grant for his sister, the assistant teacher, may have been a factor.

Master Patrick Marron
In 1876, when Patrick Marron was a monitor, second class, he went forward for the monitors' examination, but was deemed to have been unsuccessful and could not be promoted to monitor, first class. The Commissioners advised Mr Cowley, the then district inspector, that a recommendation for promotion

could not be acted upon 'until there was evidence that he had improved in the branches in which he failed at the oral examination'.[19] However, in February of the following year, Mr Marron was successful in the examinations and was promoted. Later in 1879, he completed the one-year teacher training course at the Central Training College at Marlborough Street in Dublin.[20] Family records show that Mr Marron taught at Ballynagearn national school in Magheracloone parish from July 1881 to March 1883.[21]

After Master McBride left Coolfore national school in 1883, Mr Marron was appointed as the school principal. Then in his mid-twenties, his appointment was at the grade of second class, second division, and five years later in 1888, he was promoted to first class, second division. In 1891, Master Marron took the teacher examinations and passed management, electricity and mechanics, but was unsuccessful in hydrostatics and hydraulics. Later in 1904, the Commissioners advised the school manger that Master Marron could not be promoted beyond his present grade, so long as the average pupil attendance remained below seventy.

Other teachers and monitors at Coolfore
Brigid Mee remained as a monitress until February 1877 and her replacement was Mary Keenan, then aged thirteen. Other monitors subsequently appointed included Owen Marron in 1884 and James Callan in 1886. Owen Marron was successful in the monitor examination in 1887 and in the following year was promoted as monitor, second class. In 1896 Kate Daly was appointed monitress and remained in the post until 1901, when she was replaced by Mary Brennan. Miss Brennan was, in turn, replaced as monitress by Annie Marron in 1906, and she remained at Coolfore until 1911, when she transferred to Sreenty national school.

Other monitors to be appointed included Mary McEnaney and John Marron; both were appointed in 1891. Marron passed the Commissioners' examinations for teachers in 1896, and an article in the *Dundalk Democrat* noted his success, reporting: 'John Marron, Coolfore National School, Carrickmacross, passed his fifth year's examination in July last, scoring 80% on all the subjects of the third-class teachers' programme.'[22] Mr Marron left Coolfore national school in that same year and Commissioners' records in the National Archives show that in 1905, then aged twenty-nine, he was the principal teacher at Cloughfin national school near Lifford in Co. Donegal.[23] The history of Cloughfin records that in 1900 there were sixty-five children at the school under John Marron, and that he served as 'headmaster' in the school for twenty-eight years.[24]

The list of teachers in the service of the Commissioners in 1905 also included another Patrick Marron, then aged thirty-four years, who was edu-cated at Coolfore and was employed as the principal teacher at John-street monastery school in Co. Down. Marron completed teacher training at De La Salle College in Co. Waterford.[25] The fact that there were three school-masters named Marron and associated with Coolfore national school is un-remarkable, since there were multiple Marron families in the district.

In January 1890, Miss Mary Mullins was appointed assistant teacher on a salary of £27. Then aged twenty-one and a native of Co. Laois, she had under-taken teacher training at Damastown national school near Balbriggan in north Co. Dublin. After completing the one-year teacher training course at Our Lady of Mercy College in Dublin in 1894, she was awarded a 'first' in her examinations, and later in 1897, she obtained the Commissioners' Diploma for Teachers.[26] At around that time she married John Mee of Greaghnaroog and was thereafter listed as Mrs Mary Mee in the Commissioners' records.[27] Mrs Mee went on to give many long years of service as the assistant teacher at Coolfore.

The district inspector for District 24 visited Coolfore national school once a year and also made incidental visits, and his reports to the Commissioners generally included updates on the teachers' efficiency, the management and upkeep of the school and the pupils' proficiency in the subjects examined.[28] For example, in 1879, the report for Coolfore noted that the efficiency of the teacher was good, the accounts and school stock were satisfactory, the state of repair of the school was good and the Board's rules were being observed. In addition, the pupils' proficiency was recorded as being 'on the whole good'. In 1898 the district inspector admonished Master Marron for 'serious defects in proficiency, especially on neglect to instruct 6th class in Agriculture', and he also admonished an assistant monitor for late attendance.[29] Some years later in 1911, Mrs Mee was admonished 'for failure to comply with the rules' due to her being 'absent with no authority'.[30]

In its first four decades, the school had stability in having just two principal teachers, James McBride and his successor Patrick Marron. Although the Commissioners withdrew funding for the assistant teacher for a brief period, there was a ready supply of monitors and monitresses, further ensuring sta-bility for the school.

While the pupils were mainly Roman Catholic, the school was under the patronage of Shirley and under the management of his incumbent agent, both of whom were members of the Church of Ireland. Hence, formal communi-cations between the school and the local Catholic clergy were channelled through the school manager. While E.P. Shirley, his successors and their suc-cessive agents were members of the Church of Ireland, there is no evidence of proselytising on their part. Indeed, it is probable that the local Catholic clergy and Master Marron communicated regularly, and that the clergy visited the school for the purpose of cathectic instruction and to prepare children for the sacraments of First Communion and Confirmation.

The pupils

The annual report of the Commissioners of National Education for 1872 recorded 120 boys and 121 girls on the Coolfore school register.[31] Two years later, the Commissioners' annual report recorded sixty-five boys and fifty girls, with an average daily attendance of seventy-nine pupils.[32] The large fall in the number of pupils enrolled over the two-year period is unclear. As a schoolhouse with just a single schoolroom at the time, it did not have the capacity to accommodate large numbers of pupils. Additionally, it may be that several parents initially enrolled their children at the school when it first opened, but subsequently withdrew them in favour of an alternative school.

School records for the 1890s show that girls were generally younger than boys when commencing their schooling; the average age for girls was 4.7 years, while that of boys was 5.4 years. Most of the pupils were the sons and daughters of local farming families, with a small number recorded as the sons or daughters of labourers. With the exception of three Presbyterian pupils, all the pupils were Roman Catholic. The children were drawn from Coolfore and the adjacent townlands of Lisnaguiveragh, Greaghnaroog, Drumgowna, Drumbroagh, Greaghadromnisk and Peaste. Children also attended from several other nearby townlands, including Legghimore, Aghalile, Tiragarvan, Greaghdrumit, Beaghmagheross, Creevy, Lattylanigan and Killarue. The pupils' family names on the register included Agnew, Callan, Finnegan, Keenan, Malone, Mee, Marron, Murtagh, Nelson and Ward, names common in the district.

To comply with the Commissioners' rules, the school was expected to devote at least four hours each day to 'secular instruction' and the district inspector examined the pupils in reading, spelling, writing, arithmetic, grammar and geography. Boys were also examined in agriculture, while the girls were examined in needlework. The infant class was examined in reading only.

In the school year 1877–78, the district inspector examined seventy-six pupils at Coolfore.[33] By way of comparison, fifty-one pupils were examined at Sreenty, twenty-one at Corcreagh and 107 at Corduff male and female schools combined. These numbers indicate that, relative to most of the rural schools in the parish of Magheross, Coolfore was serving a large proportion of the population of schoolchildren in the parish. Initially constructed as a schoolhouse with a single upstairs schoolroom, the boys and girls at Coolfore were instructed together, and the numbers examined suggest that the children were taking their lessons in a very crowded space.

In 1902, while the average daily attendance was just fifty-nine pupils, the school register contained the names of 121 pupils, sixty-six boys and fifty-five girls.[34] Later in 1908, the Commissioners advised Mr William Pierce, who was then Shirley's agent and the school manager, of the need to provide additional accommodation for the large number of pupils at the school. At that time, Master Marron was residing in the nearby townland of Drumgowna. However, space remained limited until 1912, when the main downstairs' room was made available as a classroom. With the additional room, it was possible to introduce cookery classes for the female pupils. The change also resulted in additional cost in heating, and the Commissioners reminded Mr Pierce of his responsibility to 'make every school comfortable by having it properly furnished, lighted, cleaned, ventilated, and adequately heated in cold weather'. At that time, the teacher was responsible for part of the cost of heating the school, although this responsibility was later removed.

Scarlet fever
In the late nineteenth century before mass vaccinations were available, infectious diseases were common in the towns and cities. In 1889, the *Northern Standard* reported that the poor sanitary arrangements in Monaghan town, due to imperfect drains, had caused a scarlet fever epidemic that created 'widespread panic, filled the fever hospital and closed our schools'.[35] Infections and associated fevers were also common in rural national schools, and inevitably, infections spread quickly among the children in small, crowded schoolrooms. Virus illnesses like measles and mumps and bacterial infections like typhus and scarlet fever could result in several children being infected at the same time. Also known as scarlatina, scarlet fever was one of the commonest bacterial infections in children of school-going age; it presented with a fever, sore throat and a rash, and was associated with poor hygiene and unpasteurised milk.

Scarlet fever and measles were highly contagious and could be fatal, and for that reason, the public health response demanded that when an outbreak occurred in a school, the school should close. When there was an outbreak of scarlet fever in several schools in west Farney in 1875, the local sanitary authorities acted quickly and closed Coolfore national school and the schools of Corcreagh and Corduff. At the time, Coolfore school was closed from 11 May to 1 July, a period of about seven weeks, and as a result, the school holidays were dispensed with that year. Corcreagh national school was also closed that year for a period of three weeks, and like Coolfore, the school holidays were dispensed with.[36] At Corduff schools the district inspector's examinations planned in May were postponed until the end of the year.[37]

'A County Monaghan sensation'

In 1908, a number of national and regional newspapers reported on a shooting and its aftermath involving Master Patrick Marron.[38] *The Evening Herald* carried the report from its Carrickmacross correspondent, writing that 'a rather sensational shooting affair occurred in the neighbourhood of Coolfore' on the evening of Monday, 22 June. The report described the incident:

> Mr Patrick Marron, national teacher, was leaving his school after the day's course when he was shot by his brother Michael and is said to be at present in a precarious condition. It is understood that some dispute exists among the parties in reference to a farm of land. The injured man, who was attended by Dr McCaul, is held in much esteem in the district. His assailant has been placed under arrest.[39]

The Freeman's Journal reported that the incident happened 'at a place called Drumgowna' and that 'the extent of the unfortunate man's injuries is not known'. The *Journal* advised its readers that 'the injured man was treated by Dr M. McCaul, Carrickmacross, who found him suffered from an extensive gunshot wound'.[40] The affair had caused 'a widespread sensation in the locality', where 'great sympathy is felt for Mr Marron, whose teaching abilities and sociable qualities have won for him public respect and esteem'.[41]

Most newspapers that reported on the shooting used the phrase 'A County Monaghan sensation' in their banner headline.[42] *The Northern Standard* reported on the court hearing at Carrickmacross courthouse, which took place on the day after the shooting.[43] *The Standard* opened its report with a comment that both Patrick Marron and Michael Marron were married men and both were well known locally, and the reporter noted that 'the tragic event has occasioned widespread excitement in a most peaceable district'.

The details of the shooting were presented before the court. The main witness was Patrick Farrelly, an employee of Master Marron, and in his evidence, he said that he heard a shot and found Master Marron lying by a ditch on the roadside crying 'Paddy, he killed me!' Michael Marron was standing close by shouting angrily. The schoolmaster was surrounded by some of the schoolchildren, one of whom was his son Philip, who was crying 'My father is shot!' Other schoolchildren gave evidence to the court; Bridget Brennan witnessed the shooting and saw Michael strike his brother with the gun while he lay on the ground, while another pupil said that Michael called his brother 'a dirty old hound'. In court, Michael Marron refused to give evidence in his defence, declaring: 'I know nothing about it'.

Patrick Farrelly helped the schoolmaster to his home, all the while accompanied by Michael, who was described as being 'in a rage'. Although the victim of a serious assault, Master Marron declined to make a statement against his brother, saying instead that 'there were facts under the case which none of them knew anything about'. Some few days later, the *Irish Independent* carried a brief report that Patrick Marron's condition 'continues to improve'.[44]

Michael Marron was sent to Dundalk jail and later brought before a court in Belfast where he pleaded guilty to attempted murder.[45] At the hearing, evidence was given to suggest that Michael had been unwell and drinking at the time of the shooting and was 'brooding about a farm being given to his brother Bernard in America'. It appears that Patrick received compensation in the will, but Michael did not. In the event, the judge passed a sentence of twelve months in prison. At the Belfast court, it was reported that Master Marron had made a recovery but had lost the use of his right arm. He later returned to teaching at Coolfore.

The tragic affair of brother in conflict with brother shows how disputes over inheritance could be emotionally charged with feelings of anger and resentment, which could escalate into violence.[46] Land inheritance, in particular, had the power to generate strong emotions in Ireland, and the tragic events of June 1908 showed this to be especially true of a June afternoon in rural west Farney.

The shooting of Master Marron at Drumgowna in 1908 was a highly unusual event in the life of a rural farming community and its national school. Aside from the trauma of the gunshot wound to Master Marron, it is probable that some of the schoolchildren also experienced emotional trauma on witnessing the shooting. Michael Marron was also a victim of the tragedy insofar as his emotional response to a family inheritance resulted in his incarceration. Within a decade and a half, however, some members of the local community, including Patrick Marron's son Philip, would be bearing arms in the War of Independence and the Civil War that followed.[47]

8

Rural schools and their teachers in west Farney

The Commissioners of National Education maintained records on each national school. The records were based on district inspectors' annual reports, which included details of school attendance and pupils' levels of proficiency, and reports of teachers' competence and alleged transgressions of the rules by individual teachers. Reported transgressions included irregularities in school accounts or inaccurate recording of daily school attendance, and the records documented sanctions imposed on teachers for such transgressions.

Communications from the Commissioners to the district inspectors also included strict instructions on how they should oversee the schools in their respective districts. For example, in March 1855, the Commissioners issued a strongly-worded circular to the district inspectors, warning them that they should ensure that the teachers that they sent up for examination were adequately prepared.[1] Some communications also concerned matters that were not directly related to regular school business, but instead concerned the general conduct of teachers and their moral welfare. Hence, in 1871, the Commissioners communicated with Mr A. Simpson Esq., of District 24, about teachers at Bailieboro national school, writing: 'We have to inform you that the Commissioners disapprove of their teachers having any concern with a shop in which the sale of spiritous liquors is carried on.'[2]

Despite these restrictions, rural schoolteachers were an integral part of their local community, and they were expected to organise and participate in community events like concerts, local dances, and Gaelic sports. They were also expected to support and participate in religious events in their parish, such as First Communion, fund-raising concerts and other parochial activities.[3]

District inspectors' reports

The district inspectors' reports to the Commissioners provide evidence of the state of schools and schooling in their respective districts, and they also provide some information on the local circumstances of the people. During the 1880s, J.B. Skeffington was the district inspector for District 24, which included south Co. Monaghan. He reported on conditions that were 'very unfavourable to attendance at schools' in the years 1879 and 1880.[4] These conditions were due to the near-famine conditions that affected the rural poor in counties Monaghan and Cavan, when successive severe winters in 1877, 1878 and 1879 had resulted in crop failures and poor potato yields. The bad winter of 1879 and the following poor summer had resulted in 'general poverty and especial want of fuel and clothing' among the population.

Skeffington also reported that there were 'too many unsuitable or inferior schoolhouses, very many without proper out-offices, a large number but in-differently fitted out and furnished'.[5] He bemoaned the lack of attention to the upkeep of some schoolhouses and the supply of school materials. He also remarked on the difficulty in achieving high standards of instruction in small schools or where teachers were themselves of a low standard.

In 1881, Mr H. Worsley succeeded Mr Skeffington, and he too reported similar concerns to his predecessor regarding the upkeep of schoolhouses and schoolrooms, writing that 'in too many cases mending and whitewashing of walls and painting of woodwork had been neglected' and he declared that 'damp is a great enemy in this district'.[6] Worsley also commented on the very low level of training among the teachers in his district, where just one-third were trained.

These district inspectors' reports convey something of the state of the schools in District 24, which contained 135 schools, including the schools on the Shirley estate in rural west Farney. In the highly regulated system, the district inspectors maintained close supervision of the national schools, in particular, the pupils' proficiency, the quality of teaching and the general management and upkeep of the schools. It is unsurprising that the principal teacher should be subject to the closest scrutiny during inspection visits, and inspectors' annual reports tended to focus more on teachers' shortcomings and less on their teaching effectiveness.

Rural schools in west Farney in the parish of Magheross

Although E.J. Shirley granted leases on the chapel grounds at Corduff, Corcreagh, Lisdoonan and Magheracloone to the Board of National Education in 1841, it was not always possible for local trustees, who wished to build a schoolhouse, to secure suitable sites.[7] This difficulty was overcome when the

Schools' Act of 1881 provided the legal means by which suitable sites could be made available for the building of national schools. The Act enabled land-owners or their tenants to grant leases of ninety-nine years for the purpose of constructing a national school.

In addition to Coolfore national school, the children of west Farney could attend one of the other schools supported by E.J. Shirley; these were at Sreenty, which Shirley re-built in 1856, the Presbyterian school at Carrick-maclim and the Protestant school at Corvally, both of which were connected with the Board in the latter half of the nineteenth century. Other available schools were those in Carrickmacross town, and the rural schools at Corduff and Corcreagh and at Lisdoonan in the neighbouring parish of Donagh-moyne, all of which were connected with the Board.

Corduff male and female schools

During the 1830s, E.J. Shirley granted a plot of ground to build a sacristy be-side the thatched chapel at Corduff Mountain where schooling could be con-ducted.[8] The sacristy was the site of religious tensions when Shirley's agent Sandy Mitchell insisted that the children should read the Protestant Bible.[9] In response, as has been discussed in an earlier chapter, the Catholic Bishop of Clogher withdrew the children from Corduff school and the local people revolted, tearing down the sacristy, and in defiance of Mitchell, they con-structed a stone schoolhouse for the Catholic children on the chapel grounds. After Shirley granted the chapel grounds to the Board of National Education in 1841, the school at Corduff could operate without menaces from Mit-chell.[10]

The newly-erected school at Corduff Mountain was first approved as a national school in connection with the Board in 1840 and received grant aid of £127 1s. 4d.[11] The initial application for grant aid listed the Bishop of Clogher as the patron and Rev. Felix Keown, curate at Carrickmacross, as the school manager. The new schoolhouse was a two-storey building, with the male school on the ground floor and the female school on the upper floor. Built of stone and mortar with a slated roof and boarded floors, it measured forty-eight feet by twenty feet. Although new, the out-offices were of bad construction and in bad repair.

Approved as two separate schools, the male and female schools were each assigned a separate roll number.[12] Secular instruction was conducted on five days each week from 10 a.m. until 3 p.m., and religious instruction was con-ducted on Saturdays from 10 a.m. to 12 p.m. In 1845, there were 134 boys and 117 girls enrolled at the schools.[13] At that time the male teachers were Peter Kelaghan, John McGinn and P. McGinn, and the female teachers were

Mary Duffy and May Gormley. Mary Duffy was dismissed as incompetent in 1847, and the female school was closed that year though it reopened again in 1849 when Sarah Kane was appointed.[14] Kane herself was later dismissed.

Most of the pupils at the Corduff schools were Roman Catholic, with just one Presbyterian boy and three Protestant boys. Successive school managers in the late nineteenth century included Rev. Thomas McNally, Rev. J.J. Mac-Mahon and Rev. Peter Bermingham. In 1889, the chapel and grounds were leased to diocesan trustees for a period of ninety-nine years; the named trustees included the Bishop of Clogher and the local Catholic clergy.[15] Thomas Mee, a farmer from Corcashyduff, was a named grantor of the lease. This arrangement allowed for the building of a new schoolhouse, and the Commissioners granted £467 15s. towards the cost of constructing the schoolhouse, which was completed in 1890.[16] Constructed from plans prepared by the OPW, the new schoolhouse was designed to accommodate up to a maximum of 200 children, with separate departments for boys and girls.

While the schools were closed on occasion for events like confirmations and fairs, in common with other schools in the district, Corduff schools were also closed several times due to outbreaks of infectious diseases. Fever outbreaks included scarlet fever in 1875 and 1917 and measles in 1899 and 1914.[17]

Some early teachers at Corduff male and female schools
All the teachers at Corduff schools were Roman Catholic. Among the principal teachers at the male school were Peter Keleghan and his successor Edward McEnaney. Master McEnaney retired in 1881 and was replaced by Francis McKeown, who was previously the principal at nearby Corcreagh national school; however, Master McKeown retired due to poor health in 1885, and was replaced by Michael Nulty in January 1886. Appointed at a young age, Mr Nulty went on to act as the principal at the Corduff male school for over forty years.[18] In the late nineteenth century, the assistant teacher at the male school was James Keleghan, and the monitors included James Marron (1882), Peter McQuillan (1887), James Keenan (1888) and Thomas Callan (1893).

The principals at the female school included Bridget Marron (née Brennan) and her successor, Mary Ann McCluskey, who was appointed in 1900 and who later married James McKittrick, a local farmer from Corduff.[19] Mrs McKittrick continued as principal during the 1920s. Assistant teachers at the female school included Mary McEnaney and Elizabeth Daly (née Callaghan), who gave long years of service until 1911, when she retired and was replaced by Miss Annie Marron, who was previously the monitress at Coolfore national school. Two years later in December 1913, Annie Marron died, and Miss Mary Marron was her successor. Other assistant teachers included Miss Bridget Smith and Mrs Mary Flood, and the monitresses included Alice Hanratty and Julia Fox, who was later appointed assistant teacher at Sreenty national school.

'Meagre preparation'

Successive district inspectors for Corduff schools examined the pupils' proficiency in the various subjects, and based on this, judged the competence of the teachers, and imposed sanctions on them for pupils' poor proficiency or breaches of the rules. Sanctions could include a reprimand, a fine, loss of a gratuity for service, demotion or even the threat of dismissal. Like many school principals, Michael Nulty was the subject of unfavourable comments from district inspectors, including reports that his teaching lacked 'system and thoroughness' and showed only 'meagre preparation'. One district inspector admonished him for neglect in keeping the school account books, and in 1893, he was fined £1 and demoted 'for continued failure to keep his school account [...] and for irregularities in [the] record of pupils' attendance'.[20] Given the many reported transgressions, in 1897 the district inspector requested the local curate, who resided at the parochial house beside the school, to 'keep a sharp eye' on Master Nulty.

Other teachers were also the subject of inspectors' reprimands. In 1870, Bridget Brennan was denied a gratuity on the grounds that the pupils' answering was 'quite insufficient'; however, in the following year, the district inspector reported 'very favourable testimony to the zeal and general efficiency' of the female teacher.[21] Later in 1894, based on the pupils' 'low answering', Thomas Callan's salary was withdrawn. On a number of occasions, individual teachers were admonished for their late attendance in the schoolroom. From time to time during the early 1900s Master Nulty's performance was reported as unsatisfactory; however, in 1919, the district inspector reported that he had now made a 'faithful effort to carry out the Inspector's suggestions' in reducing irregularities and omissions in his work and no further action was required.

Master Nulty pursued interests outside of his school duties. He was an accomplished gardener who advertised and sold his prize-winning sweet peas and was an active member of the Carrickmacross branch of the Irish National Federation, a nationalist political party.[22] In 1904, he published a school textbook on grammar with the very long title of *Graduate Drill Exercise in Etymology and Syntax, being for the most part a Collection of Grammatical Errors as actually heard in speaking and found in the written composition exercises of children, including, with copious examples all points in which grammatical errors are likely to be made, and arranged according to an original plan by Michael Nulty, Corduff Na-*

tional School, Carrickmacross.[23] Described as 'a neat booklet of forty pages, well printed and divided into 33 crisp chapters', it cost 2*d.* per copy or 2*s.* per dozen copies and was available post free on request from Mr Nulty. Welcoming its publication, a reporter for the *Dundalk Democrat* commented: 'It is our confirmed opinion that there are no persons more qualified to write textbooks for the Irish National Schools than the Irish national teachers themselves.'[24] Why Master Nulty should write a textbook on grammar is unclear, since the Commissioners supplied schools with a recommended textbook on this subject, entitled *English Grammar*. It is also unclear if his book was used widely among schoolteachers. In January 1929, Michael McEvoy succeeded Master Nulty as the school principal.

The schoolhouse

Lack of attention to the upkeep of the schoolhouse, neglect in keeping the school accounts and irregularities in recording pupils' attendance were recurring themes in inspectors' reports on Corduff schools well into the early years of the twentieth century. The district inspectors reported on 'the careless and untidy way' in which the school was kept, including a lack of cleanliness of the schoolrooms and the general untidy appearance of the pupils. Part of the ceiling was falling down, and the out-offices and the boundary wall had fallen into disrepair.

In 1913, the average attendance was forty-five pupils at the male school and sixty-eight at the female school, and in the 1920s, the possibility of enlarging the schoolhouse was considered; however, the work to extend it was not carried out, and in January 1935, Corduff male and female schools were combined into a single school.[25]

Serving a large rural district, by the early 1950s, Corduff national school had sixty-three pupils enrolled and three teachers were employed, Mr Patrick McNally, Miss Kathleen Marron, and Mrs McEnaney.[26] Later in the century, it was customary for the parish priest to submit a report to the Bishop of Clogher on the condition of the national schools in the parish, and in 1967, Fr L. Marron reported on the condition of Corduff national school:

> Built in 1890; three teachers; building in very good condition, well-kept and clean. Open fires. Dry closets clean. Grounds clean and dry. A heap of cinders block the bottom of one of the down-pipes at the rear wall.[27]

In 1986, both Corduff national school and Sreenty national school closed and a new school, dedicated as Scoil Phádraig, was established at Corduff village to accommodate the children of the district. Today Scoil Phádraig is a flourishing rural national school. It remains under the patronage of the Diocese of Clogher as a Catholic school; however, it is described as 'inclusive of all regardless of background, religion or ability'.[28]

Sreenty national school
The townland of Sreenty lies two and a half miles to the north of Corduff village and at the extreme north-west end of the parish of Magheross, close to the Cavan border. Occupying a one-room slated building, the school there was first connected with the Board of National Education in 1846.[29] Thomas Maguire was the principal and Fr J. Mulligan was the school manager. In 1848 there were 145 children enrolled, with almost equal numbers of boys and girls.[30]

In 1851, the schoolhouse was destroyed by fire.[31] Some few years later in 1857, E.P. Shirley, who had succeeded his father as landlord in the previous year, provided funds to construct a new schoolhouse, and it was again connected with the Board in 1858.[32] While the former school was under Catholic patronage, E.P. Shirley was the patron of the new school and Shirley's agent George Morant was the named school manager; however, soon after it opened, John T. Holland succeeded Morant as Shirley's agent and school manager.[33]

The new schoolhouse was a large two-storey building; the upper floor was used as the schoolroom, while the ground floor was used as the teacher's residence at a rental cost of 2s. per annum.[34] The same architectural plan for the school would later be used to construct new schoolhouses at Ballynagearne in the parish of Magheracloone in 1862 and at Coolfore in 1871.

Teachers and pupils
When Sreenty national school was re-connected with the Board in 1858, James Duffy was appointed principal on an annual salary of £20, made up from the annual grant from the Board and local contributions.[35] While there were 166 pupils enrolled, 101 males and sixty-five females, the average daily attendance was just sixty-one. Commenting on the school attendance in 1863, the district inspector wrote: 'Attendance is low on account of the pressure of harvest work, and unusually low today [18 September], this being the last day before vacation.'[36] Despite the low attendance, Ellen Duffy was appointed as junior monitress that same year and James McBride was appointed junior monitor the following year; McBride was later appointed as principal at Coolfore school in 1871. When Ellen Duffy was promoted to assitant teacher, Mary Duffy succeeded her as monitress.

In 1875, Ellen Duffy left 'without giving the required notice' and two years later she was replaced as assistant by Julia Fox, who was previously monitress at Corduff female school. When the school manager proposed the appointment of a male assistant, the Commissioners responded that 'in schools attended by children of both sexes, the Commissioners prefer that the assistant should be a female'.[37]

Successive district inspectors' annual returns to the Commissioners included occasional reports of pupils' 'discreditable proficiency' and teachers' unsatisfactory performance. In 1862, the district inspector directed Master Duffy to 'exert himself for the improvement of his pupils in grammar and explanation and to correct their faulty pronounciation', and later in 1871, both Master Duffy and Ellen Duffy were admonished for their pupils' low marks.[38] From time to time, teachers were also reprimanded for breaches of the rules, including marking pupils present when they were absent and delayed completion of the calling of the daily roll.

Master James Duffy reached retirement age in 1881 and the Commissioners recommended him for pension.[39] James Kelly replaced Duffy, and some few years later in 1894, he and Julia Fox were married. At that time, the average attendance was 100 pupils, and in the following year, two monitresses were appointed, Mary McDonald and Mary McBride, who had lately been the assistant at Coolfore school.

In 1883, the Commissioners learned that a Carrickmacross court had issued Master Kelly with a 'Certificate of order' and a fine of 3s. 6d., for disorderly conduct on the street in Carrickmacross.[40] Despite testimonials of good character from the parish priest and the local church curate, Master Kelly was temporarily withdrawn from his duties and required to attend the Board's training college at his own expense. He later returned to Sreenty school in 1886, when he was again given charge of the school. James Murray replaced Master Kelly as the principal in 1909.

Patronage of the school

In 1914, Mr R.C. Heron, the district inspector, prepared a report on Sreenty national school, where 'order was very good' and 'the weekly syllabus and progress record were kept for all classes'. On the organisation and methods of instruction, he reported:

> The pupils answer very intelligently and read very distinctly and with expression. Object lesson very well taught using science equipment [...] Needlework generally good. Drawing of juniors good – taught by principal. Small blackboard would suit the infants.[41]

Mr Heron noted that, contrary to the rules of the Board, the school manager, William Pierce Esq., had visited Sreenty national school only once since his appointment as Shirley's agent in 1908.[42] At the time, the school had ninety-five pupils, all Roman Catholic, and Heron remarked that it was over-crowded. He described the physical state of the schoolhouse: 'One chimney is leaning outwards and may fall. One out-office is in bad repair.' Mr Heron also remarked that Mr Pierce 'was not inclined to spend money on the school as the [Shirley] estate has been sold', but he was willing to hand over the school to trustees, as agreed under the terms of the sale of the estate to the tenants.[43]

However, two barriers existed to the transfer of patronage at that time. Major Evelyn Charles Shirley was absent on military duties in the Great War and did not wish to attend to the matter until the end of the war, and Fr McKenna, the parish priest, did not wish to assume patronage, due to a very large debt incurred in the repair of several churches in his parish. Besides, Fr McKenna was delaying in the hope that Mr Pierce would pay for the necessary repairs to the schoolhouse. In the event, it appears that the building was not repaired, and patronage of the school was not transferred from Shirley to diocesan trustees until 1921. The building that E.P. Shirley provided continued to function as the Sreenty schoolhouse, until it was replaced by a single-storey building in 1935, which was located just north of the Five Crossroads.

In the early 1950s, there were fifty-two pupils enrolled and the teachers were Mrs Bríd McCabe and Miss Elizabeth O'Connor, who was appointed in the early 1940s.[44] In a report to the Bishop of Clogher in 1967, Fr L. Marron described the condition of Sreenty school: 'Built in 1935; two teachers; solid and well-built structure; very well maintained; neat and clean; open fires. Dry closets clean. Grounds very well kept and include a shrubbery and flower plot.'[45]

Miss O'Connor retired in 1974, after many long years of service.[46] At that time, Sreenty school was at risk of being reduced to a single-teacher school due to falling numbers; however, it secured a second teacher, Mrs Bridget McNally.[47] This appointment was much to the relief of the then principal Mr Brian McDermott and the parents of the district. The school was subsequently merged with Corduff national school in 1986, to form Scoil Phádraig, a new school at Corduff village. Both Mr McDermott and Mrs McNally transferred to the new school, where Mr McDermott was appointed principal.[48] Reflecting on his time at Sreenty, Mr McDermott recalled how, on warm summer mornings, the children, on arrival at the school, placed their bottles of milk in the little stream that ran through the schoolyard to keep it cool and fresh. The schoolhouse at Sreenty was subsequently sold and today is a private dwelling house.

Corcreagh national school[49]

Although there is evidence of a hedge school at Corcreagh in 1826 when Bernard Larkin held a school in a barn there, a national school was later established in connection with the Board of National Education sometime after 1845, when E.J. Shirley granted the Corcreagh chapel grounds to the Board for the purpose of establishing a schoolhouse.[50] As with Sreenty national school, the original schoolhouse at Corcreagh was a two-storey house, with the schoolmaster's residence on the ground floor and the schoolroom on the upper floor.[51] In the early years, the school was non-vested and the manager was Rev. J.J. McMahon, Catholic curate at Carrickmacross. While there were 125 pupils on the roll in 1870, the average daily attendance was just thirty pupils and remained low over subsequent years.

Schoolteachers at Corcreagh

Like the other rural schools in the district, the Commissioners' records for Corcreagh national school contain reports of teachers' proficiency and of sanctions applied for poor proficiency or transgressions of rules. Sanctions typically involved a reprimand. For example, Francis McKeown, who was the principal during the 1870s, was occasionally reprimanded for breaches of the rules, including failing to record the names of absent pupils, failing to comply with the school timetable and closing the window shutters, thereby interfering with the light and ventilation in the schoolroom.[52] Master McKeown resigned in March 1881 to become the principal at Corduff boys' school, and in what appears to have been a direct exchange with Corduff, was replaced by Edward McEneany, the then principal at Corduff. However, Master McEnaney's tenure at Corcreagh was short-lived; six months after his appointment, he was dismissed as unqualified and was succeeded by Peter Carroll, who was previously at the rural Tunnyduff national school near Bailieboro.

By the late 1880s, the building was considered no longer suitable, and the Commissioners made a grant of £290. 8s. 10d. to the diocesan trustees towards the construction of a new schoolhouse, which was completed in 1890 on the chapel grounds at Corcreagh.[53] With growing pupil numbers in the early 1890s, Alice Marron, formerly of Lossets national school, was appointed as assistant and two monitors, Bernard Hand and James Finnegan, were also appointed; a third monitor, Thomas Carroll, was later appointed in 1893. At that time, the average attendance was seventy pupils.

Master Carroll resigned in 1901 and Miss Marron was the temporary principal until John Keenan was appointed the following year. Later in the decade Catherine (Katie) Clinton replaced Miss Marron as assistant and she, in turn, was replaced by Rose Ann McGee in 1914. Master Keenan continued as the principle until his retirement in 1929. A number of monitresses were appointed in the period after 1911, including Alice Hand, Brigid Duffy and Brigid Marron.

Although the Commissioners paid schoolteachers' salaries, the administrative arrangements required that payment depended on a school submitting the correct and accurate information on the teachers and monitors employed. Therefore, in 1906 when the teachers at Corcreagh complained that their salaries were not paid at the usual time, Rev. Bermingham sought an explanation from the Commissioners. The matter was raised in parliament when John McKean, the MP for Monaghan South, asked the Chief Secretary to the Lord-Lieutenant of Ireland why the Corcreagh teachers' salaries had not been paid.[54] In response, McKean was informed that the quarterly returns, on which the payments depended, were irregular and were sent back to the school manager for completion. Consistent with the strict bureaucracy of the civil service, only when the returns were re-submitted 'in a complete state' could the salaries be paid.

During the mid-twentieth century, there was a succession of teachers at the Corcreagh national school. Seamus McHugh, who completed his training in 1956, was appointed school principal in that same year. Mrs Murray was the assistant at that time. Several years later, when reflecting on his time at Corcreagh, Master McHugh remembered his first monthly salary cheque of £22, out of which he was expected to purchase coal for the school, make repairs to the schoolhouse and pay for lodgings. He also remembered Mrs Murray for her 'efficiency and friendship' and he recalled how the children at the school were 'bright, industrious, alert and respectful'.[55]

Although in the townland of Corcreagh, the schoolhouse is located on the road bordering the townland of Raferagh, and hence, it is known locally as Raferagh national school. Reporting on the condition of the school in 1967, Fr L. Marron wrote: 'Built in 1890; two teachers. Recently decorated attractive and clean. Grounds very well kept. Dry closets clean.'[56] Like the neighbouring school at Corduff, today Corcreagh is a thriving rural national school. It continues to function as a two-teacher school with approximately thirty pupils on the rolls.[57]

Carrickmaclim and Corvally schools
Between 1820 and 1840, there was a major growth in the population of Presbyterians in Co. Monaghan, including in the hinterland to the west and northwest of Carrickmacross, in the townlands of Carrickmaclim, Corvally, Shanco and some adjacent townlands.[58] Earlier in about 1812, Robert Winning, the minister of Ervey in Co. Meath, established a Presbyterian congregation at

Carrickmaclim.[59] Described as 'an old and settled Presbyterian community', Carrickmaclim served the local area and the nearby town of Carrickmacross. The headstones at the little churchyard at Carrickmaclim include the names of the early settlers in south Monaghan, whose ancestors came from Scotland, escaping persecution.[60]

In 1849, the church at Carrickmaclim was replaced with a new church at Shanco, some two and a half miles further to the west of Carrickmacross.[61] Although built in Shanco townland, the new church (or meeting house) is generally known as Corvally Presbyterian church, since it is located at the intersection of Shanco and Corvally townlands.

Carrickmaclim and Corvally schools were the two rural schools that served mainly the Presbyterian and Protestant communities, respectively, in the Carrickmacross rural hinterland, although some Catholic children also attended. The schools were originally conducted in their respective schoolmaster's own houses, which in each case, was a thatched house.

In the period 1837 to 1839, Carrickmaclim school was one of several scriptural schools located on the Shirley estate and supported by E.J. Shirley. At that time Peter Ward was the schoolmaster, and the school was not connected with the Board of National Education.[62] George Sudden's reports on the schools on the Shirley estate in the late 1840s included both Carrickmaclim and Corvally schools.[63] At that time, Mrs McDonald was the schoolmistress at Carrickmaclim, where there were fifty-four pupils, forty-four girls and ten boys. At Corvally, Mr Gorden was the schoolmaster and Mrs Gorden the schoolmistress, and there were fifty-seven boys and thirty-seven girls.

E.J. Shirley supported the building of schoolhouses at Carrickmaclim and Corvally, and when later connected with the Board, both schools were under Shirley's patronage. The new schoolhouse at Carrickmaclim was a single-storey slated house, located beside the old Presbyterian church and cemetery.[64] Built in about 1850, the schoolhouse at Corvally was described as a 'detached U-plan three-bay single-storey school [...] with lean-to canopy to middle of front façade [...] pitched slate roofs with kneelered gables and cut-stone copings with profiled ridge, cut-stone chimneystacks with cornices, and cast-iron rainwater goods.'[65] Although located beside the Corvally Presbyterian church, Corvally school served mainly the Protestant families who worshipped at the nearby Ardragh church, which Shirley also endowed.[66]

Carrickmaclim national school
The school at Carrickmaclim was connected with the Board for a period in the late nineteenth century. The original applicant for grant aid was E.P. Shirley's agent J.T. Holland, and the school manager was Rev. Alex Hurst Ross,

the Church of Ireland clergyman at St Finbarr's church, Carrickmacross. Rev. Hurst Ross was also the school manager at Corvally, and in 1881, he was succeeded as manager of both schools by Rev. Charles Joseph Hill Tardy. Later in the nineteenth century, Shirley's agent John T. Gibbings took over the school managership from the clergyman.

During the 1860s and early 1870s, James Reburn was the principal and Margaret Reburn was the assistant. While there were fifty-seven boys and fifty-three girls enrolled in 1872, the average daily attendance was just forty-six pupils.[67] It appears that Mr Reburn was not qualified as a teacher, and in 1874, the school manager sought the Commissioners' permission to retain him as schoolmaster, on the ground that he had been a teacher at the school for a considerable time, writing that 'his knowledge, though elementary, is sufficient for the wants of the children attending the School [and] that he is energetic and attentive'.[68] The Commissioners refused the request. Despite this, the school manager retained Mr Reburn's services, and in response, the Commissioners withdrew the grant to Carrickmaclim national school, and in October 1875 the school was struck off the roll of national schools.[69] At that time, the average attendance was just eleven pupils.

Corvally national school
Corvally national school provided an important place for the education of local Protestant and Presbyterian children; in 1872, there were thirty-seven boys and thirty-seven girls enrolled.[70] John Willis was the principal, and like other rural schoolmasters in the district, he was under the watchful supervision of the district inspector. In 1874, Mr Willis was 'severely admonished' for violating the Commissioners' rule on the teaching of religious instruction during school hours, and he was again reprimanded the following year for inaccuracy in marking the school roll.

Later in 1881, when the average attendance was twenty-eight pupils, Mary Eakin was appointed as assistant. In early 1883, the school failed to command a sufficient number of pupils and it was temporarily struck off the Commissioners' roll of schools; however, the district inspector and school manager appealed the decision, claiming that the fall in pupil numbers was due to 'exceptional circumstances', and they assured the Commissioners that the required number of pupils would be maintained in the future.[71] The school was reinstated some few months later.

Mr John Patterson succeeded Mr Willis in 1886 and Mrs Agnes Patterson was appointed workmistress at that time. Like his predecessor, Mr Patterson was admonished on occasion, including for carelessness in marking the record of attendance and lack of a system of teaching. In 1904, the district inspector reported that 'the pupils answered most unintelligently in arithmetic and read with very little intelligence' and the teacher was requested 'to make careful and systematic preparation for [his] work'.[72]

While the school remained under Shirley's patronage, with Shirley's agent acting as the school manager, in 1906 the local Protestant and Presbyterian clergymen requested that they be nominated as the joint managers of the school; however, it appears that their request was declined, and Shirley's successive agents remained as the named school manager at Corvally.

Both John and Agnes Patterson continued as teachers at Corvally well into the early decades of the twentieth century. Mr Patterson was active in the Carrickmacross branch of the National Teachers' Association and the Farney National Teacher's Association, and he partook in debates concerning teachers' salaries and the school curriculum. In 1914, the average attendance was twenty-seven male and twelve female pupils. At that time and reflecting the profile of the local population, the majority of pupils were Presbyterian, with just five Protestant children and five children of 'other' denominations. The Corvally schoolhouse also operated as a post office and Mr Patterson was the postmaster; however, he performed his postmaster duties out of school hours.

Miss Sarah J. Hogan succeeded Mr Patterson as principal in 1918, and on her appointment, she sought permission to apply for the position of postmistress at Corvally; the Commissioners had no objection, so long as it did not interfere with her duties as a teacher, and to comply with this, Miss Hogan's sister carried out the duties of postmistress during school hours. Miss Hogan remained as principal until around 1951, when Mr J. Pierce, Shirley's agent, placed an advertisement in a national newspaper, which read: 'Principal required for Corvally N.S. (C of I), 12 on roll; residence attached'.[73] A second advertisement for a principal was published in October 1956, and it appears that the position was not filled since it was re-advertised in August 1957; on that occasion and perhaps indicating a level of desperation to secure a teacher, the advertisement read 'J.A.M. would be considered'.[74]

Department of Education records show that two teachers, Miss Johnson and Miss Hillis, were employed in 1957.[75] However, given the very small number of pupils enrolled, the appointments were temporary and conditional on the Department's decision regarding the continuance of the grant to Corvally national school. In the event, the Department withdrew the grant to Corvally in September of that year and the two teachers' services were discontinued. Despite this, the school reopened in the early 1960s and continued to operate until it finally closed in 1972.[76]

9

'Cultivation of intelligence
and the training of the senses':
The revised programme of instruction

By the turn of the twentieth century, the number of national schools
had greatly increased, and there were 8,684 national schools connected with the Board of National Education, with 770,622 pupils
enrolled.[1] In the parish of Magheross, there were eleven national schools connected with the Board.[2] The great proliferation of schools in the country and
a plan to address it would lead to controversy and conflict between the Commissioners of National Education and school managers and teachers.

Some seventy years after the original plan to establish a 'unified system of
education', about two-thirds of the national schools were attended by pupils
of a single religious denomination.[3] The national school system was effectively
a religiously segregated system, and in addition, a great many schools under
Catholic management were also segregated into separate boys' and girls'
schools.

With separate denominational teacher training colleges, teacher training
had also become segregated along denominational lines and also along mostly
gender lines.[4] Teachers took a two-year training course to become fully
trained, and in the seven training colleges, females outnumbered males by
three to one.[5] At that time, about half of all teachers were formally trained.[6]
Many of the untrained teachers were school principals and assistants who
were considered unsuitable for training 'owing to age or married condition'.

The general state of primary education
In 1904, Mr F.H. Dale, His Majesty's Inspector of Schools, reported on the
general state of primary education in Ireland.[7] Dale examined the conditions
of schools, including school premises, school equipment, staffing and instruction, and in his report, he compared the administration of schools and school

practices in Ireland with that of England. Along with the annual reports of the Commissioners of National Education in the period, Dale's report offers a window on schools and schooling at the turn of the twentieth century, albeit from the perspective of senior civil servants and other state officials.

Dale observed that schools in Irish towns were 'markedly inferior to those of the English [towns] both in the requirements essential for proper sanitation and in their convenience for the purposes of effective teaching'. He attributed these defects to 'excessive economy in building' and the absence of a local authority with the power to raise rates for the building and upkeep of schools. On rural schools, Dale was less critical, writing that they compared 'not unfavourably' with those in England. Nevertheless, he wrote that the premises of a few schools were 'extremely unsuitable and fall below the standard of the worst English Schools', a situation he partly attributed to poverty in some rural districts. He also observed that the chief defects in rural schools were 'want of cleanliness, the neglect of repairs, and the insufficient heating', defects which were the responsibility of the school managers, and which could also be remedied 'by arousing a general local interest in elementary education'.[8]

Reporting on school equipment, Dale wrote that although most schools were 'tolerably well supplied with the absolutely necessary equipment for School work', the number of desks was insufficient for all the children and chalk and slates were widely used. When compared with schools in England, Irish schools were also deficient in 'attractiveness of appearance and in all equipment other than necessaries', and in a veiled criticism of the Irish in their attitudes to their children and schooling, he commented:

> This deficiency is partly due to poverty, partly to the fact that public opinion in Ireland has not hitherto attached much importance to the maintenance of a high standard as regards the comfort and attractiveness of Primary Schools as in England.[9]

Dale reported on some positive aspects of staffing in Irish schools. For example, he noted that, unlike in England, only a fully trained teacher could be appointed as a head teacher in an Irish school, and monitors were not officially recognised as part of the complement of school staff.[10] With the exception of teachers in very small schools, teachers' salaries compared favourably with those in England. However, the system of selection for promotion rested with the district inspectors and not with the local school managers, a situation which could lead to discontent among teachers.

The arrangement that required all teachers to enter the profession at the lowest grade of salary was, Dale believed, 'not well calculated to attract men and women of marked ability'. Nevertheless, the supply of teachers was much in excess of the demand, and the competition to enter the teaching profession in primary schools was very keen, and he noted that the prospect for promotion to a headship, especially for men, was higher in Ireland than in England.

'A gross extravagance': Too many schools
According to Dale, the quality of instruction in Irish schools was adversely affected by several factors. These were: the very large number of small schools, many unsuitably staffed and poorly organised; the lack of local interest, except among the clergy; the faulty distribution of staff in large schools; and irregularity of attendance. In addition, the unsuitablilty of school premises and faulty organisation in teaching certain subjects had resulted in poor school discipline. He concluded that the lack of local interest in schools was partly the result of the failure to devolve financial responsibility to local school managers or to involve the local community in the management of schools.

Dale found several instances of small separate boys' and girls' schools located in the same district. He commented on the organising of teaching in small schools, criticising as 'most objectionable on educational grounds' the practice of sub-dividing schools into male and female divisions. In this arrangement, each teacher within a division was responsible for teaching pupils from the youngest to the oldest, which impaired 'the efficiency of his work'. The practice of separating boys and girls was especially prevalent under Catholic school managers, and he considered this form of organisation a 'gross extravagance'. Such arrangements meant that the teachers tended to focus on the older pupils, and he questioned the male teacher's ability to teach the very junior pupils:

> Nor can it be reasonably expected that a man should possess the patience and sympathy with very young children which are natural to even an unskilled woman Teacher, and which are the indispensable prerequisites for any teaching of infants.[11]

As a way of addressing this and thereby reducing the proliferation of small schools, he recommended that 'no child under seven years of age shall be placed in the boys' department, save under exceptional circumstances'.

While the Commissioners controlled the administration of the national schools in a rigid and inflexible way, Dale believed that they had failed to exercise strict control over the supply and organisation of schools, thereby resulting in their proliferation. The system of state funding of schools based on the salaries of individual teachers, instead of a capitation grant based on pupil attendance, had also facilitated 'the multiplication of unnecessary schools'. Only convent schools were funded by a capitation grant and were found to be less expensive than other national schools.

Dale concluded that the Irish school system had too many small schools and was generally poorly maintained and underfunded, particularly because of a lack of local involvement and local funding.[12] He made several recommendations to the Commissioners. Pending the transfer of financial responsibility to local communities, he recommended that the Commissioners should exercise closer supervision over the supply and organisation of schools. The Board of National Education should also be given greater powers to discontinue 'unnecessary schools' and the salary of teachers should be based on school size. Schools with an average attendance of sixty pupils should be adequately staffed, and manual instructresses should be employed in smaller schools. Dale also recommended improved supply of school equipment, including desks and books.

Junior assistant mistress
In response to Dale's recommendation to reduce the number of small schools, the Commissioners introduced a new rule, Rule 127(b), which stipulated that 'boys under eight years of age are ineligible for enrolment in a boys' school where there is not an assistant mistress, unless there is no suitable school under a mistress available in the locality'. The rule signified that female teachers were considered to be best suited to teaching younger pupils. In practice, it meant that if younger boys were no longer enrolled in small schools, the average attendance would fall, and many male assistant teachers could be made redundant.[13]

While the aim of Rule 127(b) was to reduce the number of small schools by amalgamating the smaller boys' and girls' schools, school managers and teachers saw it as a move to reduce state spending on education. The Irish National Teachers' Organisation (INTO) was concerned for the position of male teachers and assistants, and the Catholic school managers objected on the grounds that the new rule was a threat to their authority over how to manage their schools.[14]

Despite the opposition, Rule 127(b) was implemented and one outcome was the establishment of a new grade of teacher, the junior assistant mistress (JAM). After 1906, JAMs were employed in small schools with an average attendance of between thirty-five and fifty pupils, whether attended by boys and girls or just one sex, to teach the junior classes and to instruct all the girls in needlework.[15] The Commissioners believed that the new class of teacher would 'prove very valuable, especially in regard to the care and education of children of very tender years' and they considered the new grade of teacher to be 'one of the most important educational reforms introduced into Ireland in recent years'.[16]

The hand, the eye, and the ear: The revised programme of instruction

When William Starkie was appointed Resident Commissioner of National Education in 1899, he introduced several reforms in the administration of the national schools, including a new system for grading, promoting and paying teachers and a reduction in the number of school inspectorate districts from sixty to twenty-two.[17] Starkie was also responsible for introducing radical new changes in the national school curriculum.

In 1900, some few short years before Mr Dale's report, the school curriculum had remained largely unchanged since 1870, when the Powis Commission introduced the system of payment of teachers by results. That system meant that in addition to a teacher's standard salary, a bonus payment could be made, based on pupils showing satisfactory progress in subjects like reading, writing, spelling and arithmetic.[18] With its emphasis on pupils' proficiency at inspectors' examinations, the payment-by-results system was seen as leading to superficial learning, with pupils' knowledge considered to be 'very largely of the "parrot" order'.[19] It also meant that in small single-teacher schools, teachers tended to focus their efforts on teaching the more senior classes to the detriment of the junior classes. Described as being 'too bookish', the curriculum, the payment-by-results system and the method of school inspections were all seen as needing 'radical change'.[20]

Based on a number of considerations, the Commissioners decided to reform the national school curriculum at the end of the nineteenth century. These considerations included the belief that payment-by-results was out of date, the desire to emphasise the development of the child by including manual and practical subjects, and the general agreement among all interested parties, including the denominational churches, that reform was needed.[21] In addition, new thinking on childhood, schooling and teaching methods had emerged in the nineteenth century.[22] The German educationalists, Friedrich Fröbel, believed in the uniqueness of each child and emphasised learning through activity and play. Fröbel established a learning institute, which he termed a kindergarten.[23] Mindful of wider political developments at the time, especially the Irish cultural revival movement associated with the Irish language and Gaelic sports, the Commissioners also felt pressured to revise the national school curriculum to include elements of Irish culture and heritage.[24]

Practical subjects

Proposals to reform the school curriculum were set out in two documents, the *Commission on Manual and Practical Instruction*, published in 1898, and the Commissioners' *Revised Programme of Instruction in National Schools*, published in 1900.[25] In a detailed investigation into the national school curriculum, the *Commission on Manual and Practical Instruction* concluded that there was an over emphasis on literary subjects and expressed a 'strong conviction' that manual and practical instruction should be introduced into schools where it did not already exist. The Commission recommended the inclusion of a range of practical subjects, to include educational handwork, drawing, elementary science, singing, drill and physical exercise, as well as kindergarten for infants, and cookery, laundry work and domestic science for girls. It also recommended that practical subjects should be examined in ways other than by examination. Elementary science should replace agriculture but could include 'the more simple scientific principles that underlie the art and industry of Agriculture'.

Recognising that individual schools differed in their ability to implement the recommended new subjects, the Commission suggested that new subjects should be introduced 'gradually and tentatively'.[26] The Commission's recommendations formed the basis for the *Revised Programme of Instruction*, and in their preamble to the Programme, the Commissioners of National Education wrote:

The general Programme is designed with the object of affording scope within its limits for an adequate amount of education for the average child attending primary schools, and at the same time of giving a child whose intelligence is above the average opportunities of developing it to the best advantage.

The cultivation of intelligence, and the training of the senses, as represented by the hand, the eye, and the ear, are provided for, while the development of the physical faculties that are so important to all children, but especially to the children of primary schools, forms a copious feature of the revised curriculum.[27]

The revised curriculum consisted of subjects like handwork for junior classes, to include paper folding, cardboard work, wire work, brick-laying, and clay modelling and woodwork for older boys 'to train them in habits of accurate observation, careful measurement, and exact workmanship'.[28] The aim of elementary science was to impart 'an intelligent knowledge of the common facts of nature, and the rudimentary principles of science', which could be illustrated in higher classes by simple experiments. The Commissioners wrote that singing should be within the reach of all children, since it had 'a cultivating and refining influence', and drill and exercise should be introduced as a way of contributing to 'the health, the spirits and the general well-being of the children'. After 1904, instrumental music was introduced as one of a number of optional subjects.

Since the school curriculum had consisted 'largely of the study of books' and was therefore considered to be 'one-sided in character', the Commissioners reasoned that the addition of practical subjects would have practical benefits for the children:

> Children should be taught not merely to take in knowledge from books, but to observe with intelligence the material world around them [...] The great bulk of children attending primary schools under the National Board will have to earn their bread by the work of their hand; it is therefore important that they should be trained, from the beginning, to use their hands with dexterity and intelligence.[29]

The Commissioners confidently predicted that the revised programme of instruction would 'lead to great educational advancement and mark the commencement of a new era in the history of National Education'.[30]

Challenges

Despite the lofty ideals of the revised programme of instruction, which emphasised the active participation of children in their own learning, it failed to recognise the reality of the national schools; for example, 60 per cent of schools had just one teacher and there would be costs involved in providing additional space, equipment, and teacher training.[31] Fewer than half of all teachers were formally trained at the time of the publication of the revised programme, and for those who attended a teacher training college, the focus of their training was on teaching literary subjects using traditional teaching methods.[32] The revised programme was accompanied by changes in teachers' conditions of employment, with a new grading system based on an inspector's report replacing the system of payment-by-results. This change reduced teachers' opportunities for promotion and greatly angered them.

Notwithstanding the challenges, the revised programme was implemented in September 1900, and the subjects that required no additional space or little additional equipment, such as singing and drawing, were introduced across the majority of the national schools.[33] With its mix of literary and practical subjects and its emphasis on new child-centred teaching methods, the revised programme improved the learning experience of pupils. Singing, drawing, object lessons and physical exercises were seen as essential elements of the primary school curriculum and were viewed as most beneficial to the pupils since their introduction.[34]

Despite the positive benefits, the widespread implementation of the new programme was ultimately limited for several reasons. These included the fact that many schools were simply too small to introduce the new subjects, many teachers were not trained in the new methods, parents were not enthusiastic and school attendance rates were low.[35] Many teachers did not initially embrace the new curriculum, and in 1903, one district inspector explained teachers' difficulties in implementing it, since many were 'imperfectly educated' and were otherwise 'distracted by considerations of salary'. The inspector wrote:

> It is not easy for men trained in the tyranny of the results system and accustomed to 'prepare' pupils for [...] narrowly defined Inspectors' tests to work efficiently a programme intended to cultivate observation and develop thought rather than to store a memory with facts.[36]

After the revised programme was introduced, the trainee teachers' diploma examinations soon included questions on childhood and new methods of teaching, such as questions about 'the characteristics of early childhood', kindergarten teaching method, and the value of physical drill. While younger teachers were reported to be more competent at teaching the new subjects and in the new teaching methods, some older teachers had 'worked too long in the groove prescribed by the results programme to easily introduce new subjects or adapt themselves to new methods', and many teachers were said to 'still teach their pupils with a view to passing an examination'.[37]

A significant cause of the failure to fully introduce the revised curriculum with its new practical subjects was the person of Dr William Starkie. As the Resident Commissioner of Education and the man responsible for overseeing its introduction, Starkie had failed to consult teachers and school managers and had consulted only a few school inspectors.[38] By changing teachers' and school inspectors' conditions of employment without consulting them, Starkie caused bitterness and alienation among them.[39] With his 'autocratic and aloof' leadership style, it is unsurprising that there was resistance to the new curriculum from the very people charged with its introduction.[40]

Despite the challenges, some inspectors reported positive benefits for pupils. One commented on the 'marked improvement in the general intelligence of the children' and another reported on how composition had improved 'under the more broadening influences of the revised programme'.[41] However, the national schools failed to fully introduce the curriculum changes as the Commissioners had intended, due to the large number of small schools, the high proportion of teachers who were not fully trained, the large class sizes and low average attendance, and the magnitude of the change itself, which left many teachers overwhelmed.[42]

Farney teachers respond
While the new system of grading teachers was the most contentious aspect of the new revised programme of instruction, the educational aspects were less contentious. Addressing a meeting of the Carrickmacross National Teachers' Association at O'Neill's Hotel in Carrickmacross in April 1903, Master Patrick Marron of Coolfore national school gave a guarded welcome to the revised programme, saying that although 'not perfect', there was much to be grateful for in the new system, since the 'intellect of the child can be developed by educating, and not stunted by cramming'.[43] He set out the attitude of the Farney teachers to the revised programme, and showed how the teachers of the district were independent-minded in their position on the curriculum reforms, which they had adopted:

> The members [of our Branch] saw that their duty was to give the New Programme an honest trial, and instead of imitating a great many people who at once find fault with every attempt at reformation, the teachers of Farney, at much personal expense and worry, set themselves to cooperate with the reformers. We have not said anything so far, that could even in the smallest way tend to embarrass those responsible for the great change. Even now, with three years' experience of the working of the system, we wish to say we are not actuated by any fault-finding spirit.[44]

Despite his stated welcome for the new school programme, Marron commented on aspects of the programme's structure and organisation; he remarked that geography was 'a most important subject in all competitive examinations' but was given 'only negative recognition' in the new programme, and arithmetic was 'not well arranged'.

Master Marron also welcomed the ending of the system of payment by results, which was not favoured by the INTO but warned that the new system of grading teachers would prevent many from ever attaining the highest rank in their profession, commenting: 'This, I submit, will have an injurious effect upon the profession, and a still more injurious effect upon education.' In his view, the injurious effect was already evident in the fall in applications for teacher training among men since the new rules were introduced, and he cautioned that fewer trained teachers would result in a deterioration in quality. Master Marron also complained about the very low level of grants available for the upkeep of schools, and he argued that the successful implementation of the new revised programme depended on the schools being properly equipped.

The Irish language in the national schools

Throughout the nineteenth century, the Irish language was in decline, especially after the Great Famine, which had a particularly severe impact on the population of the Irish-speaking districts. The decline was also related to the fact that English was the language of business, commerce and trade.[45] Since the establishment of the national school system in 1831, English had been the language of instruction in all schools, including schools in districts where Irish was the native tongue. In the national schools, languages like Latin and French were permitted, but only as extra subjects to be taught outside of normal school hours. Irish was not permitted until after 1878, when it could be taught to senior pupils, but only in the same limited way as other languages. By the century's end, it remained a minority subject, when it was taught in just 105 schools to fewer than 2,000 pupils.[46]

In 1901, the Commissioners of National Education published *New Rules and Regulations 1900–1*, which permitted the teaching of Irish as an optional subject during 'ordinary school hours', provided that the teaching of the ordinary subjects was 'not impaired or hampered'.[47] Teachers who gave 'systematic instruction' in Irish outside of regular school hours received payment of 10s. per pupil. Later in 1904 in Irish-speaking or bilingual districts, the Commissioners permitted schools to teach Irish to all classes and to teach all other school subjects, including English, through the Irish language. Since few teachers outside of Irish-speaking districts were competent to teach through Irish or to teach Irish as an optional subject, instruction in the language was only gradually introduced. After 1907, the Commissioners established evening training courses in Irish for teachers who wished to teach the subject.[48]

Despite the Irish language being an important expression of cultural nationalism, its introduction in the curriculum was not entirely welcomed by some parents and school managers, even in Irish-speaking districts; after all, the Irish language in these districts was associated with poverty, while English was associated with work and opportunity.[49] Nevertheless, in the Irish-speaking districts the number of schools teaching the bilingual programme grew, and in the period 1907–8 the bilingual programme was being taught in 110 schools, including at fifty-five schools in Co. Donegal.[50] In addition, Irish was being taught as a subject in 2,831 national schools across Ireland, with about two-thirds of these schools located in Connaught and Munster. While district inspectors reported on the number of schools in which Irish was being taught, it is questionable if it was being taught effectively or learnt effectively. Many schools employed 'extern' teachers to teach the subject, and commenting on the quality of their teaching, one district inspector in Co. Kerry remarked:

Their work is not satisfactory, partly because their methods are not good, partly because the time available for instruction in the subject is insufficient, and the intervals between the lessons are too long. They succeed in teaching the pupils the correct pronunciation of Irish, but the progress made in speaking, and in composition, written and oral, is poor.[51]

Yet there were positive reports, as one district inspector in Co. Sligo observed: 'A good deal of time and attention are devoted to the teaching of bilingual Irish, and the enthusiasm shown in the matter bids fair to produce lasting results.'[52] In 1908, Mr D. Lehane, the Commissioners' inspector in Irish, reported that, while most of the teaching was elementary, he was optimistic, writing: 'On the whole, the prospects of Irish at present are hopeful [and] its record has been one of steady progress.'[53] He also remarked that those promoting the teaching of the Irish language were 'numerous and zealous' and he wished them success.

After Irish Independence in 1922, the Government of the Irish Free State made Irish a compulsory subject in all national schools. This was part of the strategy to establish the new Irish state with a distinctly *Gaelic* identity, and the status of the Irish language was confirmed in the Constitution of 1937, which recognised it as the first official national language. However, throughout the twentieth century and beyond, the relationship between the state, the Irish language and the education system would become complex and controversial.[54] As if to foretell the challenges of teaching, learning and speaking the language, a district inspector in an English-speaking district of Co. Cork observed in 1908: 'The enthusiasm for Irish appears to wax and wane in a fitful manner. So far as I can judge, it is learnt too much as a foreign language.'[55]

10

'Safeguarding the interests of primary education': Teachers and their pupils, 1900–1946

Introduced into primary schools in 1900, the revised programme of instruction brought changes to teachers' conditions of employment, specifically, a new system of grading teachers based on an inspector's report. This replaced the payment-by-results system that had operated since 1870.[1] This meant that the role of the school inspector remained central to the primary school system and to the life of the teacher.

Teachers carried a heavy burden from the close monitoring by inspectors, and they lived with the threat of penalties, including dismissal for poor performance. Aside from inspectors' reports, teachers could also be dismissed by their school manager, and this could happen without a right of appeal. Additionally, being ultimately accountable to the Commissioners of National Education, teachers were expected to refrain from engaging in any political movements and avoid controversy of any kind. Teachers were not well paid, and given these constraints and vulnerabilities, they began to organise.

As early as 1868, teachers established the Irish National Teachers' Organisation (INTO) and made representations to the Commissioners and to parliament on several matters of concern to their members, including the threat of instant dismissal, teachers' salaries and the administration of the teachers' pension fund.[2] They also campaigned and lobbied on other teachers' grievances, including teacher training and improved grants for the upkeep of schools.[3] The INTO was an all-Ireland movement and its branches in Co. Monaghan were particularly active. Women members were active during the early years of the twentieth century, especially under the leadership of Catherine Mahon, the Association's first woman president (1902–16), who campaigned for equal pay for female teachers and female representation on the INTO executive.[4]

'The welfare and advancement of the teaching body': Teachers' grievances

In 1900, there were 12,875 national schoolteachers, of whom about two thirds (8,244) were at the principal grade and one-third (3,684) at the assistant grade. Well over half of the principals were male. Relative to the number of principals and assistants, there were few other grades of teacher at that time (Table 10.1).[5]

Table 10.1 Teacher numbers in 1900

Principals		Assistants		Junior Assistants	Work Mistresses*	Temp. Assistants		Temp. Work Mistresses
Males	Females	Males	Females			Males	Females	
4,697	3,547	1,078	2,606	13	897	14	18	5
8,244		3,684				22		
Gross total: 12,875		*Includes industrial teachers						

In 1900, Mr A. Purser, the Chief Inspector for Education in the northern part of Ireland, referred to improvements in teachers' conditions of employment and better opportunities for career advancement:

> The improvement in the teachers is […] as might be expected from the superior inducements held out by higher scales of salaries […] and from greater facilities for reaching the higher grades of classification.[6]

If the Chief Inspector believed that teachers enjoyed good conditions of employment, teachers themselves did not share this view, and they discussed their grievances at regular meetings of their Association.

'Unfair and unjust treatment': Concerns of the County Monaghan branch

Established in 1893, the County Monaghan Teachers' Association was a representative body for national schoolteachers in the county and was affiliated with the INTO. The Association held regular meetings at which resolutions on matters of concern to teachers were passed. Aimed at 'safeguarding the interests of primary education' and at 'the welfare and advancement of the teaching body, and the consequent progress of the children entrusted to their charge', the Association discussed teachers' grievances, including the 'deprival of our civil rights'.[7]

To coincide with the establishment of the County Monaghan Teachers'

Association in 1893, the Farney Teachers' Association was reconstituted as the Carrickmacross National Teachers' Association in that same year. Later in 1896, Master Patrick Marron of Coolfore national school was elected secretary of the Carrickmacross branch and was subsequently elected chairman in 1903.[8]

A particular concern of the County Monaghan Association was the high number of dismissals of schoolteachers. Under the payment-by-results system, few teachers were dismissed since sanctions for poor results generally resulted in reduced income only. In 1899, the Commissioners introduced new penalties for teacher inefficiency, which 'neither fines nor reprimands could remedy', and by 1905, there was an average of fifty teacher dismissals per year.[9] In a resolution passed at a meeting in Ballybay in July 1908, the Monaghan Association expressed its concern at this high level of arbitrary removals of teachers:

> That as the dismissals for alleged inefficiency have increased since 1900 and still continue, and as such dismissals in the majority of cases are of teachers who have given long and faithful service, and are approaching the period of retirement on pension, we hereby protest against this deplorable state of affairs.[10]

The issue of teacher sackings was also an abiding concern for the wider INTO; for example, the Association intervened in the case of Bridget Carey, who was dismissed after twenty years of service at Leighlinbridge national school in Co. Carlow in 1892. Dr John E. Kenny, the MP for Dublin College Green, raised the case of Mrs Carey in parliament, where he stated that the school manager, Fr J. Connolly, had dismissed Mrs Carey and had threatened to dismiss her husband who was the schoolmaster at Leighlinbridge.[11] It was reported that Mrs Carey was in a lunatic asylum, although this fact was disputed.

After 1900, a teacher's pay and prospects of promotion rested solely on the reports of the district inspector, and to merit a promotion, a teacher needed to obtain good reports on three consecutive years.[12] In practice many teachers were left with lower salaries, even on promotion to a principalship, and this greatly angered them. The Monaghan Association called on the Commissioners to end the 'unfair and unjust treatment' of teachers.[13]

The system of deciding teachers' grade and pay came under close scrutiny in 1913, when teacher dismissals led to a parliamentary inquiry into the entire school inspections system.[14] The outcome of the inquiry resulted in only minor changes to the school inspectorate, including a new appeals procedure for teachers dissatisfied with an inspector's report; however, the teachers remained unhappy with the system.[15]

A more thorough investigation into teachers' salaries, pensions and conditions of service was undertaken between 1918 and 1919 under a vice-regal committee chaired by Lord Killanin.[16] The committee declared that education was so important that it should not be 'left dependent upon local inclination, varying according to means, energy or public spirit'.[17] Rather, it should be universally available, with teachers' salaries funded by the state and additional funding to come from local rates to support the upkeep of schools. Lord Killanin's committee also recommended that teachers should have more opportunities for promotion and receive an allowance for additional qualifications. Naturally, the INTO welcomed the report, and following negotiations, secured the salary increases recommended by Killanin's committee.

Another concern of the Monaghan Association was the requirements for entry to the National University of Ireland, which was established in 1908. In 1909 the Association discussed a resolution, which read: 'that we support the demand of the Irish Nation, that Irish be made an essential subject for entrance into the National University'.[18] There was much debate on, what was termed, the 'Gaelic League resolution', with the debate fixated on the phrase 'Irish Nation', a term that one delegate argued was used on political platforms and implied two nations, 'an Irish and a non-Irish [Nation]'. While the resolution was carried, several members disassociated themselves from it, and it appears that the Association was divided along nationalist and unionist lines. The tension within the Monaghan Association was a portent of future tensions between pro- and anti-home rule factions in the county, which were split along largely denominational lines.

James Farmer of Annaglough national school was the Monaghan Association president, and at the same meeting he complained of a 'deplorable state of affairs' regarding schoolrooms, saying that 'the great barrier to education at present was the insanitary and unheated schoolroom with its clay floor and rickety desks that should have been discarded years ago'.[19] However, in a letter to *The Freeman's Journal* some days later, Canon Smyth, the parish priest of Ballybay, who was manager of six national schools in his parish, refuted the claim, writing that Mr Farmer was indulging in 'rhetorical flourishes' and his statement was 'a libel on every school manager in County Monaghan'.[20]

'A striking incident'

In 1905, the INTO was the subject of a reprimand from the Commissioners of National Education over an alleged display of disloyalty to the King and a disregard for the Commissioners' rules among some teachers.[21] The allegation arose out of a report in the *Sligo Champion*, printed on 29 April, which described the events surrounding a banquet held at Sligo Town Hall as part of the INTO's Annual Congress. Among the 140 delegates and guests present were Catholic and Protestant clergymen and Dr Douglas Hyde, president of the Gaelic League. The newspaper reported that 'a striking incident' occurred when the President of the Association, J.J. Hazlett proposed the customary toast to 'The King':

> A number of the invited guests, including some clergymen, having observed that the first toast was that of 'The King', decided to leave immediately, and they did so, being unwilling to participate in a function of which the toast was a feature [...] Others disassociated themselves from the toast by leaving the dining hall and remaining outside until it had been disposed of. When the toast was actually given by the President, the majority of those present, guests and Congress delegates, remained seated, choosing this third method of indicating their non-participation in this particular item of the programme.[22]

The newspaper also reported that there were cries of 'seats!' from the hall and that most of those present remained seated. Having been informed of the incident at Sligo, the Commissioners wrote to Mr Hazlett, requesting him to furnish a report of the proceedings in connection with the toast to the King. In reply, Mr Hazlett stated that he was approached by several persons, 'presumably guests', wishing to know if he proposed to proceed with the toast, and in reply, he advised them that he had 'no intention of departing from the usual custom'.[23] He commented that the press report of the incident was 'considerably exaggerated', although he confirmed, with regret, that several persons remained seated during the toast. Mr Hazlett reported himself convinced that those who showed their objection to the toast were guests and he wrote that the INTO would, 'in the name of the whole body of teachers, entirely dissociate themselves from, and repudiate, the regrettable and unpardonable conduct of a section of those who attended the dinner in Sligo'.

Despite Mr Hazlett's explanation and his organisation's declared rejection of the conduct of some guests at the banquet, the Commissioners felt it necessary to issue a circular to all teachers of national schools, reminding them of the Commissioners' 'practical rules that must be strictly observed', including the rule that forbade teachers from attending 'political meetings of any kind [...] to abstain from any controversy; to be imbued with a spirit of obedience to the law and loyalty to Sovereign'.[24] In the circular, the Commissioners warned that while teachers were 'free to have their own political views [...] any teacher who may be proved to have taken part in disloyal demonstrations will receive the severest penalty which the Regulations permit'.[25]

While the INTO was bound by the Commissioners' rules and sought to uphold them, at meetings of the INTO, such as those at Sligo in 1905 and at Ballybay in 1909, some teachers took the opportunity to express nationalist views. Beyond the immediate concerns of the INTO and despite the threat of sanction for breaches of the Commissioners' rules, many teachers, whether of a nationalist or unionist persuasion, were swept up in the political fervour that was growing in the early years of the twentieth century. The national teachers of Ireland were, after all, an integral part of their local community.

Marriage ban and strike

After Irish Independence, the INTO continued to work to promote the interests of national schoolteachers, including teachers in Northern Ireland. In the early 1930s, Ireland experienced the economic effects of the major global depression after the Wall Street Crash, and the depression was compounded by the economic war with Britain.[26] The fledgling state was caught in an cycle of economic depression, and in 1932, the government introduced a budget that included proposals for spending cuts in the form of pay cuts for public servants, including teachers.[27] Hence, a particular concern for teachers was the proposed 'economy cut' to their salaries, which the INTO resisted, believing teachers' salaries to be already 'altogether insufficient' at that time.[28] Despite teachers' opposition, the salary cuts were introduced.

In the same year, the government introduced the marriage ban on female teachers as another measure to address the severe economic depression of the period. The ban required female national schoolteachers to resign on marriage, and this decision was not just about economic policy, but was also informed by the prevailing beliefs and assumptions about the role of women in society, and in particular, their role in the home.[29] The INTO strongly objected to the proposal, writing:

> The proposed regulation requiring women teachers to retire on marriage deserves condemnation, whether regarded from an educational, ethical, or economic standpoint [...] The rule cuts across the constitutional and social rights of women teachers and is bound to react harmfully on the schools, and the status of the profession and will ultimately have the effect of seriously lowering the standard of education in rural areas.[30]

Despite strong opposition from the INTO, the marriage ban was introduced and remained in effect until 1958, thereby demonstrating the relative powerlessness of national teachers, and women teachers in particular, against prevailing political, social and religious forces operating in Ireland at that time. The power of these forces was evident in the wording of Article 40 of the

Irish Constitution of 1937, which assigned the woman's role to the domestic sphere:

> The State recognises that by her life within the home, woman gives to the State a support without which the common good cannot be achieved. The State shall, therefore, endeavour to ensure that mothers shall not be obliged by economic necessity to engage in labour to the neglect of their duties in the home.[31]

Although national teachers were often powerless in their efforts to achieve improved conditions of employment, they were prepared to take a stand. In March 1946, the INTO led the teachers into a national strike to demand better pay and to resist what they saw as outmoded teaching methods associated with the teaching of Irish as the sole medium of instruction in infant classes.[32] They also objected to the introduction of the Primary Cert as a compulsory examination. The strike lasted for thirty weeks, and despite support from the Catholic Church, and from parents and the public, the teachers' demands were not met, and they returned to work on 31 October at the behest of the Catholic Archbishop of Dublin, John Charles McQuaid.[33] The decision to return to work caused internal discord within the INTO at the time.

While the INTO strike demonstrated the teachers' impotence against the intransigence of Éamon De Valera's government, the strike and its aftermath also showed that national teachers were no longer deferential to their government masters. Although unsuccessful, their action in striking ultimately made the INTO politicised and stronger, and inspired other professional groups who would later pursue their grievances with the government.[34]

While the Catholic hierarchy supported the INTO's efforts to secure better pay and better conditions of employment, it could be just as powerful an adversary as the government in facing down teachers. Having consolidated control over the patronage and management of the majority of national schools, the Church could influence the direction of the new state through its control over childhood itself. As Duggan writes: 'the Catholic hierarchy viewed the educational landscape as their fiefdom and any measures perceived to threaten their interests were stoutly resisted'.[35] This resistance was clearly demonstrated in the 1930s, when the INTO attempted to establish an Educational Advisory Council to give lay schoolteachers a voice in school policy and school management; fearing this as a threat to its influence, the hierarchy blocked the INTO.[36]

In Catholic schools, catechism was the principal means of religious instruction and the local clergy paid very close attention to catechetic instruction and its assessment, and later in the 1960s, some teachers complained of interference from their local clergy, a complaint that was frequently discussed at INTO meetings.[37] Teachers' willingness to question the Catholic Church in educational matters somehow foretold the advent of the social protest movements in the late 1960s and early 1970s that began to challenge the conservative and traditional social order, including the power and authority of the Catholic Church.[38]

School attendance

Since the establishment of the national school system, the records of the Commissioners of National Education indicate a consistent pattern of low average pupil attendance. This pattern was evident in most national schools in the nineteenth century and was replicated across all the schools in the parish of Magheross in west Farney, where attendance in 1874 at both rural schools and in the schools in Carrickmacross was well below 50 per cent.[39]

While historically Irish parents keenly supported their children's education, the pattern of attendance suggested that not all parents were committed to sending their children to school on a regular basis, and it also reflected the importance of children as labourers in the rural economy. From time to time, as has been discussed in an earlier chapter, school attendance could also be impacted by epidemics of infectious diseases, notably scarlet fever and measles. Although education remained a valued commodity in Ireland, in the very poor rural districts, it was not always a priority.[40]

As a way of addressing the problem, in 1892 the Westminster government introduced legislation to compel parents to send their children to school; the *Education Act 1892* introduced compulsory school attendance. Representing a substantial state intervention in the family, the Act required all children over six and under fourteen years of age to attend school and to make seventy-five attendances in each half-year.[41] However, the Act applied to urban areas only and allowed for exceptions in rural areas. In practice, it was also limited, partly because the Catholic hierarchy disapproved of such legislation, seeing it as an interference with the principle of absolute parental authority.[42] In the last decade of the nineteenth century, the average daily attendance remained low, but relatively stable at between 61 and 63 per cent nationally.[43]

At the start of the twentieth century school attendance continued to be relatively poor, and where attendance was recorded as low, it meant smaller average class sizes, resulting in enforced dismissals or retirements of assistant teachers. In 1900 Mr E. Dowling, Chief Inspector for the southern part of Ireland, reported that there was no 'material improvement in the *regularity* of school attendance' and that attendance had 'seriously declined', which he partly attributed to epidemics of infectious diseases among children.[44]

School attendance was also a concern for teachers themselves, including teachers from the Carrickmacross National Teachers' Association. Addressing a meeting of the Association in 1903, Master Patrick Marron said:

It is deplorable to think that the vast bulk of the children at the National Schools, owing to the irregularity of attendance are receiving an education that can be of no practical utility to them in after life [...] The poor pupils are in blissful ignorance of their misfortune. It is only in later years, when they enter into competition in the battle of life with children in other lands, who have the benefits conferred by regular attendance at school, that they will realise the magnitude of their lost opportunities.[45]

Commenting on school attendance at a large girls' school in 1904, one teacher said: 'One-third of the children are almost always here; about half of the rest come fairly regularly; the remainder we hardly ever see.'[46] One district inspector laid some of the blame for poor attendance on teachers:

It is surprising to what a small extent ordinary wet weather deters little children from attending school. The perseverance of such pupils, badly clad as they often are, should be a powerful appeal for punctuality on the teacher's part, so that the lighting of fires and other arrangements for their comfort might be completed before the arrival of the earliest of the weather-beaten little travellers.[47]

In his report on the state of schools in 1904, Mr F.H. Dale reasoned that irregular attendance was partly due to 'greater poverty of the population, the more inclement weather, especially in the West of Ireland, and the more widely spread indifference to education among the parents'.[48] He questioned whether compulsory school attendance in rural districts was desirable, due to the difficulty in enforcing the law and given the circumstances of rural farming families:

It would be unreasonable in my judgement to expect that under existing conditions the country Schools in Ireland should exhibit the same regularity of attendance throughout the year [...] The exigencies of the parents' work on the land and their poverty render the employment of the older children inevitable during certain parts of the year.[49]

Dale suggested that attendance in rural districts might be improved if arrangements could be made to transport children to school in covered carts.

In the early twentieth century, a number of official government reports on national education considered, among other things, school attendance. The Vice-Regal Committee of Inquiry into Primary Education in 1913 heard evidence that 'a great number of children were leaving school in the fourth standard'.[50] Following Independence, the new Dáil Éireann debated the 1892 Act, and in 1922, it was noted that 'the attendance of children at school has of late been notoriously irregular and [...] the present compulsory attendance law has proved to be inadequate to deal with the situation'.[51] The government later passed the *School Attendance Act 1926*, which required school attendance for every day of the school year for children aged six to fourteen years, and the responsibility for enforcing the obligation was largely in the hands of local Garda Síochána.[52]

School discipline
In the nineteenth century and for much of the twentieth century, children occupied a subordinate position in society and in the family, and their behaviour was strictly controlled in the home and in school.[53] Parents instilled in their children respect for authority, and children were expected to accept without question the roles that their parents assigned to them.[54] In rural Ireland, children played an important role as a source of cheap labour, and this often meant working on the family farm or being hired out to other farmers or town merchants.[55]

The Catholic clergy also exerted considerable control over children, largely through schooling, where children were expected to exercise self-control.[56] While schools also controlled children's behaviour, the Commissioners of National Education urged that control should be exercised with due regard to the child's welfare. Under the Commissioners' rules, teachers were required to strictly observe the following 'practical rule':

To evince a regard for the improvement and general welfare of their pupils; to treat them with kindness combined with firmness; and to aim at governing them by their affections and reason, rather than by harshness and severity.[57]

On 'governing' pupils' behaviour, the Commissioners issued *Instructions in regard to the infliction of corporal punishment in national schools*, which explicitly permitted the practice, stating that 'only a light cane or rod may be used for the purpose of corporal punishment, which should be inflicted only on the open hand'.[58] Nevertheless, the Commissioners cautioned teachers that 'punishment should be administered only for grave transgression – never failure in lessons' and that 'frequent recourse to corporal punishment will be considered by the Commissioners as indicating bad tone and ineffective discipline'.

District inspectors reported on school discipline, usually commenting on how well teachers maintained 'good order and discipline' in their schools. Corporal punishment was an integral part of schoolroom practice, as the following question in the 'Theory of [Teaching] Method' examination of 1904 indicated: 'Discuss the propriety of allowing children to be punished by the natural consequences of their acts.'[59]

Following Irish Independence, the Department of Education's *Rules for National Schools* also addressed school discipline; Rule 130(1) contained the earlier rule on treating children 'with kindness, combined with firmness', and added: 'ridicule, sarcasm, or remarks likely to undermine a pupil's self-confidence should be avoided'.[60] Rule 130 also set down the strict condition that corporal punishment should be administered 'only in cases of severe misbehaviour and not mere failure at lessons', and it should be administered 'only by the principal teacher or other member of the school staff authorised by the manager for the purpose'. The rule also decreed: 'Any teacher who inflicts improper or excessive punishment will be regarded as guilty of conduct unbefitting a teacher and will be subject to severe disciplinary action.'[61]

Corporal punishment in schools was also referred to as 'physical chastisement of pupils', and since the rules permitted corporal punishment, the practice was common. Schools were required to maintain a 'punishment book'; however, there is little evidence of these books having survived or if indeed schools maintained them.[62]

Dating from the period 1905 to 1927, one surviving punishment book from a Co. Wicklow national school lists the names of the pupils punished, the offence committed, the 'nature and amount of punishment' administered and the teacher's signature.[63] The book contains examples of pupils' alleged offences and the precise punishments dispensed, including: 'disobedience: 2 slaps; beating other children on the way home from school: 4 slaps; fighting during playtime: 2 slaps; refusing to attend school for guardian: 3 slaps; and leaving school premises without permission: 2 slaps'.[64] At a school in west Co. Dublin in the period 1908–12, the punishment book contained records of punishments for similar offences, including: 'disobedience and impertinence: 2 slaps; copying repeatedly: 2 slaps; inattention and stubbornness: 1 slap'.[65] Teachers at the same school also used detention after school hours as a punishment for offences like 'disobedience'.

Where a punishment became the subject of complaints from parents or a civil or legal case, teachers tended to defend and justify their action and maintain their absolute authority to use corporal punishment.[66] In October 1935, a court in Castleblaney, Co. Monaghan, heard the case of a female school-teacher who was defending a charge of assault on a pupil, brought by the boy's mother. The alleged assault involved the teacher striking the pupil about the head with an ash plant for 'bad writing', causing him to bleed.[67] In response to the charge, the teacher gave evidence that the injury sustained was the result of the boy accidentally hitting his head on the desk and causing a previous injury to bleed. The parish priest, who was the school manager, and a number of the pupils gave evidence that corroborated the teacher's account. The school principal and the local doctor also gave evidence. However, the complaint of assault was upheld and the teacher in question, who was reported to have had twenty-eight years' experience, was fined £100. In closing remarks, the judge said:

> [I have] great sympathy with teachers, for their's was a trying task, especially in cases where parents objected to their children being punished in the regular and proper manner, but in that case a proper instrument should have been used. It was surprising that proper canes were not supplied to teachers instead of ones they themselves cut from hedges.[68]

The judge also concluded that he 'was satisfied that the children who had given evidence for [the] defendant had been intimidated and that the teacher was unfit to be in charge of young children'. The fact that the judge referenced the use of 'a proper instrument' for punishing in a 'regular and proper manner' indicates how much the practice of corporal punishment was a taken-for-granted practice in national schools in mid-twentieth century Ireland.

In the 1950s, the School-Children's Protection Organisation, a voluntary child welfare group, recorded examples of punishments in primary schools, including teachers' excessive use of the cane on pupils' hands and legs, pulling of hair or ears, having pupils kneel for long periods or stand facing the wall, and refusing pupils' permission to use the toilet.[69] It was only when the rights and status of children began to be formally recognised and set down in international and Irish law and when parents demonstrated opposition to the practice, some through the School-Children's Protection Organisation, that corporal punishment was finally ended. In 1982 the Minister for Education issued a circular to all school managers and school principals. The circular re-stated Rule 130(1) in the 1965 Rules regarding the teacher's responsibility to treat pupils 'with kindness, combined with firmness', and it replaced Rule 130(2), which permitted corporal punishment 'in cases of severe misbehaviour' with the following: 'The use of corporal punishment is forbidden.'[70]

11

'Until the war is over': Patrons, managers and pupils at Coolfore, 1916–1966

The events of the Revolutionary Period 1916–23, which ultimately resulted in the creation of the state of Northern Ireland, meant that the number of schools, pupils and teachers, for which the new Free State government was responsible, was significantly reduced. Well over one third of schools came under the local education authorities that were set up in each of the six counties of Northern Ireland.[1] In the Free State, the office of the Secretary for Education replaced the Board of National Education in Ireland as the state authority responsible for national schools.

The Board held its last meeting on 31 January 1922. At the meeting, Pádraic Ó Brolcháin, the acting Chief Executive Officer, read a statement on behalf of the Minister for Education of the Provisional Government, Mr Finian Lynch, in which he advised the Board that the Minister was to take full control of and responsibility for primary education in Ireland.[2] This meant that after ninety years, the Board would cease to exist.[3] Subsequently in 1924, the *Ministers and Secretaries Act* established the Department of Education, which remained the body responsible for national schools throughout the twentieth century.

'A scholar named Marron'
Coolfore national school's principal of long-standing, Master Patrick Marron, died on 17 November 1916. Aged fifty-eight when he died, Master Marron had given over forty years of service at Coolfore, including his time as a paid monitor.[4] He was succeeded by his wife Annie (née Callan), then aged thirty-four, and eight children: Philip, Patrick A. (Alf), Lawerence J., John E., Mary J. (May), Annie, Tommie and Rose.[5] Master Marron's wife Annie died in 1962.[6]

Some few days after Master Marron's death, Mr William Pierce, the school

manager and Shirley's agent, wrote to the Commissioners of National Education, enquiring if it would be possible 'to keep the school for his son, who
is about eighteen years of age and [...] being trained for a Teacher'.[7] The son
in question was most probably Philip, Master Marron's eldest son, who was
born in 1898. Mr Pierce made the inquiry at the behest of the Marron family
and the Commissioners, in turn, sought confirmation from the teacher training colleges as to whether a 'scholar named Marron' was in training at the
time. Having contacted the various training colleges, the Commissioners' reply
advised that 'no case of name [Marron] is at present in training'. Instead, they
provided Mr Pierce with details of a Mr James Marron, who had trained at
St Patrick's College, Drumcondra, from 1914–16, and who had already passed
the final examinations, including the examinations in Irish and Music.[8] At
the time, James Marron was connected with the Patrician Brothers' monastery
boys' school in Carrickmacross.

Regarding the request to have the school 'kept' for Master Marron's son,
the Commissioners called Mr Pierce's attention to Rule 165e, which stated:

> A King's scholar is not eligible for employment in any capacity dur-
> ing the time which he may have contracted to remain as a student in
> a Training College, unless the Commissioners are satisfied that the in-
> fraction of the contract is justified by illness or other satisfactory
> cause.[9]

The Commissioners' reply meant that Master Marron's son could not be
appointed. Instead, in December 1916, Mr Pierce advised the Commissioners
that he had appointed James Marron, subject to the Commissioners' approval.
James Marron, then aged twenty of Evelyn St, Carrickmacross, had previously
completed his monitorship at the monastery national school in Carrickmacross in June 1914. He had also previously acted as a substitute at Killark national school in the parish of Magheracloone and had successfully completed
his teacher examinations.[10] James Marron's appointment was confirmed, and
he took up the post of principal teacher at Coolfore national school on a
provisional basis on 8 January 1917.

At the time of Patrick Marron's death, Mrs Mary Mee remained as the
assistant teacher at Coolfore. She had reached the age of sixty in December
1928; however, the Department of Education policy at that time was 'to retain
efficient women teachers in the service beyond the completion of their six-
tieth year'.[11] On that basis, Mrs Mee continued to teach at Coolfore until her
death at age sixty-two in June 1930, following a brief illness. She had completed over thirty-eight years' teaching service at Coolfore.

Difficult circumstances

When S.E. Shirley died in 1904, his heir Evelyn Charles (E.C.) Shirley, then aged fifteen, was a minor and so the patronage of Coolfore national school came under the Shirley estate trustees.[12] In the following year, Mr William Pierce Esq. succeeded Mr Gibbings as Shirley's agent and was the named school manager.[13]

In 1906, during the later years of the land reforms, tenants of the Shirley estate had entered into negotiations with the trustees of the estate to purchase their holdings.[14] These negotiations and the subsequent transfer of ownership took place over a number of years, culminating in its completion by about 1910. In that year the Commissioners of National Education informed Rev. Dean McGlone, who was then the parish priest of Carrickmacross, that since Coolfore and Sreenty national schools were located on a portion of the Shirley estate that was sold or was being sold to the tenants, the trustees of the estate 'did not wish to incur further expenditure upon them'.[15] This implied that no tenant would be required to purchase a schoolhouse that was located on a part of their newly-acquired farm holding.

At the commencement of the Great War in 1914, E.C. Shirley, then aged twenty-five, became the High Sheriff of Monaghan, and by then, he had also become the school patron of Coolfore. At that time the Shirley family had moved to live permanently at Lough Fea House near Carrickmacross. In addition to Coolfore, the rural national schools at Sreenty and Corvally, along with the school at Ballaghnagearn in Magheracloone parish, remained under the patronage of the Shirley estate. Although E.C. Shirley was patron of the schools, the greater part of the Shirley estate, including the lands on which the school premises were located, had been sold to the tenants under the land purchase arrangements that followed the land reform acts of the late nineteenth and early twentieth centuries. This somewhat irregular arrangement led to difficulties for the schools at that time.

These difficulties were demonstrated in the case of Sreenty national school, when in 1914, the district inspector reported that the chimney of the school was leaning outward and risked falling and the out-offices needed repair. In response, Mr Pierce advised the district inspector that Mr Shirley 'was not inclined to spend any money on the School as the Estate has been sold' but was willing to hand it over to trustees 'as agreed at the sale of the estate'.[16] However, the handover to trustees was delayed with the outbreak of the Great War, when Shirley, then a commissioned officer in the British Army, was abroad on military duties. Shirley was aged about twenty-five at the commencement of the war and was a Major in the Warwickshire Yeomanry. He was posted to Gallipoli, where he led C Squadron in 1915.[17] Major Shirley remained on active service abroad throughout the war and visited his demesne at Lough Fea only occasionally when on leave. His absence resulted in delays in completing the transfer of patronage of the schools. The delay, in turn, presented difficulties for all the schools, including Coolfore school, which like Sreenty school, also needed financial support for the maintenance and upkeep of its premises.

Patronage of Coolfore national school

Sreenty national school was the focus of the initial communications on the transfer of patronage of the schools, and the plan was to first resolve the patronage of that school and then deal with the other schools. Following the final completion of the sale of the Shirley estate to the estate tenants in 1910, Shirley and Mr Pierce were obligated and willing to relinquish patronage and managership of the schools in question, under the terms of the sale of the estate, and were willing to transfer the three Catholic schools to Catholic diocesan trustees.[18] Corvally national school was then a school for Protestant and Presbyterian children and was also under Shirley's patronage.

For a change in the patronage to occur, the Commissioners required a written statement nominating the parish priest as Mr Pierce's successor as school manager. While he was willing to take over the management of Sreenty national school and the other schools, Fr McKenna, the then parish priest, was not in a position to do so at that time, citing physical and financial inability to take over the schools. Besides, having repaired several churches in the parish, he had a very large debt to pay. Fr McKenna was also anxious that Sreenty and the other schoolhouses should be improved and implying that Shirley might take on the cost of the improvements, he requested that 'at present a burden beyond what he (Fr McKenna) is able to bear should not be forced upon him'.[19]

Negotiations regarding the transfer of the patronage of Coolfore national school were first entered into with the relevant interested parties, including Mr Pierce and the Commissioners of National Education, through the senior school inspector, Mr W.R. Hughes. Major Shirley's solicitors, Fottrell and Sons of Fleet Street in Dublin, were also advising on the matter. The initial communications took place in 1914 and concerned the four rural national schools of Sreenty, Coolfore, Corvally and Ballaghnagearn.

In 1915, Coolfore national school had eighty-one pupils on the rolls, and all but one were Roman Catholic, and the average attendance was fifty-five pupils.[20] At the time, the district inspector reported that the school needed new desks in the downstairs classroom and the replacement of writing slates with paper. The walls in the out-offices were neglected and these also needed repair. However, Mr Pierce was unable to attend to these expenses since the land on which the school was located was no longer part of the Shirley estate. Pierce suggested that 'a local fund should be organised for such repairs'.[21] However, since no funds for repairs were provided by either Shirley or the local community, the recommended improvements to the out-offices were not made at that time.

Later in November 1916, in anticipation of the change of patronage of Coolfore school, the local Catholic curate, Fr P. McCleary, wrote to the Commissioners concerning the appointment of Master Patrick Marron's successor. He advised the Commissioners that if Mr Pierce were to make an immediate appointment of a school principal, it must be made with the 'previous sanction' of Dean O'Connor, the then parish priest of Carrickmacross.[22] In his letter to the Commissioners, Fr McCleary reminded them of the prior agreement regarding school patronage after the sale of the Shirley estate lands:

> About ten years ago, terms of sale of the Shirley Estate were arranged between the Trustees of the Estate and Corduff and Raferagh Tenants Committee, of which I was then Chairman. One of the conditions of sale was that the patronage and managership of Sreenty and Coolfore Schools, then as now in the hands of the landlord, should be handed over to the PP [of] Carrickmacross. The present PP is now Very Rev. Dean O'Connor. The Estate is now vested, but I have, since Mr Marron's death, learned that the landlord and his agent still retain management and patronage of these schools. Myself and the Tenants' Committee intend to fight this matter out through appeal to the Estates' Commissioners in view of a new appointment [of a principal teacher] to Coolfore NS having to be made.[23]

The Estates' Commissioners, to which Fr McCleary referred, was a statutory body responsible for purchasing untenanted land to be later resold to tenants.[24] Soon after Fr McCleary wrote to the Commissioners of National Education regarding the appointment of a new principal at Coolfore, Mr Pierce wrote to the Commissioners in early December, informing them of the appointment of James Marron as the new principal. Given the timing of Mr Pierce's communication to the Commissioners, it is doubtful whether he consulted or even informed Dean O'Connor in advance of the new appointment at Coolfore.

The patronage of the four schools remained unresolved in 1916, and the matter could not be resolved as long as Major Shirley was abroad on military duties and unavailable.[25] The district inspector, Mr Hughes, advised the Commissioners of the respective positions of Mr Pierce and Rev. Dean O'Connor, who had succeeded Fr McKenna, regarding the patronage of the schools. Throughout 1917, with Fottrell and Sons acting as intermediaries, there were efforts to secure Major Shirley's consent to hand over the national schools. However, it appears that Shirley considered the patronage of the schools on his estate as unimportant, when compared with the worldly events in which he was then engaged. While on leave at Lough Fea in January 1918, Shirley informed Mr Pierce that he wished 'to leave the matter over until the war is over [and] he does not care to deal with matters of this kind at present'.

In the following year, the district inspector again noted that repairs and upkeep of Coolfore school premises were needed. Specifically, the side wall of the out-office had partly fallen, leaving a piece of masonry loose and a danger to the children. In addition, pointing and plastering of the school stonework was also needed, and some trees on the school grounds needed to be cut down. The school floor had been cleaned just once in the previous year and was in much need of cleaning, and a cloakroom was required, which could be provided in a spare room downstairs. A fireguard was also needed for the upstairs' stove, and smaller desks were needed for the younger children.[26] As long as Shirley remained the school patron but was no longer the owner of the land on which the school stood, the state of uncertainty regarding responsibility for the school's upkeep and maintenance would continue, resulting in ongoing neglect of the school premises.

After several communications with Major Shirley's solicitors, the patronage of Coolfore national school was finally settled when it was transferred to Catholic diocesan trustees in September 1921.[27] The trustees were named as Most Rev. Patrick McKenna, the Bishop of Clogher; Archdeacon Patrick Keown; and Canon Andrew J. Maguire. Shirley's agent Mr Pierce relinquished the post of school manager to Archdeacon Keown, who was the parish priest at Carrickmacross.[28] Thereafter, Coolfore and Sreenty national schools came under the patronage of the Catholic diocese and under the management of the local Catholic clergy. The patronage of Ballynagearn national school was also transferred to Catholic diocesan trustees and came under the management of the parish priest at Magheracloone.

Cordial relations

In 1922 the Bishop of Clogher made an episcopal visit to the parish of Carrickmacross, and to coincide with the visit, the Catholic priests submitted a written statement to Bishop McKenna on 'the condition of religion' in the parish.[29] Signed by four priests, including Archdeacon Keown, who was the manager of all the Catholic national schools in the parish, the statement set out the circumstances of the parish in respect of religious observance, the conduct of masses and other liturgical events in the various churches and the conduct of schooling in the parish. The priests' statement opened with the following:

> We are happy to inform your Lordship that the condition of religion in the parish is satisfactory, and that the harmonious relations which have, we understand, from time immemorial between the priests and the people of Carrickmacross are well maintained [*sic*]. There are no abuses in the parish. The people are respectful towards their priests and amendable in all things that appertain to their spiritual welfare.
>
> The people of the parish as a body approach the Sacraments regularly and many of them frequently [...] The people in all districts of the parish are very faithful in attending to Mass on days of obligation, and daily Mass, especially in Lent and October, is well attended in St Joseph's [...] The Total Abstinence Pledge is annually renewed in all Churches of the Parish.[30]

The statement included details of the masses and other religious services held in each of the churches in the parish, and the priests also reported on schools and schooling in the parish, writing:

> The teachers of the parish are a hardworking, conscientious body, and the most cordial relations exist between them and the [School] Manager. We regret, however, to be obliged to state that the parents, especially in the rural districts, have not hitherto corresponded with the efforts of the teachers as earnestly as might be expected. After due allowance has been made for defective attendance due to the prevalence of epidemics in the district, it must be admitted that there is considerable negligence on the part of parents in sending their children to school.[31]

In their statement, the priests provided information, which seemed to bear out their concerns regarding school attendance. For example, when compared with the monastery and the convent schools in Carrickmacross town, where the level of attendance in 1921 was 75 and 76 per cent, respectively, at Coolfore school, it was 62 per cent and at Sreenty it was just 60 per cent. Relative to the urban schools, attendance at the other rural schools in the parish was also low.[32] In their report the priests appeared to ignore the fact that there were differences in school attendance between urban and rural schools, differences that could be accounted for in factors like distance to travel, weather and children's farming responsibilities.

Referring to the changed circumstances of the schools that were formerly under Shirley's patronage, the priests wrote: 'During the past year, the owner-ship of the School premises in Sreenty and Coolfore has been acquired on behalf of the Catholics of the district, and the PP of Carrickmacross is now Manager of the Schools.' On the state of repair of the schools, the priests re-marked that, with the exception of Sreenty, all the schools were 'in a state of good repair', and they advised that 'a new school at Sreenty will be a necessity in the near future'. In the event, Sreenty acquired a new school in 1935.

School managers under Catholic diocesan trustees

Monsignor Keown was the school manager for Coolfore and Sreenty schools after 1921 and had served as the manager of the other Catholic schools in Carrickmacross parish since 1919.[33] On the occasion of his Golden Jubilee in the priesthood in November 1938, the national schoolteachers of the parish made a presentation to him of a Ciborium in gratitude for his service and contribution to their schools. Master Cooney and Miss Rushe of Coolfore national school and several other teachers attended, and Master McEvoy of Corduff school gave an address, which included the following tribute:

> We, your teachers [...] express to you our deepest gratitude for the kindness, help and encouragement we have ever experienced at your hands. We are especially grateful to you for the freedom accorded to us in our work in the schools, and for the trust you have always re-posed in us. You have not only been our Manager, but a kindly coun-sellor and friend. We never fear any harsh interpretation of Educational Codes so long as we have a champion so eager and able to defend us as you.[34]

The teachers also thanked Monsignor Keown for his efforts in providing suitable school accommodation for the children of the parish. A strong advo-cate for the education of Catholic children by Catholic teachers in Catholic schools, Monsignor Keown was a member of the Central Association of the Catholic Clerical Managers. Speaking at Coolfore in 1937, he remarked that 'it was especially gratifying that the religious training of the children formed an important part of the curriculum'.[35] He held strictly to the primacy and absolute authority of Rome and demanded that the people of the parish should do likewise by submitting to hierarchical authority, advising his con-gregation that 'every Catholic should obey the Bishops in their teachings'.[36]

Monsignor Keown's most visible legacy are the stained-glass windows at St Joseph's church, which he commissioned from the famous Harry Clarke studio in 1924. Influenced by the European modernist styles of the early twentieth century, the window lights at St Joseph's are full of deep rich colours and Celtic and medieval symbolism.[37] He continued to act as the school manager for the national schools in the parish until his death at age eighty-five in October 1946. As a measure of his standing and that of the Church hierarchy at the time, those attending his funeral included Church dignitaries and senior government members, including An Taoiseach Éamon de Valera; Sean McEntee, the Minister for Finance; and Conor Maguire, the Chief Justice.

Monsignor Keown's successor as parish priest and the school manager of Coolfore was Monsignor Hugh Finnegan.[38] During his tenure at Carrickmacross, Monsignor Finnegan commissioned the famous Irish liturgical artist Richard King to paint the Stations of the Cross, a series of fourteen oil paintings which adorn the walls of St Joseph's church.[39] A former pupil of Harry Clarke, King completed the paintings in *c.* 1950–51, and with their rich colours, the paintings complement Clarke's windows.[40] Framed monochrome copies of the fourteen paintings were placed on the walls of the upstairs classroom at Coolfore sometime in the 1950s. King was also an illustrator who designed commemorative Irish stamps but was best known as an artist in stained glass.[41] Monsignor Finnegan died in October 1966 and was succeeded by Monsignor Patrick Mulligan, who later became Bishop of Clogher, and was the school's last manager at the time of its closure in 1968.

School subjects at Coolfore after 1922

After 1922 the Free State government positioned children and their schooling as important in the pursuit of its mission to forge a distinctly Irish cultural identity for the newly-independent nation. In this nationhood-building mission, the ideals of child-centred education, as espoused in the curriculum reforms of 1900, were relegated in importance, in favour of more traditional didactic instruction aimed at forming the child's knowledge, skills and character for a future role in the new nation.[42] For boys, this future role was productive work, and for girls it was motherhood and domesticity, and the school curriculum reflected this gendered division of subjects.[43]

Developed by the National Programme Conference in 1922 and 1926, the revised national school curriculum reflected the Irish language, culture and tradition, and it marked a renewed focus on the 'three Rs' and other literary subjects.[44] After 1926, the schoolteachers at Coolfore and other national schools were required to teach compulsory subjects, including Irish, English, mathematics, history, geography, music, rural science/nature study and needlework for girls. Needlework received three hours each week and domestic science was also added for girls. Algebra and geometry were taught to boys only and became optional in classes taught by women teachers and in single-teacher schools.[45]

In 1928, the Department of Education introduced the Primary School Certificate examination, which would 'testify to the successful completion by the pupil of Standard VI Course of the School Programme'.[46] The 'Primary Cert' examination became compulsory in 1943 and would continue for all pupils completing primary school education up until 1967; its ending coincided with the introduction of free secondary education.

Religion was also compulsory as an extra-curricular subject and was held to be 'by far the most important [subject]'. For the majority of national schools, religion meant Catholic teaching, and through its management of the schools and its wider influence among local and national politicians, the Catholic Church now held a central and controlling role in education. The new state and the Catholic Church were engaged in an effective power-sharing arrangement in areas of public life like education, healthcare and social care. In this way, the state accorded the Church a privileged position in the national schools, accepting its authority in matters related to education and schooling.[47] As an indication of the number of Catholic religious congregations involved in the establishment and management of national schools, in 1926 there were twenty-two separate orders of religious sisters managing 334 convent schools and five male religious orders managing 117 monastery schools. In addition, the majority of national schools in the country were under the patronage of diocesan trustees and were managed locally by Catholic clerics.

To underline the essential role of the school as an ecclesiastical extension of the church parochial hall, Catholic schools were regularly used as venues for parochial activities. For example, during the 1930s, Coolfore national school was the venue for a bazaar and concert in aid of the Society for the Propagation of the Faith.[48] School pupils were frequently at the forefront of such events. At a concert performed by the children at Coolfore in January 1937, each 'little artist' was asked to respond to the question, presumably addressed to the male pupils only: 'What he would like to be when he became a man.' The standard response was 'to be good Catholics, good Irishmen and industrious citizens'.[49] Such set pieces and other Church-sponsored devotional and recreational activities were organised by the teachers.

As if to foretell Éamon de Valera's much derided and much analysed 1943 'cosy homesteads' speech, in which he valorised the idea of Ireland as a rural idyll, at the same Coolfore concert in 1937, Monsignor Keown said that 'he wished that the craze for abandoning rural life in favour of town and city should have no place in the parish', and apparently overlooking the economic realities of rural life, he hoped that the people would 'settle on the land, the natural life for them, a life that conduces most to health, happiness, and length of days'.[50] Catechism held a prominent place in the school curriculum, underlining the central role of religion in the schooling experience in the new state. Through catechism, children learned the articles of Catholic faith by heart and the parish priest examined them in their knowledge of the subject.

Following independence, national schools were also places of learning about the Irish nation and its traditions and folklore, and teachers were expected to inculcate a pride of nationhood. This was especially evident in 1966, when the Golden Jubilee of the 1916 Rising was being commemorated. Several national and local events took place in that year, including a great parade through Carrickmacross, involving several local brass and pipe bands, scouts and guides, town councillors, Catholic clergy and members of the Old IRA.[51] In their April 1966 editions, national newspapers carried colour supplements, which celebrated the Rising and its fallen revolutionaries. At Coolfore, the senior classes learned the opening passage of the Proclamation of the Irish Republic by heart, and pictures of Pearse, Connolly and the other executed revolutionaries were placed on the walls of the upstairs schoolroom.

In pursuit of its policy to promote the Irish language in national schools, the Department of Education instructed teachers of infant classes not to use English in their lessons if they were able to use Irish.[52] Additionally, in Irish-speaking districts and in some English-speaking districts, children up to the age of eight were taught entirely through Irish and this was continued in about half of the schools up to the age of ten, and in about a third of schools until the pupils left school. The success or otherwise of teaching through Irish depended on the ability of the teacher to speak and understand the language. In 1934, as a way of arresting the decline in the use of Irish in the Irish-speaking districts, the Department of Education gave a monetary incentive of £2 to parents or guardians if they could demonstrate that their children were fluent in Irish.[53]

Events at the schoolhouse

Coolfore national school was a prominent local landmark on the road connecting the Ballybay and Aghalile roads. The schoolhouse was the site of an act of vandalism in late November 1932, when windows were broken, fences broken down and there were attempts to remove the large iron entrance gates from their pillars.[54] Although the Gardaí at Carrickmacross conducted investigations, no offenders were identified, and the motive for the damage was also not identified.

Some years later in November 1950, parts of the interior of the schoolhouse were damaged by a fire, which occurred when the school was closed for a period of ten days to facilitate the potato harvest. On the Monday morning following the ten-day 'vacation', Master Cooney opened up the school-house and was greeted by smoke, which poured out of the door. A newspaper report described the damage:

> Until the door was opened and smoke gushed through, there were no signs of the fire, which had made a large hole in the upper floor, through which the burnt furniture, including book presses, fell through to the stone floor of the cloakroom underneath [...] The thickened smoke blackened the interior of the school.[55]

The report noted that the fire originated from sparks in the chimney of the fireplace in the upstairs room, and spread to the wooden floor and nearby presses, and the entire school building was saved by the fact that the windows were closed. A cast iron potbelly stove was subsequently used to heat the upstairs classroom.

The act of vandalism and the destructive fire contrasted with the pleasantries that were associated with planned events at the school. The schoolhouse acted as a local community venue, usually for activities related to the school itself or the parish. For example, a bazaar in aid of the Propagation of the Faith was held in November 1934, at which a large attendance contributed £20 to the fund.[56] Some years later on a Sunday evening in January 1937, the School hosted a concert in aid of the school repair fund, where the pupils provided the entertainment. Addressing the large audience, Monsignor Keown remarked that 'the people of the locality were singularly blessed in having such competent teachers as Mr Cooney and Miss Rushe', and he added that 'the efficiency of the teaching was clearly manifest in the high-class entertainment', which the children provided.[57]

In April of that same year, a large audience attended a second concert in aid of the school repair fund, and on that occasion, the audience was treated to step dances, three- and four-hand reels, songs and storytelling. A local Coolfore dramatic club gave a debut stage performance of a three-act comedy, which had the audience 'laughing heartily from start to finish'.[58] Later in December 1937, a second concert, again featuring the Coolfore dramatic club, was held at the school; on that occasion the concert was held in aid of the Society for the Propagation of the Faith.[59]

At a packed Catholic Hall in Carrickmacross in January 1938, the Coolfore dramatic club was again on stage and had the audience 'in fits of laughter'. Three members of the Coolfore troupe, Miss K. McNally, James Fealy and seventy-eight-year-old Tom Ward – 'who showed a spirit and lightness of foot that would do credit to a youngster' – performed a three-hand reel.[60] Involving a 'blend of town and country talent', the concert at Carrickmacross was also held in aid of the Society for Propagation of the Faith, and the pupils of the Patrician Brothers' monastery school and the St Louis convent school sang songs and gave recitations, while the Patrician boys opened the concert, singing 'Faith of our Fathers'.

Aside from parochial events, from time to time, schoolhouses like Coolfore and Sreenty were the venues for lectures given by agricultural instructors on a range of topics related to farming and animal husbandry, including pig rearing and poultry keeping.[61]

Dúchas: The Irish Folklore Commission

In the late 1930s, the Irish Folklore Commission enlisted pupils to collect, record and write short essays on local folklore, based on interviews with their parents, grandparents and neighbours. The aim was to preserve stories in the oral tradition, including stories about the locality, its old customs, folktales and legends, proverbs, games and pastimes.[62] At Coolfore national school, under the guidance of Miss Rushe and Master Cooney, fifty-four essays were collected between 1937 and 1939 and donated to the the Dúchas Schools' Collection, part of the national folklore archive. Essay titles included 'My home district', 'Proverbs', 'Local cures', 'Old schools' and 'Famine times'. Among the pupils who contributed essays were James Murtagh, Legghimore; Lawerence McMahon, Coolfore; Tom Ward, Coolfore; Margaret Shankey, Rakeeragh; Bridget Raferty, Greaghnaroog; Michael Hamilton, Greaghnaroog; John James Tumelty, Coolfore; and James Dowdall, Killarue.

A number of the pupils wrote essays on the subject of 'Old schools', a topic that recorded short stories of former hedge schools in the district.[63] Among the pupils to contribute an essay on the subject was James Dowdall of Killarue who wrote of two hedge schools, one at Laragh and one at Creevy, where the teacher was Bessie Costello.[64] Margaret Shankey of Rakeeragh wrote about Owen Mc Kitterick who conducted a hedge school in a barn; although blind, 'he could [recognise] everyone who came to the school as he was gifted, and he could therefore know them by their breathing'.[65] Margaret also wrote on the topic of 'local cures', including cures for common childhood illnesses:

When the children would have the mumps, the father would put an ass's winkers on them and lead them three times into a pig sty. This was done three times in the morning before sunrise and three times in the evening after sunset. Long ago the godfather would buy a red ribbon and tie it on the child's neck as a cure for the whooping cough. Another cure for whooping cough was to drink 'ferret's leaving's'. Still another was to drink ass's milk.[66]

Michael Hamilton of Greaghnarogue also contributed an essay on the local cure for the mumps, writing:

The remedy […] was, to get a horse's halter and put it on the patient's head and to lead him in and out on the pigsty door for three mornings in succession. Then the person while leading the patient in and out on the pigsty door would pronounce the words, 'Tugad na mucna leicnea, leicne,' and these words would cure the disease.[67]

Loosely translated, the Irish incantation declared that the pigs bring the mumps, and perhaps it also called on the pigs to take away the mumps.

Writing essays about 'my home district', a number of the pupils gave a brief sketch of their own townland. James Murtagh wrote that the land in Legghimore 'is dry and some of it is hilly but none of it is boggy [and] it grows an average crop'. Laurence McMahon wrote that in Coolfore townland: 'Most of the land is tilled. The crops mostly grown are potatoes and oats and a couple acres of flax. The farmers say that the ground is good for oats and grass-seed.' Rose Quigley of Drumgowna wrote that the land 'is very good although it is rather wet and heavy' and she wrote that Marron was the name most common is the townland.[68]

Miss Rushe also contributed a number of essays to the folklore archive, including essays on 'The Penal days', 'Hedge schools' and 'The local landlords'. She also contributed several poems to the collection, which her neighbour Patrick Marron, aged seventy-eight of Drumgowna, had supplied. One poem was written by Peter McDaniel of Corkashybane in 1842, and Marron explained to Miss Rushe that, when writing home to his parents from Dublin, McDaniel always wrote in poetry and never wished his poems to be published. Entitled 'Letter to parents', McDaniel's short poem captures the names of some of the locals in the district of the period:

It's a glorious day in summer in 1842.
Oh! father dear and mother fond I'm thinking now of you.
I hope you're hale and hearty and feel no ache or pain
Since I bade goodbye to all I loved in dear old Curkishbane.
How is all the family and my dear sister one
Not forgetting my brothers all, that's Hughie, James and John
How is Daniel Hanlon, from my native Irish town
And fearless brave Tom Dwyer, the scholar of renown
How is Johnny Dally or does he deal in hogs,
And likewise Barney Callan, or does he rule the bogs.[69]
Marron also explained to Miss Rushe that McDaniel was a clever boy

who attended a local hedge school, and when coming home from school with his companions, he met sappers who were out mapping the district. When one of the men asked him where he got his education, the young McDaniel replied: 'The side of the hedge where the most shelter was.'[70]

24—Master Patrick Marron and wife Annie, 1899 (Courtesy St Louis Convent, Carrickmacross)

25—*Coolfore girls 1911 (Courtesy Monaghan County Museum). Back row (l. to r.):* ——, Nan Murphy, Teedie Murphy, Maggie Fox (?), Rose Hanlon, ——, Nannie Rooney. *Middle row:* Annie Marron (Monitress), Rosie Murtagh, Mary Murphy, Nan Mee, ——, Mary Daly (Boston), Mary Daly (Bocks), Rose Ann Callaghan, Katie Ward. *Front row:* Bridgie Mee, Mary Connor, Katie Malone, ——, Linn Mee, Babby Callan, Bridgie Murphy (Cormoy), Rosie Mee, Katie Keaskin, ——

26—*Coolfore boys 1911 (Courtesy Monaghan County Museum). Back row (l. to r.):* James O'Neill, Frank Murphy, Thomas Malone, Paddy Hanlon, Jimmy Keaskin, Tommy Gilsenan, Phil Marron, Pete Ward. *Middle row:* Willie Reilly, Jimmy Dowdall, Pete Callan, Hugh Murtagh, Jimmy Ward, Jim Marron, Packie Marron, Pete O'Neill (tbc), John O'Neill, Mick Farmer. *Third row:* Packie Marron (Sally), Walter Eakin, Alf Marron, Larry Murtagh, Jim Daly, Jack Gilsenan, Packie Ward, Gene Ward, James Malone, Josie Marron. *Front row:* Paddy Ward, L. Marron, Tom Finnegan

27—*Coolfore boys 1914 (Courtesy Monaghan County Museum). Back row (l. to r.):* Paddy Keenan, Frank Mohan, Peter Mohan, Willie Reilly, Tommy Finnegan, Jimmy Rooney, Tommy Ward. *Middle row:* Paddy Hanlon, Walter Eakin, Larry Murtagh, Josie Marron, Alf Marron, L. Marron, Josie McEnaney, Fran Marron. *Front row:* James Malone, Rory O'Carroll, Nicky O'Carroll, John Marron, Joe O'Connor, Peter Boylan, Packie Sherry, Frank O'Connor, Packie Mee

28—*Coolfore girls 1914 (Courtesy Monaghan County Museum). Back row (l. to r.):* ——, Rosie Mee, Kate Ann Gillick, Bridgie Murtagh. *Middle row:* ——, Nan Mee, Mary Kate McDaniel, Rose Ann McDaniel, Mary Connor, Mary Gillick, Katie Brennan, Kate Malone. *Front row:* Alice Gillick, Bridgie Mee, Nora Mee, Mary Marron, Julia Connor, … McDaniel, … McDaniel, Maggie Callan

161

30—Corduff National School, 1930 (Courtesy 'Corduff Calling' 1983). Back row (l. to r.): Margaret Marron, Maura Traynor, Rose Marron, Nellie Callan, Alice Mooney, Molly Sheridan, Annie McGrother, Nan Marron, Katie Traynor, Bridgie Ward, Kate Ann Rushe, Lizzie Rushe, Bridgie Marron, Rosaleen Marron. *Second row:* Trodda McGee, Mary Ann O'Connor, Ellie Keenan (Sreenty), Teresa O'Connor, Maggie Marron, Sally Traynor, Annie Corrigan, Ellie Keenan (Corkisbane), Philomena Hanratty, Kathleen Murray, Cassie Fealy. *Third row:* Patsy McGee, John McGee, Patsy Marron, Kathleen O'Connor, Bridgie Reilly, Kate Reilly, Mary Kelly, Rose Traynor, Kathleen Marron, Dermot Peddigrew, Vincent Peddigrew, Frank Flood. *Front row:* Peter McGee, Michael McGee, Cissie Fox, Nellie Marron, James Keenan, Connolly sisters, Joe Flood *(opposite page, top) —Coolfore boys 1927 (courtesy Monaghan County Museum). Back (l. to r.):* Packie Garvey, Pat McCabe, Pat [?]key, Gene Malone, Tommy J. McGinnity, Tommie [?]nbers. *Second row:* Bennie Costello, John [?]naney, Pierce Finnegan, Padge Keenan RIP (died [?]nkirk), John Marron, James Keenan, Arthur [?]an, Bennie Meehan. *Third row:* Bennie Shankey, [?]omiskey, Peter McEnaney, Seamus Garvey, Peter [?]abe, Jemmy McCabe, J.V. McGinnity, John [?]abe, James Gollogly. *Front row:* James Marron, [?]y McMahon, Phil McMahon, Eoin Garvey, Jim [?]key, Tom Callan, Leo McGinnity, Owen Ward, [?]nie Begley

31 (right)—Coolfore school concert poster, 1937 (Courtesy B. McGinnity)

32—Section of window light in St Joseph's RC church, Carrickmacross (Image © the author)

163

33—*Carrickmacross girls' national school (date and list of names unavailable)* (Courtesy Ms Ronnie Buick)

34—*Carrickmacross Monastery boys' national school (date unknown) (Courtesy Monaghan County Museum). Back row:* Johnny McMahon, S. Downey, John Rafferty, Brian Walsh, P. Farrelly, Gerard Hand, Sean Reilly. *Middle row:* Brother Philip, M. Swinburne, —— ——, Brendan Walsh, ——, Pat Allen, ——, Gerry McDermott, John McDonald, ——, Manus Daly, Dominic McCartney. *Front row:* K. O'Brien, J. Murphy, Jack Connolly, Philip Reilly, P. Woods, Frank Rooney, John Jones, Tom Loughran, F.J. McDonald, Paddy Roche, K. McCartney. *Seated:* ——

35—Former residence of Master Patrick Marron, Drumgowna (Courtesy E. Sherry)

36—Sample of old Gaelic script, Miss Rushe papers (Courtesy G&R Callan)

37—Main Street Carrickmacross, c. 1950 (Courtesy Monaghan County Museum)

38—May Eucharistic procession Carrickmacross (Courtesy Monaghan County Museum)

39—Blackrock seaside village, Co. Louth (Courtesy Irish Historic Picture Company)

40—Fane Valley jam factory, Shercock Road Carrickmacross, c. 1950, view towards Mullinary (Courtesy Monaghan County Museum)

41—Coolfore boys c. 1958 (Courtesy B. McGinnity). Back row (l. to r.): Kieran Daly, James Tumelty, Thomas McKeown, Thomas Ward, John Murtagh. *Front row:* Francis Connor, John Henry Keenan, Bernard McGinnity, Eugene Ward, Joseph Murtagh, Laurence Murtagh

42—Coolfore boys c. 1963 (Courtesy J. Meehan). Back row (l. to r.): Martin Farrell, Patrick Meehan, Frank Ward, Patrick Callan, Michael Malone, Philip Malone, Michael Reilly. *Front row:* Gerard Fealy, Michael Mee, Paul Hand, Alfie Mee, James (Jem) Meehan, Eugene McKenna, Michael Connolly, James Fealy (Standing on school steps: Anne Mary (Anna May) Meehan (RIP))

43—*First day at school: Joseph Callan, Drumbroagh, one of the last pupils enrolled at Coolfore (Courtesy J. Callan)*

44—*'I stood upon the little bridge … at the old school in Coolfore' (Image © the author)*

45—*Primary Certificate 1930 awarded to Mary Boylan, late mother of the author (Image © the author)*

46—*'Nestled in rolling drumlins': The former Coolfore schoolhouse (Image © the author)*

12

'Tastefully and with expression': Teachers and pupils at Coolfore national school, 1924–1968

Following Irish Independence, the government of the new Free State set about establishing the structures of national government and public administration. This included the establishment of government ministries, including a Minister for Education. The nationalist fervour that preceded the War of Independence was now channelled into developing and promoting a distinct *Gaelic* identity for the new state, and the national schools, their teachers and the Irish language became important in this effort.

In the drive to revive the Irish language, pupils in infant classes were taught through the medium of Irish and teachers were expected to spend at least one hour on the teaching of Irish in all other classes.[1] At national schools like Coolfore, where English was the pupils' first language, Irish began to feature on the curriculum. At nearby Lisdoonan national school, the local teacher, scholar and folklorist, Henry Morris, was active in promoting the Irish language in south Monaghan and across south Ulster. As the schoolmaster at Lisdoonan in the early years of the twentieth century, Morris taught through the medium of Irish and he founded the first Co. Monaghan branch of the Gaelic League in Lisdoonan. A Co. Monaghan native, Morris later became an inspector for the Department of Education.[2]

After Independence, lessons in history featured stories of ancient Gaelic Ireland, and teachers in training were expected to study works, including *Irish Nationality* and the *Life of Hugh O'Neill*.[3] Despite the introduction of the new revised curriculum in 1900, which emphasised practical subjects and activity-based learning, by the early 1920s, the pupils continued to be taught mainly numeracy and literacy subjects through traditional teaching methods.

For most of the years after Independence until its closure in 1968, two teachers were the dominant figures at Coolfore, Master Cooney and Miss

Rushe. Both teachers had completed their teacher training within a few years of each other, Master Cooney in 1916 and Miss Rushe in 1923, and each gave over forty years' service to teaching. Both attended teacher training in Dublin training colleges, where their training emphasised traditional teaching methods, although they also studied kindergarten and practical subjects.[4] By the time the more progressive child-centred curriculum was introduced in the late 1960s, both Master Cooney and Miss Rushe had retired.[5]

Master Cooney

Master James Marron remained as principal until the end of 1923, when the Commissioners noted that he could not be reappointed as principal, since he had not obtained the teacher's diploma.[6] Although eligible to be appointed as assistant at Coolfore, Mr Marron resigned in December 1923.[7] Mr Francis Cooney, who was previously assistant at St Michael's boys' school at Cootehill, was appointed principal in January 1924.[8] Then aged twenty-nine, Master Cooney had completed his teacher training at St Patrick's College, Drumcondra, in the period 1914–16, and he also held an ordinary certificate in Irish.[9] A native of Cox's Mill in the parish of Donaghmoyne, Cooney was the son of a farmer and RIC officer.

Like all national schoolteachers, Master Cooney was under the watchful eye of the district inspector, and his efficiency as a teacher was judged by the proficiency of the pupils, as reported in the inspector's examinations. The inspector could also make unannounced visits to the school, typically in the morning when school lessons were about to commence. The inspector's reports for Coolfore national school included reports of Master Cooney's teaching methods, his timekeeping, accuracy in monitoring and recording school attendance, and his management of the school accounts.[10]

Literary organiser

When a district inspector found inefficiencies in teaching and the organisation of a school, the Department of Education could appoint a 'literary organiser' to visit the school to give guidance and advice to the school principal. This could involve spending a number of days at a school to observe the teaching and the organisation of the school curriculum and to give advice on how the school timetable could be efficiently organised. Following a visit to a school, the literary organiser prepared a report for the divisional inspector, which was communicated back to the school manager.

In September 1932, Miss E.M. Brady, the literary organiser for the Senior Division, visited Coolfore national school, and having spent a number of days at the school, submitted a detailed report of her findings and recommendations. She found that the arrangements for teaching Irish involved grouping the junior classes together into a single junior division and teaching them all the same material, and similarly, grouping the senior classes into a single senior division and teaching them the same material. In place of this arrangement, Miss Brady re-drafted the timetables for the junior and senior divisions on a 'bi-partite arrangement [with] the underlying aim being direct teaching of one group during an entire half hour, while the other group is engaged in independent desk work, under general supervision'.[11] This arrangement would ensure 'separate teaching of Irish for pupils of unequal attainments'.

Miss Brady found a low standard of proficiency in geography among the senior pupils, which she attributed to the fact that the subject was taught through Irish, when the pupils had only 'a very limited knowledge of the language'. She also believed that the standard of proficiency resulted from 'mechanical methods' of teaching without the use of a blank map and sketch to be used in conjunction with printed maps, and she also remarked on the lack of textbooks in geography:

[The] absence of pupils' textbooks in these subjects has deprived the scholars of a means of supplementing and consolidating the instruction given and has denied them an excellent training in industrious habits by not taking an active interested part in their own education.[12]

She added that the pupils in third and fourth classes, who had 'gone through the Junior classes under care of the present Assistant [Miss Rushe] show promise'.

On English composition, Miss Brady recommended that the teacher should read weekly a model essay to the class, and it should then be 'discussed as to language, ideas, structure etc.' The pupils should then be required to use the model essay in writing 'on a *kindred*, but not identical topic'.[13] On English reading, she recommended that it should be taught 'by the Paragraph Method', which she described in her report: '[The] pupils should be trained to recognize the central idea in a paragraph and to use this central idea with its emphasising points in giving an oral summary of the piece – This is the basis of all intelligent study.'

She found that penmanship was 'in general defective' and she advised Master Cooney to give periodically a blackboard demonstration on 'the essentials – stroke, size, space'. Miss Brady also recommended that the school should acquire a clock, a blackboard and easel and some 'handwork' equipment for infant training.

Excellent moral character

In the course of her visit, she took charge of Master Cooney's classes to demonstrate effective teaching, so as to remedy any faults in the schoolmaster's teaching methods. She closed her report with the following remarks:

> I was impressed by Mr Cooney's intelligence, earnestness, and courtesy. The [School] Manager states that he bears an excellent moral character, and although the pupils' proficiency is understandably subnormal, their politeness and the general cultural tone of the School is much above that usually found in country districts.

Like the local doctor, priest, clergyman and local councillor, the schoolmaster was held in high esteem in the community. He frequently took part in the activities of the INTO or in local politics, the GAA and parish events. Master Cooney was no exception and was a founding member of the Committee of the Carrickmacross branch of the INTO. He was also a member of the Carrickmacross Savings Committee, which was established in October 1930 as part of a wider national thrift movement.[14] As a teacher, he had definite ideas on teaching and was a strong supporter of the Irish language.

A skilled Gaelic footballer, Master Cooney coached the boys in football in the school playground, and he was also an accomplished athlete in track and field sports, notably the long jump and sprinting; he held the title of Ulster Champion in the 100 yards' dash for several years.[15] His fitness for sports was, no doubt, helped by his daily cycle to and from Coolfore, a round trip of six miles from his home in Carrickmacross. Master Cooney, who lived with his wife at Farney Street, cycled to Coolfore via the Aghalile Road and up the steep incline of Neil's (or Becka) Brae. On wet mornings he was well prepared, arriving at the school in a pair of rainproof leggings, a parka and a cape that covered the handlebars on his bicycle.[16] He wore a moustache and was remembered for his loud voice, which he could use to good effect when encouraging or admonishing a pupil.

He was also remembered as a very nice man, and this author remembers being rewarded with a threepenny bit for proficiency in spelling. Master Cooney also took a keen interest in horse racing and enjoyed trips to the races with his Farney Street neighbour Dr Moran.[17] In September 1960, he reached the age of sixty-five years, but he continued teaching until his retirement in January 1962.

Miss Rushe

When Mrs Mary Mee died in June 1930, Monsignor Keown, the parish priest, advised the Department of Education that he had appointed Miss Mary

Anne Rushe as her successor. Aged about twenty-nine years when she was appointed, Miss Rushe was then the assistant monitress at the Clones convent national school, and she was previously a monitress at Carrickmacross convent national school between 1918 and 1921.[18] She completed her teacher training diploma course at the College of Our Lady of Mercy at Carysfort in the period 1921 to 1923.[19] When she was appointed at Coolfore on 1 July 1930, the average attendance remained fairly constant at around fifty-five pupils. Like Master Cooney, Miss Rushe was a member of the INTO, but there is no evidence of her taking part in meetings of the local branch of the organisation. Known as 'Minnie' Rushe, she was the daughter of a local farming family from the townland of Corkashybane.

Miss Rushe's teacher training course
Miss Rushe's teacher training at Carysfort coincided with the War of Independence and the Civil War, and her training ended after Irish Independence had been achieved. At that time, all the teacher training colleges were single-denomination institutions, and all were single-sex, with the exception of the Church of Ireland College at Rathmines.[20] Catholic all-female colleges like Carysfort were boarding colleges. Like a girls' secondary boarding school, the student's life was highly structured around set times for classes, meals, religious services and dormitory, and the training was intended to socialise the student into a role that involved completing well-defined tasks in the schools.[21]

Miss Rushe studied subjects that were prescribed in the *Programme for Students in Training* and included Irish, English, history, geography, arithmetic and mensuration, theory and method of kindergarten, practice of teaching, drawing, vocal music and physical drill.[22] The course in practice of teaching required students to demonstrate teaching in their practising schools; for Miss Rushe, this was the St Louis convent school at Clones. She also studied needlework, domestic economy, cookery and laundry work, subjects that were prescribed for female students only. In the male colleges, the students studied algebra, geometry and rural science.

At Carysfort, Miss Rushe and her fellow student teachers also studied catechism and were examined on Church doctrine and Church history. For example, the examination of 1923 included questions on 'the elements of a mortal sin', 'proof of the Resurrection' and a question that asked: 'Why does the Church forbid mixed marriages so sternly?' All students were required to read 'a standard' *Life of Christ*, and the *Programme for Students in Training* included recommendations for talks to be given to student teachers, including:

The life of the individual; duties of the individual; personal dignity;

the idea of honour; uprightness; integrity; equable temperament; moral energy [...] the rights and duties of the teacher; the relations of parent and teacher, of teacher and pupil; personal and professional dignity and self-respect [...] The idea of the nation and of patriotism.[23]

The list of recommended talks was compiled by Pádraic Ó Brolcháin, the acting Chief Executive Officer of the Board of National Education. Ó Brolcháin also recommended that student teachers should be given talks on 'the drink evils – its baneful effects on the social, economic and national life'.[24]

The teacher training course at Carysfort emphasised the teacher's responsibility to know and teach the primary school curriculum, as laid down by the state, and the teacher was expected to avoid any criticism of the school curriculum or to avoid introducing new subjects or new teaching methods that were not prescribed.[25] The course was regarded as an intensive, instructional type of training, which emphasised learning the methods of teaching, including how to prepare and present a lesson.[26] The available textbooks and notebooks from Miss Rushe's personal papers indicate that the course at Carysfort emphasised learning the methods of classroom instruction.[27] On teaching children how to read, her educational notebook included the following maxim: 'All explanations in reading lessons must be brief, definite and necessary.'

Miss Rushe learned the steps in the 'look and say' method of teaching reading to infant classes, and the method of teaching the children how to memorise and appreciate 'the beautiful ideas' in a poem and how to recite a poem 'tastefully and with expression'. She learned the step-by-step procedure in the method of teaching senior classes the skills of sewing on gathers and flannel patch and knitting a long stocking. This included the methods of teaching 'thimble drill' and 'needle drill'. Miss Rushe faithfully recorded these and other teaching methods in her notebook, which also contained the following maxim: '[The] child's tendency to ask questions is due to natural instinct of curiosity and should be encouraged.' Along with teaching the standard lessons in reading, writing, arithmetic and religious instruction, Miss Rushe also taught singing and one of the songs in her repertoire was 'Singing bird': 'I have seen the lark soar high at morn. Heard his song up in the blue. I have heard the blackbird pipe his note. The thrush and the linnet too.'

'Very religious woman'

Former pupils at Coolfore remembered Miss Rushe as a slight, bespectaled woman who always wore black, including a beret when arriving at and leaving the school, and she kept her small lady's watch in a silver metal box that she placed at the front of her desk.[28] In the early days, she was brought to the school by pony and trap, and from time to time, she cycled to and from the school. Given the location of her home in Corkashybane, a journey of almost three miles via several steep hills, her homeward cycle must have been a great test of her stamina. In later years, she travelled to and from the school with her brother Johnny in his Ford Prefect.

On Master Cooney's retirement in 1962, the school manager, Monsignor Finnegan, recommended Miss Rushe as a teacher 'capable and worthy of the office of Principal'. The Department of Education confirmed her appointment, and Miss Rushe moved to the upstairs schoolroom, where she took over the teaching of the senior classes.

Miss Rushe was a devout Catholic, and as a young woman, she indicated her Catholic testimonials by sometimes inserting into her college exercise books the initials 'EdeM' after her name.[29] Denoting 'Enfante de Marie', the title was most likely conferred on her by the sisters at St Louis convent girls' school. She also inserted the phrase 'Noblesse oblige' into the front page of her exercise books, a phrase that indicated a self-declared commitment to act honourably and generously to others.[30] Miss Rushe's textbooks also contained occasional insertions of religious pamphlets and leaflets containing daily prayers to be recited; her daily prayer for the month of March 1922 was 'A prayer for Ireland', which included the invocation: 'May Ireland ever remain the seat of religion and learning.'[31]

Best remembered as 'a very religious woman', several former pupils recalled her daily routine of prayers, including Friday afternoon prayers at the little Marian grotto in the schoolyard. She conducted morning prayers to start the day, devotion to the Stations of the Cross at the mid-morning break and a recital of the Rosary at the lunchtime break.[32] Such was her religious dedication that she was sometimes heard reciting a prayer to herself as she arrived at the school gate.[33] She often spoke to the children about the end of the world and warned them that when they slept in their bed at night, they should place their hands across their chest in a sign of the cross, so that they might be prepared to meet God, who could come 'like a thief in the night'.[34] Aside from her religious devotion, Miss Rushe was also remembered as a very kind woman.

Miss Rushe retires
Having commenced her teaching service at Clones in 1924, Miss Rushe had completed forty years of service in 1964 and was scheduled to retire that year. However, the Department of Education retained her services for a further two years, after which time, she was obliged to retire. She was then aged sixty-

six. Despite her age and long years of service, Miss Rushe did not wish to retire and was determined to remain in her post. At the time, the acting parish
priest, Fr Thomas McCarvill, appointed Mr Fergus Lane to succeed Miss
Rushe.

Then a young lay teacher at St Joseph's boys' monastery school in Carrickmacross and with three years' teaching service completed, Mr Lane was
scheduled to take up his post at Coolfore on 1 July 1966. However, when he
learned of Miss Rushe's strong desire to remain in her teaching post, Mr Lane,
who was then an active member of the INTO, did not wish to interfere in
the case of a fellow teacher until the matter of her retirement was settled. He
advised Fr McCarvill of his position in the matter, and rather than going to
Coolfore, presented for work at St Joseph's school instead. Mr Lane recalled
the events of the morning of 1 July:

> At approximately 10:30, Fr McCarvill arrives up at the school and he
> says: 'Why aren't you out in Coolfore?' and I said: 'I told you I am not
> going out.' He said: 'I told you that school is going to be amalgamated
> [with St Joseph's]. And in two years' time, whoever is principal is
> going to be amalgamated with this school, and some fellow' – and the
> words he said, 'some fellow from the arsehole of Kerry' – 'will get that
> job and he will come in here and he will be superior to you in this
> school, because he will be, as they were called at the time, a privileged
> assistant.' So, he said: 'Get into that car!' and I said: 'You will just have
> to settle this with the principal here [at St Joseph's].'[35]

Following the conversation, Fr McCarvill accompanied Mr Lane to Coolfore, by which time, Miss Rushe had arrived at the school. Although the precise details of what next transpired are not recorded, one account suggests
that Miss Rushe was already teaching the pupils when Mr Lane arrived, and
she insisted that she was not leaving.[36] In the event, it appears that Fr McCarvill persuaded Miss Rushe to leave the school. At that point, Mr Lane and
Miss Rushe exchanged pleasant words, and when Mr Lane then gave the instruction 'Suas Leat'[37] to the pupils standing at the bottom of the school steps,
Miss Rushe gently reminded him that, in the interest of preserving the female
pupils' modesty, he should let the boys go up the steps first. The events of the
morning of 1 July were doubtless difficult for both Miss Rushe and Mr Lane.
Upon her retirement, the children presented Miss Rushe with a small gift of
a bedside lamp.[38] She enjoyed a long retirement, spending her final years living
with her brother and sister at Killanny where she died in May 1986.

Mrs Donnelly and Master Lane

When Miss Rushe was appointed principal at Coolfore in 1962, Mrs Bridget McGrane was appointed for a brief period as junior assistant mistress, pending the appointment of Miss Rushe's successor as assistant. In the event, Ms Rushe's successor was Mrs Kathleen Donnelly, who was appointed in April 1962.[39] She was formerly a junior assistant mistress at St Brigid's national school, Newbliss, in north Co. Monaghan.

Former pupils spoke of Mrs Donnelly as a gentle woman and a good teacher, who took time to instruct individual pupils who did not understand what was being taught.[40] In the spring and summer months, she took the younger pupils on nature walks along the road to study the local flora.[41] Mrs Donnelly remained at Coolfore, teaching the junior classes until the school closed in 1968, and after the female pupils transferred to St Louis convent girls' school in Carrickmacross, she was also posted there. While she was no longer teaching the pupils who transferred from Coolfore, she looked out for them, as one former pupil remembered:

> She would always come out into the yard at playtime, and she would call us over and talk to us and make sure our necks was clean […] She was always looking out for us, and she would always say: 'If you have any bother, just come to the door and knock at the door, I am here.' She was always good like that.[42]

Fergus Lane attended primary school at St Joseph's boys' school in Carrickmacross and completed his secondary education at St Macartan's College. He completed his teacher training diploma at St Patrick's College, Drumcondra, and commenced teaching at St Joseph's in 1963. During training, he was expected to demonstrate high standards in the way he planned and conducted lessons, and the school inspector assessed his performance in meeting these expectations. He first encountered the inspector at the end of his first year of training, when he underwent a major assessment. This involved the inspector sitting in the classroom for a whole day, observing and assessing his performance, as Mr Lane recalled:

> He would scrutinise every single one your notes, every single one of your reports, and if anything was out of place, and you got various things [like] 'go maith', 'an-mhaith', 'míshásúil', which was unsatisfactory; you didn't want unsatisfactory.[43]

As a newly qualified teacher, Master Lane continued to experience the highly bureaucratic system of school inspections, requiring him to set out clearly his teaching plans and to record all lessons given, as he explained:

> You had to draw a plan for the year, and you had to do one of those for each class [...] and then you had to draw up the monthly plan. And then you had to draw up a weekly plan and that wasn't good enough [...] You had to fill in again another report of what you did every week and every month and what you had done for the year.

This meticulous planning and recording was done more to satisfy the school inspector and less to meet the needs of the pupils and their learning:

> The inspectors were very strict on those [reports], you had to have them [and] they were far more strict on those than they were on records of pupils or records of anything else. Once you had your notices done – we used to call them the 'notices' – that was all that mattered to the inspector.[44]

After two years of teaching and having satisfied the inspector, the close scrutiny of the teacher ended. The school was then subject to a general inspection every five years. The focus of school inspections was the teacher, and as Mr Lane explained, a teacher's performance was judged on what the pupils did or did not know. Aside from the Primary Cert examination, which ended in 1967, pupils did not sit formal examinations, but instead, were continually assessed, and the teacher prepared a report for the parents at the end of the school year.[45]

While the school inspector had authority and oversight over academic matters at the school, the parish priest, acting as the school manager, had absolute authority over the running of the school. The introduction of boards of management in primary schools was an important step in improving the experience of teachers. This change meant that individual teachers or the INTO were no longer dealing with a single priest as their school manager, but with a management structure that had wider public representation, including parents.

As a member of the local branch of the INTO, Master Lane was active in trade union matters, and while still a young teacher, he was elected chairman of his local union branch. Teachers' salaries were a major concern for the INTO at that time, and the union managed to secure substantial increases on what, at the time, was a very low salary.

Master Lane was remembered as a very good teacher. His arrival at Coolfore heralded a big change for the senior pupils in the upstairs room, where he brought a more progressive teaching style to that of his predecessor. Like

Mrs Donnelly, he also took the pupils on nature walks in the summertime, where they collected and identified samples of wildflowers and placed them in a scrapbook.[46] On very wet days when school ended, he occasionally packed some of the children into his Morris Minor and delivered them home safe and dry. As a Gaelic footballer and associated with Carrickmacross Emmets GAA club, he encouraged the boys to play football and coached them. Although he was the principal at Coolfore for just two school years, Master Lane remembered his time there with great fondness. He recalled how the small rural school of fewer than thirty pupils was a close-knit community where the children looked out for each other.

Pupils at Coolfore

In the decades before and after the Second World War, Coolfore national school served the rural district to the north-west of Carrickmacross. The district contained small farms and the children's parents and grandparents had farmed the land as former tenants of the Shirley estate. While a rural road network was well developed in the mid-twentieth century, the location of townlands like Peaste and Greaghdrumit meant that many of the children travelled to school across fields.

At the time of Master Cooney's appointment in 1923, the average attendance at Coolfore was fifty-five pupils, and attendance levels fluctuated to coincide with key periods in the farming year. This pattern of attendance was common in most rural schools, as the divisional inspector for Monaghan and Cavan observed in 1927: 'in practically all the rural schools [...] the attendance is adversely affected by farming operations in the spring and autumn seasons'.[47] By 1940, school attendance nationally had greatly improved to 85 per cent.[48] Similar to the nineteenth century, occasional outbreaks of infectious diseases also reduced the levels of attendance; in March 1959, Coolfore school was closed for a week due to a flu epidemic that left the children and their parents confined to bed.[49] At the same time, an epidemic of mumps combined with flu resulted in the closure of the nearby schools at Sreenty and Corcreagh.[50] Mumps was a particularly distressing condition and was a common infectious illness among the schoolchildren of the period.

Life after primary school

In the early years after Independence, the number of children progressing on to secondary education was low and more boys than girls went on to complete it. The national statistics for 1926 bear this out, with almost twice as many boys (441) as girls (231) taking the Leaving Certificate examination. At the time, access to secondary education was based largely on parents' ability to pay school tuition fees, and this meant that only children of the better-off families and those securing a scholarship attended secondary education. The number attending secondary education gradually increased but remained low; for example, in 1940, while 63,706 pupils attained the sixth standard or above, just 1,690 boys and 1,228 girls took the Leaving Certificate. In that year, there were eight secondary schools in Co. Monaghan, including three in Carrickmacross: the St Louis' secondary school (194 pupils), the Patrician Brothers' monastery school (thirty-eight pupils) and the Viscount Weymouth grammar school (twenty-nine pupils).

After the Second World War, there was a gradual expansion in secondary education.[51] In addition, many boys and girls entered vocational courses in the vocational and technical schools managed by local vocational education committees (VECs). Courses included building, mechanical engineering, electrical engineering, applied chemistry, domestic economy, and commerce. Located in the former Union workhouse on the Shercock Road and known locally as 'The Tech', a VEC technical school was established in Carrickmacross in the 1930s. A new VEC school building was completed in March 1959 and officially opened by Jack Lynch TD, Minister for Education and the future Taoiseach.[52]

Published in 1965, an Organisation of Economic Co-operation and Development (OECD) report entitled *Investment in Education* highlighted the fact that high numbers of children left education after completing primary school, and this was related to inequalities based on social class and region.[53] At that time, one-third of all children were leaving full-time education on completing primary school, and fewer than 60 per cent of all children aged fifteen were remaining in education.[54] Based on the OECD report, the Minister for Education, Donagh O'Malley, abolished tuition fees and introduced free secondary education in 1967, and a decade later, participation rates in secondary education had doubled.[55] While it was not possible to obtain reliable statistics for Coolfore national school, in the decades before the school closed in 1968, a small number of the pupils went on to complete two years' at the local VEC 'Tech', but few attended a secondary school, and fewer still attended a university. A great many emigrated to England.

The minimum age at which children could leave school was raised from fourteen to sixteen years in 1972, and hence, many of the children who transferred to the schools in Carrickmacross in 1968 went on to complete the Intermediate Certificate, or in the case of the 'Tech', the Group Certificate. However, most of the generation that completed primary school at Coolfore in the 1940s, 1950s and 1960s left school at aged fourteen. Most rural families of the period saw work on the farm or paid employment as the only options, as Alice Lavery (née Murtagh), a former pupil at Coolfore, commented:

For all the boys and girls, there was no such thing as saying you would go on to secondary school, you would go on to grammar school, like nowadays. There was no such thing as going like that, you would go home, [and] get a job.[56]

The final years, 1962–1968

In 1951, just forty-two pupils were enrolled at Coolfore, and by the early 1960s, the average daily attendance had fallen to considerably fewer than forty pupils each year. By 1965, just five boys and two girls were added to the school register, and in the following year, just one boy and one girl were added. In 1966, when Master Lane and Mrs Donnelly were the teachers, the number of pupils enrolled was falling and was as low as twenty-eight, a position that meant that the school was not viable as a two-teacher school.

In his report to the Bishop of Clogher in May 1967 on the condition of the schools in the parish, Fr L. Marron described Coolfore national school as follows: 'Very old building but in excellent repair. Well maintained. Running water and W.C. Heating by electricity and open fires.' While the schoolhouse was a fine building and in very good repair, given the falling numbers, the Department of Education determined that it should close at the end of the 1967–68 school year. With the closure, Master Lane and Mrs Donnelly would transfer to their respective boys' and girls' schools in Carrickmacross. The local parents held a meeting at the school to object to the planned closure and to petition the parish priest to retain the school; however, the falling numbers of entrants spoke for themselves and the decision to close was final. In July 1968, the doors of Coolfore school were closed for the last time, and by the end of the year, the schoolhouse was sold to Michael Ward, a local farmer, who converted the building into a fine family dwelling house.

Sometime after the school had finally closed, K. McCahey (née Ward), a former pupil and a native of Coolfore townland, remembered the old school in a nostalgic poem (Appendix IV), which included the following lines:

I stood upon the little bridge,
Where oft I stood before
But no boys and girls to join me now,
At the old school in Coolfore.

13

'Many a time': Schooldays remembered

'I did love Coolfore School, I did like going, no matter how far I walked.'[1]

Oral history is an important source of evidence for studies in local history. It offers those who lived through a particular period the opportunity to tell their own story of the period and the events of interest to the historian. Remembered accounts of experiences give personal perspectives on the past that historical documents or artefacts cannot provide. Thirteen former pupils of Coolfore national school gave generously of their time to share their memories of their schooldays, and the former school principal also kindly shared his memories.[2] Their valuable and nuanced accounts have contributed to telling a small part of the story of a rural national school in south Co. Monaghan from the late 1930s to the late 1960s.

The participants in the oral history interviews spoke about their classroom and schoolyard experiences and about their lives growing up in the school's rural district. Their accounts spoke of getting to and from school each day, learning in the classroom, games in the schoolyard, home life on the farm and family social life. Their testimonies reveal both the common and the unique experiences of schooldays and childhood in mid-twentieth century rural south Monaghan. The former pupils' personal reminiscences and their individual interpretations of past experiences may reflect the experiences of many other children who attended a rural national school in Ireland in the same period.

Schooldays remembered: Getting to and from school
Coolfore national school was located at about midway between the Shercock and Ballybay roads and close to the Aghalile road; all three roads led to Carrickmacross. The school served over a dozen townlands. This included those near or adjacent to the Shercock and Aghalile roads, including Tiragarvan,

Aghalile, Beaghmagheross, Lisnaguiveragh, Greaghdrumit, Corkashyduff and Greaghnaroog, and those near or adjacent to the Ballybay road, including Legghimore, Drumbroagh, Greaghdromneesk and Peaste. Some children lived in the townlands of Killarue and Lattylanigan in the parish of Donaghmoyne and their parish school was at Lisdoonan. Despite the local priest's efforts to persuade parents to send their children to Lisdoonan school, parents chose Coolfore school instead, partly due to proximity to Coolfore.

In rural south Monaghan in the mid-twentieth century, the phrase 'the school run' was not in people's vocabulary. Getting to school generally meant walking, and for many children, this involved crossing fields. Bernard McGinnity attended Coolfore in the 1950s and his daily journey from his home in Peaste involved crossing the river at the bottom of his garden into Coolfore townland, then crossing two hills and traversing the streets of Owen Ward and Patrick Tumelty before arriving at Ward's Brae.[3] From there he made the final part of his journey by road. Bernard remembered how the children hurried past the 'haunted laneway' near to the school; known as 'Margaret's Lane' or 'Buckle Man's Lane', a ghost was reputed to reside in the derelict house at the top of the lane.

The Reilly children also lived in Peaste, and they crossed the three fields that took them onto the road that went via Patton's, Callan's, Tumelty's and Ward's Brae and from there onto Coolfore school. Josephine, the youngest of the Reilly children, and her siblings wore wellingtons when crossing the fields, and having arrived at the road to Coolfore, they changed into their school shoes and placed their wellingtons in the hedge, there to be collected on the journey home.[4] In wet weather, their father Peter collected them and some of the neighbouring children in his taxi car.

Mary Byrne (née Ward) and her brother Peter Ward also remembered crossing the fields from their home in Greaghdrumit, through Boylan's land and across the Aghalile Road. Mary also recalled how wellingtons were worn on wet mornings:

We crossed eight fields, and we came over to the end of the Aghalile Road and we would take our wellies off and hide them in the ditch and put on our [school] shoes and then we would walk about two miles to Coolfore school, [and] now that was [in] hail, rain, or snow.[5]

On occasion on their way across the fields, they could find one of Boylan's cows stuck in a bog and the Ward boys would dig it out and release it from its muddy hold.

Although no fields were crossed, the children from Tiragarvan, Aghalile, Beaghmagheross and Legghimore townlands made the daily trek to Coolfore

185

on the gravel road that included the very steep, and at times icy, incline of the Becka (Neil's) Brae.[6] James (Jem) Meehan from Lattylanigan also recalled the dangerous ice sheets on the roads during the very cold winters. He told how his mother, while cycling home with her groceries on a bad winter's day, might meet some of the homebound children and ask them: 'Well, was there many at school today?' The children's mischievous reply was: 'Everyone [was] in school today except the Meehans!' On his journey to and from school, Jem sometimes crossed the Drumbroagh hills, or occasionally, got a lift on the back of McKenna's or Fealy's tractor, and on wet days, was transported in Peter Reilly's taxi car.[7]

When first starting school, many children were accompanied by a neighbour's older child. During his first week at school, Joseph Callan's mother took him to school on her bicycle, which was fitted with 'a little metal seat with little metal flaps on the bottom' to protect his feet from getting caught in the rear wheel spokes. Mairead Nulty (née Byrne) similarly remembered how, on her first day at school, her mother took her on the carrier of her bicycle, but after that, she was placed in the trust and care of her older neighbour Anna-May Meehan (RIP).

The teacher kept the daily roll book, and each pupil who was present answered 'anseo' when their name was called. When a pupil was absent, the teacher inserted a zero mark or 'duck egg' against their name. Fr McCarvill, the school manager, was remembered as being very strict on school attendance; when visiting the school, he always checked the absences in the roll book and warned the children: 'I don't want to see many duck eggs here!'[8]

While the journey to school could take half an hour, the homeward journey could take much longer. On the way home, children made time to 'dilly and dally' for play, or gather wild strawberries and gooseberries, leaving their parents to wonder why they were so late getting home.[9] Another reason for some of the children arriving home late was a local farmer, who leaning on his garden wall, quizzed the homebound children to get the latest news.[10]

Apple orchards were also a big distraction on the way home from school in the early autumn. Mary Byrne remembered how they stole apples from an orchard along the Aghalile Road and 'would be killed going home because we wouldn't be hungry for the dinner because we were full of apples'.[11] Her brother Peter also remembered how the orchard owner 'would run' the children if he caught them stealing apples but would happily give them apples if they knocked on his door and asked him. In the autumn, the homebound children from Beaghmagheross, Legghimore and Aghalile could be found picking the small, sweet apples that fell to the ground in Ward's orchard near the school.

186

Old class photographs of Coolfore and other schools show children in their bare feet. While the absence of shoes on children's feet was a visible sign of poverty, especially in the early years of the twentieth century, some of the former pupils who shared memories of their schooldays during the 1930s and 1940s spoke about going barefooted to school by choice in the summer months. Paddy Wallace, who commenced school in 1941, remembered how the children looked forward to summertime, when they could cast their shoes aside: 'We couldn't wait for the summer, all the young gasuns, to go barefoot.'[12] Going without shoes on gravel roads could be injurious to young feet, as Paddy recalled: 'Many a time we would have "quick toes", with stones and that.' Alice Lavery (née Murtagh) from Legghimore, who commenced school in 1935, also spoke about going barefooted to school: 'We weren't allowed to wear shoes to school in the summertime [...] we went to school in our bare feet. Shoes were only permitted when going to Mass on Sunday [...] that was the norm for all children.'[13]

Schooldays remembered: Learning the lessons
Most children attended Coolfore national school at age four or five. Infant classes included 'playtime', which involved Miss Rushe taking out several showboxes containing wooden spools and strings, wooden bricks, and other small objects. These simple, improvised teaching materials were based on the kindergarten method and were intended to promote child-led play, which in turn, supported learning social and manual skills.

Alice Lavery was aged five when she commenced school in September 1935. She recalled her first day, taking her seat at her own little desk with a line of small children of the same age beside her. They were each presented with a slate on which they wrote 'ABC and 123' in chalk and then wiped it off. Alice also recalled being taught how to spell 'cat' and 'dog', words with just three letters; she found this easy and could say the spellings by heart, since her parents had taught her to spell them before she commenced school. Josephine Marron (née Reilly) also remembered using a slate for writing and she spoke of how she was naturally left-handed and would get things done quickly, but the teacher would ask her to 'go back down and do it with the other hand'. Joseph Callan's earliest memories were also of learning his ABCs and learning to count with the Ladybird books, and like other children, his mother had taught him the alphabet and basic counting before he commenced school.

As the children got a little older, they learned to write using pen and ink, and Bernard Fealy remembered how the ink could make 'an awful blotch' on the copybook, which displeased the teacher who was very strict about tidiness. Children were also expected to take good care of their schoolbooks, and brown wrapping paper was used as a protective cover, so that books were kept clean and available for handing down to younger siblings. Alice Lavery remembered being reprimanded by the school inspector for having stains on the brown paper cover of her book:

> It was either butter or lard [stains] on the back of my paper, the brown paper, and she took it off [and said:] 'That is a disgrace [...] backing a book with greasy paper!' She took it off and I went home and told my mother, and I said 'I am not going to back a book again' [...] and I quit backing the book!

When the children progressed to fourth class, they left Miss Rushe's down-stairs' room and attended Master Cooney's upstairs' room for the final three years of school. Some children loved arithmetic, or 'sums', and some were adept at it. The children in the senior classes were expected to strictly follow Master Cooney's method of instruction. His method in arithmetic involved him writing a problem on the blackboard and expecting each pupil to copy it down and calculate the answer in their copybook. Any deviation from this approach could get a pupil into trouble, as John Joe Cunningham recalled:

> [Master] Cooney put a sum up on the board and I was watching him doing the thing on the board, but I had the answer in my head, and I couldn't do it on the paper. We were supposed to be taking the sum down. 'Any answers?' [asked Master Cooney] and I put my hand up straight away.

Despite John Joe providing the correct answer, when Master Cooney found no written answer in his copybook, he was most displeased, and turning up his moustachioed lip, said: 'I can't understand how you have the answer to this [...] and you can't do it on the paper!'

Former pupils remembered the subjects at which they were proficient and which they liked.[14] Mairead Nulty took great pride in knowing arithmetic and she also loved English poetry. Michael Ward remembered being good at spelling, while Bernard Fealy excelled at geography. Despite the emphasis on learning the Irish language in national schools, some former pupils recalled their difficulty with the language, and for that reason, greatly disliked it. Paddy Wallace recalled how he was 'hopeless at Irish' and Alice Lavery remembered how she could never pick it up. John Joe Cunningham similarly recalled how he 'couldn't handle' Irish, although English was 'no bother' to him.

If Irish was a difficult subject and poorly learnt, it seems that the state's emphasis on Irish history did not feature strongly in the Coolfore curriculum, and some former pupils lamented the fact that there was little history taught at the school.[15] Nevertheless, the Easter Rising was one aspect of Irish history that featured prominently on the curriculum during 1966, when its Golden Jubilee was being commemorated.[16] When teaching history, Master Lane favoured teaching through storytelling, rather than having the pupils remember facts like dates and places.[17]

In later years, Mrs Donnelly taught knitting and sewing to the female pupils, including the senior girls. On one occasion, while the girls were engaged in their knitting class, one young boy, James Fealy, with some bravado, declared that the boys could knit 'just as good as the girls'. In response, Mrs Donnelly set James and the other boys a challenge to learn knitting and show that they could indeed knit 'as good as the girls'. Wool and knitting needles were duly purchased and under Mrs Donnelly's guidance, the boys had soon mastered the plain and purl stitch technique. By year's end, each boy proudly sported a newly-knitted jumper.

An cigire and examinations
Remembered as a very big event when everyone at the school was 'in a heap', the visit of the inspector, or cigire, was preceded by a period of heightened anticipation for both pupils and teachers.[18] Similar to the weeks leading up to the Primary Cert examinations, preparation for the visit of the cigire was associated with an intense focus on learning.[19] In addition to the expectation that they would know the lessons, the pupils were expected to be on their best behaviour when the cigire visited. Alice Lavery recalled the visit of the cigire, and in retrospect, her recollection was tinged with some scepticism as to the benefit of the inspection for the school children:

> An inspector lady [came] and she went around every girl and every boy, and we had our book out as if we were learning but it wasn't open; we were just sitting there. I remember the inspector, yes. I don't know what she was looking for. Was she looking for to see were we educated properly to go to a grammar school? No, no![20]

Former pupils remembered having to travel to Corduff school to take the Primary Cert examinations, a distance of some three miles from Coolfore. Some made the journey on foot while others cycled. The examination was remembered less for the subjects taken and more for the setting and the circumstances of the examination. In the late 1950s, Bernard McGinnity cycled to Corduff with Mary Callan, a neighbour, to take examinations in English, Irish and Arithmetic. The title of the Irish composition in the examination was 'Poll i mo phóca' ('Hole in my pocket'); pupils wrote about going to the shop, and having lost the shopping money on the way, returning home emptyhanded. On his return to Coolfore, Bernard was asked to rewrite the essay, the reason for which he could not explain. Alice Lavery walked to Corduff where 'a neutral teacher' supervised the examinations. She passed and was awarded the Certificate with her name inscribed in the old Celtic script.

Religious instruction
In the decades after the Second World War, religious instruction held a central place on the primary school curriculum, and catechism was the principal subject through which religious instruction was conducted in Catholic schools. The subject was taught for thirty minutes each day at noon and the teacher was expected to adhere strictly to this plan, since failure to do so was considered a grave offence in the eyes of the parish priest.[21]

Catechism was especially important when pupils were preparing for First Communion and Confirmation, and also in advance of a visit from the parish priest. The children stood in a line in front of the priest, who quizzed them on their knowledge of it.[22] Some parents also participated in preparing their children for First Communion, similarly quizzing them on their knowledge.[23] Like the visit of the cigire, the pupils and teachers anticipated the priest's visit with heightened anxiety. Michael Ward recalled how the children wore their Sunday best for the visit of the priest and remembered: 'You had to stay quiet and answer what you were asked [and] you would have to be right'.[24] Mairead Nulty also remembered the fear engendered by the priest's visit: 'You were afraid of your life [of] what question was going to come at you!'

Each child who had reached seven years, the 'age of reason', could go forward for First Communion, and preparation involved the priest hearing the child's first confession in the school. Confession involved a pupil kneeling at a chair that was placed at a right-angle to the priest's chair, and with hands joined, the penitent pupil proclaimed: 'Bless me Father, for I have sinned.' One unfortunate pupil knelt on an upturned thumbtack but dared not move until the confession was heard, despite the excruciating pain and accompanying cold sweat.[25] Among the priests who made occasional informal visits to the school were Fr McHugh, Fr McCarvill and Fr Ferguson. As part of their religious formation, the pupils also learned to sing 'Hail Queen of Heaven' and other hymns.[26] Confirmation was also anticipated with some fear and trepidation, since the children feared that the Bishop's touch of confirmation on the cheek would be a hard slap.[27]

Under Miss Rushe, religious instruction did not end with classes in catechism; she also conducted prayers with the pupils on three separate occasions during the school day and brought them out to pray at the little Marian shrine to the side of the schoolhouse on Friday afternoons. Protected by a wire-framed net, the shrine contained a statue of the Blessed Virgin and a wooden butter box from Lough Egish creamery on which flowers were placed.[28]

Master Cooney also participated in religious instruction and insisted that the pupils kept their catechism reading books neat and tidy. Jem Meehan remembered how one boy who sat beside him in class experienced Master Cooney's ire during a catechism lesson:

[Master Cooney] would take up your book and he would read the questions out to you, and [the boy] knew he was going to be in trouble, you know. The [catechism] book was in flitters and there were tractors drawn on it [...] and he didn't answer any of them. [Master Cooney said]: 'Go back on them [lessons!]', and he flung the catechism down the school and made bits [of it], and pages flying everywhere.[29]

Aside from school holidays, the school calendar was arranged to coincide with events in the ecclesiastical year, and the curriculum was punctuated with activities like preparation for First Communion and significant holy days of obligation. In early springtime, children gathered rushes from the local fields to make the distinct Crios Bríd (St Bridget's Cross), and later in March, they collected shamrock to wear to mass on St Patrick's Day. The annual May Eucharistic Procession was also a major event in the Catholic calendar and pupils from Coolfore and the other parish schools attended 'the procession' in Carrickmacross, where the town was decorated in flags and bunting, and shop windows and houses were adorned with religious icons, emblems and flowers.

Children's health and welfare
While the children's spiritual wellbeing seemed to be all important, their health also mattered, particularly since childhood infectious diseases were still prevalent in rural Ireland in the post-War years. Many children at Coolfore contracted measles and mumps, both of which could be severe infections, and for which no vaccine was available by the time the school closed in 1968. Although an archaic practice after the War, some parents still resorted to a local custom for 'the cure' for mumps, which, as described in an earlier chapter, involved a neighbour placing a donkey's winkers on the young patient and leading them around a pigsty while reciting an incantation.[30] The anxiety induced by this 'cure' ritual no doubt added to the distress of the fever and painful swollen neck glands.

Earlier generations of children risked contracting other infections like tuberculosis, diphtheria, whooping cough and polio; however, by the late 1950s vaccines for these infectious diseases had become available. Flu was also endemic and the public health authorities closed the school for a week in March 1959, due to an outbreak of the flu virus among the children.[31] Coolfore schoolchildren were included in the school public health schemes, which included health checks by the local GPs and district nurses, childhood vaccinations and mass chest X-ray examinations. Among the public health professionals who visited the school were Dr Deery, Dr Creedon and Nurse Busby, and the children were always dressed in their best clothes for the visits.[32]

In the post-War years, corporal punishment was remembered as part of the everyday experience of schooling. Remembered punishments included a 'clip on the ear', five slaps, or detention after school. Punishments could be dispensed for a range of transgressions, such as lack of care in handwriting, an untidy copybook, failing to do homework, answering on behalf of another pupil, 'carrying on', or turning around to look when the door opened at the back of the classroom. Sometimes dispensed for not knowing their lessons, a pupil could be sent to the corner of the classroom; this form of punishment was remembered as more unpleasant than any corporal punishment. When a punishment was dispensed, children tended not to tell their parents, and although parents generally accepted punishments as part of schooling, since they themselves had experienced it, some did not always condone it.

Schooldays remembered: In the schoolyard and playground

The grounds of Coolfore school were surrounded on either side by a row of large Lawson Cypress trees. Joseph Callan remembered their fragrant smell as the children played around them; however, he also remembered how the grounds were not well maintained in later years: 'It was quite unkempt, there were paths through the grounds but there were clumps of briars here, there, and everywhere, and little paths running through them.'[33] This neglect of the school grounds was, perhaps, a portent of the approaching closure of the school.

On one side between the schoolhouse and the trees was a narrow garden, where the boys played football during the brief mid-morning breaks. With little time to play and even less interest in returning to the classroom, a lost ball was the perfect excuse to stretch out the breaktime, as Peter Ward recalled:

> When it would be coming close to the bell time for you to go back in, and [you would] draw a good kick on the ball and make sure it landed below in the meadow on the other side of the road. Two or

three of us would be sent down to look for it. We'd have more time down there than we would in the class.[34]

Miss Rushe became very anxious and concerned that a boy might be injured by a passing car when retrieving a ball.[35] Marbles was also a popular game among the boys, and although boys and girls were segregated in the schoolyard, when the teacher was not looking, the girls joined the boys in games of marbles.[36]

On the other side of the schoolyard, the girls played games like hopscotch, giant steps, 'tig', skipping and rounders, and they also sang songs and nursery rhymes.[37] The schoolyard also contained the 'den', a three-walled enclosure between the school gable and the outdoor toilets, and this was sometimes used for playing handball. At the time of year when farmers were testing their cattle for tuberculosis, the cattle's ears were tagged, and this was the inspiration for a game of 'tagging', which the boys played in the den. In the game, the bigger boys 'herded' the smaller ones into the den where they 'tagged' their ears with a twist of the earlobe, before releasing them with a slap on the backside as they exited.[38] Paddy Wallace told of one young lad who took delight in chasing the girls, stinging their legs with nettles, but who earned slaps from the teacher for his mischief-making. Unlike the boys, the girls were not boisterous in the schoolyard, and as Mary Byrne recalled: 'There was no badness in us in them days at school, it was all just laughter and craic.'[39]

The playground
In addition to the schoolyard, a local farmer provided a small triangular field at the nearby school crossroad for use as 'the playground'. It was used at lunchtime for games of football and other sporting activities, like jumping and running races. As a former champion athlete in field sports, Master Cooney took the bigger boys for sporting activities in the playground, including the long jump, the high jump and football.[40]

Like his brother Jim, who was also a teacher and holder of an Ulster Football Championship medal with Co. Monaghan,[41] Master Cooney was a good Gaelic footballer in his youth, and he organised football games with the boys. His method of training included running with the ball and challenging the boys to tackle him.[42] The playground fell at an incline in two different directions, so it was not ideal as a football-playing surface; nevertheless, with improvised goalposts made of large straight branches, competitive matches were organised. By convention, the two tallest boys in the playground were the team captains. They selected their respective teams, with each captain, in turn, selecting his players according to a boy's height and known footballing prowess.[43]

'Foreign' games, like soccer and rugby were frowned upon during Master Cooney's time, and when he found one boy heading a ball, he strongly reprimanded him.[44] During the War years when no football was available, the boys played with an improvised ball made of bundled-up paper and tied with a piece of string. The playground at the crossroad was generally the preserve of the boys, although the girls also came to play games from time to time, including 'roly-poly' and other games.[45] In later years Master Lane also organised Gaelic football games in the playground and he also introduced the game of rugby.

The schoolhouse

Although the schoolhouse walls were thick and built of stone and mortar, on cold winter days, the downstairs room could be cold and drafty, and the upstairs room could also be 'a cold miserable place' when unheated.[46] When one pupil complained that she was 'frozen with the cold', the teacher sent her outside to walk around the school for half an hour. Although warm when she returned, she remembered being very angry with the teacher.[47]

Coal was the main source of fuel for both the open fireplace in the downstairs room and the pot-bellied stove in the upstairs room. Coal was stored in a bunker underneath the external steps, and fires were kindled with newspapers and lighted firewood before the coal was added. Former pupils spoke of their responsibilities in cleaning out the embers, supplying fuel or fetching firewood. During the War years, Master Cooney asked each pupil to supply a bag of turf for the fire.[48] In later years, the senior pupils were sent out in the mornings to the nearby fields to gather sticks for kindling firewood.[49] Each Friday afternoon, the children were tasked with cleaning the classroom floors. This involved sprinkling water mixed with Jeyes Fluid on the floor to reduce dust during sweeping. The sweet aroma of the Jeyes Fluid remains long in the memory.

To the rear of the downstairs' classroom were two small rooms, a cloakroom at one side and 'the dairy' at the other, which contained a flagstone floor and small benches where the younger pupils sat and ate their lunch. Lunch typically involved bread and jam and either milk or cold tea in a bottle wrapped in a brown paper bag, which the children brought to school in their satchels. On very cold winter days during the late 1930s and early 1940s, Master Cooney and Miss Rushe brought potatoes and vegetables to the school and made soup for the children.[50] Later, Mrs Donnelly shared brown bread and jam with them.[51]

The male and female outdoor toilets were essentially dry latrines that had been constructed at the time when the school was first built in 1871. When used, the human waste went into a hole in the ground, which was covered with clay or ashes. Some former pupils remembered the pungent smell of the toilets and how, each summer, they were emptied in preparation for the following school year. With 'slugs of every description', nature also helped to remove the waste.[52]

Schooldays remembered: Growing up on the farm

For most young children growing up in rural south Monaghan in the mid-twentieth century, after returning home from school, farm or household chores needed to be done. Only when these chores were complete could play commence. School children carried out routine chores around the farmyard, including milking cows, cleaning out a cow byre or a hen house, spreading dung and pulling and thinning turnips.[53] Potatoes were also gathered in the field or collected in a bucket from a potato pit. While attending Coolfore school, many children were essential contributors to the farm work and to the family income.[54]

Several former pupils spoke about sowing and gathering potatoes. 'Setting spuds' was remembered as the process of sowing seed potatoes by hand, and involved wearing an apron containing the seed potatoes, and with each step taken, placing a new seed in the drill in front of the foot.[55] During potato-gathering season in September each year, Peter Ward and his brother Patsy (RIP) were taken out of school and spent two weeks gathering potatoes at Gartlan's farm at Louth Village.[56] The Ward boys also gathered potatoes at their Uncle Pat's farm at Broomfield, and in the summer, they helped him with the hay; their sister Mary would bring tea and sandwiches into the hayfield. Peter spent summer months at Hill's farm at Reilly's Cross, thinning turnips, pulling plants, and doing other chores, while Mary spent Saturdays in Carrickmacross, cleaning at the houses of Mrs Mills on the Main Street and McMahon's at Mullinary.

'Gathering spuds' involved the backbreaking work of collecting the dug-up potatoes on the ground and placing them in a bucket or basket and then building them into a potato pit.[57] Despite this gruelling work, some children received no payment, and as Paddy Wallace remembered, acknowledgement was often merely a few words of flattery from the farmer, like: 'The Lord spare you, you're a great gasun!' or 'Oh you are a great lad, I never saw a lad such a good worker as you!'[58]

In the 1960s, some farm work continued to be done in traditional ways, like cutting hay with a scythe or turning hay with a pitchfork.[59] As farm work became more mechanised, most young boys, often aged as young as ten or eleven years, learned how to drive a tractor and handle other farm machinery like tractor-drawn hay rakes or reaper-binders.[60] At busy times when crops were being harvested, farm work demanded that all hands were available, including those of schoolchildren.[61]

Harvest time and farm work
Following a long-held tradition in rural Ireland, many of the schoolchildren at Coolfore were not sent to school at busy times in the farming year, typically in early summer when hay was being harvested and during the potato and corn harvesting period in early autumn, or during market days. Absence from school for farming events was generally permitted if a parent made a written request to the teacher.

During harvest time, children were expected to help with the work, which began in around mid-August. Oats was a common crop in south Monaghan, and John Joe Cunningham and his brothers helped with harvesting them. This involved walking behind the reaping mill to gather the oats and tying them into sheafs using the correct technique. Each sheaf was tied firmly with a band made from the cut-oat's stalk and sheafs were stacked into stooks, with four to six sheafs in each stook. The stooks were later drawn into the haggard, where they were built into ricks in readiness for threshing. Ricks were carefully constructed, with the corn head side placed inwards to protect the seeds.

Threshing-mill owners like the Callans, Comiskeys and Boylans were hired for the threshing. The arrival of the big threshing mill into the haggard was a moment of great excitement for the children. All the neighbouring farmers and labourers came to help, and the young girls of the house helped their mother to prepare the dinner for the men.[62] Bernard McGinnity remembered the excitement of threshing time at his parents' farm at Peaste:

We would be rushing home from school if we knew the mill was coming that day. And when we would come to the top of the hill, we could see our haggard [...] and we would run to try and get there quick before the miller would go away, to get home before it finished.

In addition to oats and potatoes, farmers generally kept a field of seed hay. Harvesting seed hay involved the same harvesting techniques that were used for oats. Straw from the threshed hay was used as fodder for horses and cattle. When the threshing was complete and the harvest saved, some customs were observed. For example, it was traditional for each farmer to donate a bag of grain to the local priest.[63] In October, the Protestant community celebrated the 'Harvest home' service of thanksgiving, when the churches were decorated with symbols of the harvest.

Although flax harvesting had largely declined, it was still grown in parts of south Monaghan, and Paddy Wallace remembered how sowing, pulling and tying flax was 'a slavish job'. He told of how a neighbouring farmer, who having contracted out the work of sowing and harvesting his field of flax, declared that the crop had made money for everyone but himself!

Many families had little disposable income in the post-War decades, and for some, the money that their children earned while working on farms during the summer needed to be rendered up as part of the household income.[64] In addition to money earned from farm and other hire work, many children earned pocket money by selling blackberries to the Fane Valley jam factory, which was located at the former Carrickmacross workhouse on the Shercock Road. In early autumn, blackberries were found in abundance along the hedges and the children gathered and transported them to the jam factory in buckets or creamery cans. Although the money earned from the blackberries was not substantial, it was sufficient compensation for the many small thorns lodged in the blue-stained fingers and hands of the children.

Today a keen collector of vintage farm machinery, as a young boy Bernard McGinnity ploughed with horses and a wheel plough, and he remembered it as a slow, laborious task. Using a wheel plough, he could adjust the depth of the furrow and plough both uphill and downhill. Michael Ward also worked with horses, which were used to pull a plough or hay tumbling rake and to move or 'trace' stacks of hay from the field to the haggard with a chain tied around the stack base. Exchanging the horse for the tractor relieved much of the heavy burden of farm work; however, a farmer could form a close attachment to his work horses. Joseph Callan remembered the sad day when his father sold Jack, 'a big easy-going horse', and how, as the horse was being ridden away, it turned back with a plainful look at his father who cried at the sight.

Schoolchildren were also called on to assist on mart day when cattle were taken to the sales yard in Carrickmacross. While tractors and cattle trailers were available, where a farm was within a few short miles of the town, cattle were driven by road to market.[65] Farm women traded eggs for provisions like tea and bread with Mr Muckian from Dundalk, who made his weekly rounds each Friday afternoon in his red lorry. For the children, the sweet aroma of the freshly-baked batch loaves, which Mr Muckian sold, was matched only by the taste of the 'penny bars', which he handed out on his visits.

Schooldays remembered: Leisure and entertainment

In the years during and after the War, visiting a neighbour's house for a céilí was common. Neighbours gathered at a house for music and singing, and

McGinnity's of Peaste was a popular destination as a céilí house. Benny Meehan, a renowned local folklorist and musician from neighbouring Coolfore townland, played his fiddle there, and along with Packie Dowdall, another local folklorist, told stories long into the night.[66] Going on a céilí also referred to simply visiting a neighbour's house to spend an evening of chat. Children who were sent on an errand to a neighbour's house, generally did not knock before entering, such was the trust among the rural community.[67]

In addition to going on a céilí, visits to a neighbour's house were sometimes made for prayer meetings, and Paddy Wallace shared some amusing anecdotes about such events. At one meeting, 'rosary after rosary' was being recited, but with midnight fast approaching, there was no sign of the host offering tea. As the Litany was being recited with 'Holy Mary Mother of God, pray for us. St Joseph, pray for us. St Patrick pray for us', a voice from the back of the kitchen was heard to shout: 'Will you make tae for us?' As prayers were being recited at another rosary evening, the lady of the house suddenly shouted out to her husband: 'James, did you close in the gate on the pigs?'

In the period before television, newspapers and the wireless were the main sources of information about the wider world. Some radios were powered by wet batteries that were re-charged at the local chemist.[68] The All-Ireland football final was the major national sporting event and was broadcast on *Radio Éireann* each September, with Michael O'Hehir providing his distinctive fast-paced commentary. Pat Gilsenan remembered listening to the 1947 final, which Cavan and Kerry contested in New York. Sitting with other children at the doorstep of his neighbour Paddy Keenan's house, the *His Master's Voice* wireless set was placed at the open window and the broadcast could be heard loud and clear. Harry Chambers also had one of the first wireless sets, and many neighbours gathered at his house on the Aghalile Road to hear the final.[69]

The local Gaelic football team was Corduff Gaels, then a fledgling team that was reformed in 1967 after several years' absence from competitions, and it affiliated with the Monaghan GAA County Board in 1968. Several Coolfore alumni from the local area made up the team at that time, which played at Nelson's Park, a flat field near Carrickmacross, which John Nelson, a local farmer, generously provided.[70]

Another major sporting event was the World Heavyweight boxing title fight between Cassius Clay and Sonny Liston in 1964. The fight was shown on the early television sets, which began to arrive in the rural homes of south Monaghan at around that time. Children soon learned which neighbour had acquired a set and walked there to watch the big fight.[71] A number of families on the Aghalile Road were among the first to acquire a television set, including the Murtagh, Garvey, and Wallace households.[72] On Saturdays, children could arrive uninvited at a neighbour's house to watch their favourite shows, like the Flintstones and the Lone Ranger. The off switch was sometimes used if parents decided that material on the television was unsuitable for children.[73]

Another source of entertainment was 'the pictures'. Located on the Chapel Lane in Carrickmacross, the Stella Cinema was the local picture house. The Ward children were given 2s. in pocket money to go to the pictures, and with the cinema costing 'one and six', they could purchase 6d. worth of sweets at Hand's shop on the way. Peter remembered how 6d. worth of sweets 'would keep you chewing, eating the whole way through the film'. Perri Crisps and aniseed balls were also favourite treats, and Hand's shop also sold individual cigarettes.[74]

Most children pursued fun and leisure outdoors. Played on the local roads, skittles was a popular children's game.[75] Fishing by hand for brown trout and eel in the local river that ran past Coolfore school was also a popular summer pastime for many children, and on hot summer days when all the farming chores were complete, many local children also swam at Creevy Lake on the Lisdoonan Road.[76] At weekends in the summer, the lakeshore was thronged with local children. Known to the rural children as 'townies', children from Carrickmacross also swam at the lake.

Few families took summer holidays, in the modern sense of the term, although the better-off families of the district spent a week at one of the numerous boarding houses at Blackrock seaside village in Co. Louth.[77] For most rural families in the period up to the late 1960s, summer holidays consisted of the annual day trip to 'the Rocks' on 15 August. The date was significant as it was the Catholic Feast of the Assumption and Blackrock village was the site of a Marian shrine.[78] Families from the landlocked counties of Monaghan and Cavan flocked to the Rocks on 'the Fifteenth', and the day was perhaps less about a pilgrimage of religious devotion and more about a day at the seaside and an evening's entertainment in one of the local music pubs.[79] The other attraction at Blackrock were the heated salt baths that people visited, believing that the waters there had healing powers for treating rheumatism.[80]

Alice Lavery was a young girl in the 1930s, a time when trains still ran from Carrickmacross to Dundalk and onto Blackrock, and she recalled the excitement of the train journey. In later years, Danny Hughes' seafront shop was a wonderland for children, where rock candy and colourful beach toys, including windmills, buckets and spades were sold.[81] Mr Hughes sold candy with the inscription 'Blackpool', where he purchased it, and not 'Blackrock', but this fact went unnoticed to the children who consumed it with delight.[82] Other attractions at the Rocks were the skating hall and the outdoor seawater swimming pool that was constructed in the early 1960s. By the 1970s, the tradition of the 'Fifteenth' at the Rocks was in decline, as families with more disposable income sought holiday destinations further afield.[83]

Schooldays remembered: The War

Some of those who shared their memories of schooldays attended Coolfore in the years during or immediately after the Second World War, a period referred to as 'the Emergency'. The War in Europe had little meaning for the younger children attending Coolfore school at the time, as Paddy Wallace recalled: 'It didn't mean anything to us, there was a war on, and we hardly knew what the meaning of it was. You wouldn't be interested in world affairs back then.' Nevertheless, with Coolfore school less than fifty miles' distant from Belfast, the sound of the War was never far away, and for some former pupils, the War had more personal meaning in the memory.

Alice Lavery remembered hearing the rumble of the German planes that flew directly over the school on their bombing raids to Belfast: 'The big German bombers used to come over and everybody in the school had to run and pray at the grotto that they wouldn't drop a bomb on us.'[84] Although a young boy at the time, Michael Ward also remembered the war-time bombing raids on Belfast, when a squadron of four to five bombers crossed overhead:

> I remember the Germans, the planes going to bomb Belfast, I was young at that time, only about eight. I remember my father taking me out and the planes going across. You could see them; they weren't flying that high and the roars of them [...] I was afraid of my life. I wanted to go back into the house.

Michael's childhood fears were somewhat justified, as he also told of how a bomb was dropped at the nearby townland of Bocks Upper in the parish of Donaghmoyne:

> Lough Egish butter [was] got beyond in England, and they wanted to bomb all the creameries. So, they were coming around and it was at night [...] and they couldn't see because the lights were put off at night. And they kept flying around and they couldn't hold the bomb any longer, it was time to go, and they dropped her at Bocks Rock [...] and it hit the rock and it blew the windows out of a few houses around [and on] Smithy Finnegan's forge too.

The bomb in question fell on Friday, 20 December 1940, and was one of two bombs dropped at around 9 p.m. that evening. Marie McGivney, a descendant of Owen Finnegan, the local blacksmith, told how the first bomb fell beside the home of Patrick Daly, causing extensive damage to his house and farm outbuildings and creating a large crater.[85] On hearing the first explosion, Owen Finnegan emerged from his house with a Tilley lamp in hand, and was thrown to the ground by the blast of the second bomb, which exploded in the air above his house. The bomb smashed windows and removed slates from his roof and left Finnegan with just the handle of the Tilley lamp in his hand. As he emerged from his house, Patrick Daly received shoulder and arm injuries from glass and wood splinters from the air blast caused by the second bomb.[86] Daly's house, then newly-constructed, was so badly damaged that he was obliged to return to live in his old, thatched house. While his Tilley lamp was never found, Finnegan the blacksmith gathered up metal fragments from the bomb and forged working compasses and dividers that he used for measuring distances and scribing arcs and circles on metal.[87]

As Michael Ward explained, the target of the German bombs was the nearby Lough Egish creamery, since the Germans considered that Irish creameries were supporting the British war effort through the export of butter.[88] In the immediate aftermath of the bombings, there was much local interest and curiosity, and both Daly and Finnegan conducted tours of the bomb crater site, with Finnegan wearing his Sunday best for them.

Pat Gilsenan remembered the post-War rationing and the ration book which his mother used when shopping in Carrickmacross. The privations of war-time meant that coal and other fuels were expensive, and while south Monaghan is not generally regarded as a place of turf cutting, mud turf was cut and used as a fuel. Paddy Wallace spoke of cutting mud turf in the summertime at a bog located between the Aghalile and Shercock roads.[89] He explained the method, whereby the mud was cut using a slane, a special V-shaped turf-cutting spade, and the soft wet mud was carefully lifted and laid out to dry. The wet mud was shaped by hand and marked at nine-inch intervals, and when dry, the turf pieces easily broke away for gathering.[90] When spreading the mud, no shoes were worn. Paddy referred to the turf as 'slane turf' and remembered that it was a 'great burner'.

Moving to Carrickmacross schools

When the time came for Coolfore school to close in 1968, the children were naturally apprehensive and concerned that they would be behind in their lessons, when compared with their new classmates in Carrickmacross.[91] They need not have worried, since children in the lower classes at Coolfore could listen to the lessons being conducted with the higher classes in the same room, and this helped when their turn came to learn the lessons. Bernard Fealy remembered how, when he entered fifth class at St Joseph's boys' school, he was already familiar with much of what was being taught. Mairead Nulty and Mary Byrne similarly recalled how the Coolfore girls were ahead of the St Louis girls in their lessons. Mary Byrne remembered: 'I didn't realise how privileged we were to be taught in Coolfore until I went to the Louis [...] because I went into fifth class in Louis, [and] everything I had done in Coolfore [...] I already knew [it].'[92] The school cleaning duties were also familiar to Mary and the other Coolfore girls, since pupils at St Louis convent school were made to polish the schoolroom floors.

When the Coolfore boys and girls transferred to the schools in the town in 1968, they no longer had to walk to school or traverse fields and rivers, since a school bus collected them. For the girls, another positive aspect was the fact that, unlike at Coolfore, they now wore a smart uniform. With approximately fourteen boys and fourteen girls from across the junior and senior classes transferring into their respective new classes, typically just one or two pupils was added to each class in the town schools. The children left their small mixed class at Coolfore for a larger single-sex class, and for some, this was the most difficult aspect of the experience of moving school.

14

Conclusions

In 1831, Lord Stanley set out the principles by which a unified system of education should operate. In bringing children of all denominations together, such a system would promote religious tolerance and harmony among Catholic, Protestant and Presbyterian children, and it was hoped, would be acceptable to all parents and communities. The decades that followed saw the establishment of national schools supported by and connected with the Board of National Education in Ireland. By the mid-nineteenth century, the growing number of state-supported schools bearing 'national school' on a plaque on the schoolhouse wall had become a common artefact of the built environment.

Except for some large convent schools in towns and cities and some two-storey schoolhouses built to a local vernacular form, most schoolhouses in rural Ireland were constructed to a simple design, according to plans provided by the OPW.[1] Typically, the rural schoolhouse was a single-storey building, purely functional with few architectural embellishments. This uniformity of rural schoolhouse design represented the physical manifestation of a standardised, regulated, state system of education.[2] Whatever its structural form, the rural schoolhouse was central to the social and cultural life of each parish.

The development and provision of mass elementary education in Ireland in the early nineteenth century occurred in the wake of the Act of Union, when Ireland came under the direct rule of the Westminster parliament. It also followed closely on Catholic Emancipation. The national school system was an early example of direct state intervention in the lives of the people. While the system was founded on the explicit and admirable ideal of bringing together children of all religious denominations under a single unified system, its underlying impetus reflected prevailing beliefs about the role and responsibilities of Empire in civilising the people under its rule and imposing social order. While ideas about class, race and gender shaped the way that the system was planned and developed, its development was also shaped by local forces, including the denominational churches and parents who saw schooling as a means of family advancement.[3]

The national school system that followed Stanley's letter was introduced some ninety years before Independence, yet it continued to be operated in post-independence Ireland, remaining essentially unchanged until the last decade of the twentieth century, when comprehensive educational legislation was finally enacted.[4] The establishment of denominational schools under religious patronage undermined Stanley's principle of a unified education system. In this regard, Patrick O'Donovan is more direct, writing that 'vigorous episcopally-led opposition' to change and an 'unrelenting and stultifying parochial clericalism endured in the national school system', resulted in the exclusion and loss of civic and parental engagement in educational matters.[5]

Throughout the nineteenth century, the ascribed role of women in Ireland was that of housewife and mother with responsibility for childrearing and the family economy, and this limited opportunities for women in the public sphere, including in learned professions like medicine and law. Nevertheless, national school teaching, and later, hospital nursing, provided women with opportunities to secure education and meaningful and respectable roles outside the home.[6] Although nuns enjoyed a near monopoly on principalships in the larger girls' schools, many female teachers held principalships in smaller lay schools.[7]

A disunified system: State and Church control

The national schools were closely monitored and controlled by both state and Church authorities. State authorities were represented in the person of the district inspector, who enforced the Board's rules; hence, the school inspectorate was the main expression of bureaucratic monitoring and control. The district inspectors monitored the quality and practices of the teachers and the proficiency of the pupils. School principals, in particular, were subjected to close monitoring, and district inspectors tended to report more on a principal's shortcomings and less on their successes in teaching and managing their school. To that extent, and in terms of academic attainments, the real effectiveness of teaching was difficult to evaluate.

Church control was at first represented in efforts by some evangelical Protestants to promote religious instruction in local pay schools, including those schools in which the teacher and the majority of the pupils were Catholic. With the advent of the national school system and its fundamental principle that no attempt should be made to interfere with the 'peculiar religious tenets' of Christian pupils, religious and secular instruction were to be conducted separately. Despite this principle, the schools were gradually organised parochially and managed along single denominational lines, and in the case of many Catholic-managed schools, into single sex schools. This ecclesiastical control of local schools would remain a fundamental feature of the national school system.

Another feature of the national schools was the way in which the school curriculum accentuated gender differences that already existed in wider society. The schooling experience for girls was one that emphasised the acquisition of accomplishments and skills for their ascribed role in the domestic sphere.[8] Hence, girls learned needlework, cookery, laundry work and domestic science, while boys learned arithmetic, science and agriculture. In this way, the curriculum privileged boys for their assumed roles in the public sphere of work and occupations outside the home. The gendered nature of schooling also accorded with the position of the Catholic hierarchy, which saw the girl's role as belonging in the family home setting as wife and mother.[9]

Ecclesiastical control of schooling occurred in the context of a transition in the role and status of the main denominational Churches, not just in education but in wider political and social life. Having established de facto control of the education of its own community through school patronage, the Catholic Church had become more powerful socially and politically.[10] Any opportunity to bring Catholic, Protestant and Presbyterian children together in a unified national school system had been lost by the mid- to late nineteenth century.[11] In its place was a system in which teacher appointments and other school affairs were managed by the clergy of their respective denominations, with Catholic clerical managers, in particular, exercising control over all school affairs. Contrary to the principles under which the national school system had originally been established, religious instruction came to be permitted during school hours, and was an integral part of the school curriculum.[12]

Coolfore national school
Coolfore was one of a dozen national schools in the parish of Magheross, and one of seven rural schools in the townlands to the north-west of Carrickmacross on the Shirley estate. The history of the development of Coolfore school exemplified the development of the national school system more generally, which in turn, exemplified wider social, cultural and political developments. For example, in its early development, Coolfore was influenced by successive landlords and their agents on the Shirley estate. Like other national

schools in west Farney and elsewhere in Ireland, Coolfore school later came under the influence of the Catholic Church, through the local parish clergy acting as school managers. This influence was also embodied in the school-teachers, who were responsible for cathectic instruction and associated religious formation of the pupils.

At the end of the Great War, the transfer of school patronage of rural schools on the Shirley estate from Shirley to Catholic diocesan trustees was completed, and this process coincided with the wider changes in the balance of power that were occurring in Ireland at that time. These changes were a prelude to the eventual demise of the landed class and the emergence of an increasingly powerful and influential Catholic hierarchy in the political and social life of the country. In the national schools, this power was demonstrated in the way that the local clergy closely supervised the children's religious formation.

Throughout the late nineteenth and early twentieth centuries, rural schools like Coolfore provided a varied curriculum that emphasised the development of literacy and numeracy skills, which were considered essential for productive work beyond school. In the years after Independence, Coolfore continued to serve the families of several rural townlands near Carrickmacross. In addition to mandatory regular catechetic instruction, the school curriculum now included the Irish language, which was central to the government's mission to establish the new state as distinctly *Gaelic*. Coolfore school was served by committed teachers who gave long years of service and who taught a highly prescribed curriculum using highly prescribed teaching methods. Like their counterparts in other local national schools, the teachers operated under the watchful gaze of the district inspector and the parish priest.

In the face of falling enrolment, Coolfore school closed in 1968. At the time of its closure, it retained the essential characteristics of a small rural national school in mid-twentieth-century Ireland. Its pupils walked to school across fields and over roads, carrying their satchels containing schoolbooks, exercise books and a lunch of bread and jam. A place of learning and of play, the school was a social space in which pupils and their teachers lived out their respective roles, each contributing to the daily life of the school. For a great many of the children, their schooling was a preparation for work on the family farm, work for which they were well equipped on leaving school, or as labourers in England's post-War reconstruction.

Educate together

The history of the national school system is a chapter in the history of the relationship between Church and state. That relationship was represented in the initial tensions that arose over religious instruction in schools and in the way that school patronage became a branch of parish administration. After Independence, the state conferred on school patrons and managers enormous responsibility for nation building. Over a half century after Coolfore national school closed, most primary schools remain state-aided parish schools under denominational patronage and management, with almost 90 per cent under Catholic diocesan patronage.

Nevertheless, while professing a particular denominational ethos, primary schools may now not use religion as a basis for the admission of pupils. This is a requirement under the relevant provisions of the Education Act 2018 and is consistent with the principles of equality, diversity and inclusion. While some schools that provide education in a minority religion can prioritise a student of that religion, primary schools' admission policies prohibit discrimination based on religion and a range of other factors, including the child's race, gender, disability and parental characteristics, such as occupational status. These requirements also reflect the very practical need to ensure access to primary education for the increasingly diverse ethnic and religious families and communities throughout Ireland, including families that self-identify as non-religious.[13]

Even before the major inward migration that occurred in the first two decades of the twenty-first century, there have been historical precedents for the establishment of multi-denominational schools. Commencing in Dalkey in south Co. Dublin in 1974, the first state-aided, multi-denominational primary school was the prototype for a national movement to educate children together, irrespective of their social, cultural or religious background.[14] Led by parents and communities, the Educate Together movement has established upwards of a hundred primary schools.[15] The Irish government policy is to facilitate the transfer of school patronage from Catholic to multi-denominational patronage and to expand and prioritise the transfer of viable schools to multi-denominational community national schools under local education and training boards.[16]

At the time of writing, a pilot scheme to divest schools of Catholic patronage, and thereby achieve a greater plurality of primary education provision, is underway in several counties. The aim is to provide greater choice for parents and increase the overall proportion of schools that are multi-denominational. Whether and to what extent this is achieved in the twenty-first century remains to be seen. School patronage is a complex issue that involves decisions around a school's ethos, governance arrangements, management and decision-making expertise, curriculum and teaching, resources and supports for non-denominational pupils, the Irish language and parental rights. Although the ideal of a national unified system of primary education, as envisioned by Lord Stanley in 1831, was never realised, primary schools are nevertheless welcoming places for children of diverse faiths and ethnic backgrounds. Despite the demise of many rural schools in the 1960s, in the early twenty-first century, rural national schools like Scoil Phádraig at Corduff and the national schools at Corcreagh and Lisdoonan are thriving and remain central to the social and cultural life of their communities.

Appendices

APPENDIX 1
Participants in oral history interviews

I am sincerely grateful to the following, who took part in oral history interviews and generously shared their memories of their time at Coolfore National School.

Mary Byrne (née Ward) (MB), interview 28 March 2022
Joseph Callan (JC), interview 22 March 2022
John Joe Cunningham (JJC), interview 29 March 2022
Bernard Fealy (BF), interview 29 January 2022
Patrick Gilsenan (PG), interview 20 July 2022
Alice Lavery (née Murtagh) (AL), interview 15 November 2021
Fergus Lane (FL), interview 11 December 2021
Bernard McGinnity (BMcG), interview 25 March 2022
Josephine Marron (née Reilly) (JMa), interview 15 April 2022
James Meehan (JMe), interview 7 August 2022
Mairead Nulty (née Byrne) (MN), interview 29 June 2022
Paddy Wallace (PWc), interview November 2022
Michael Ward (MW), interview June 2022
Peter Ward (PWd), interview 28 March 2022

APPENDIX 2
Pay schools in the parish of Magheross, 1826

Parochial returns to the Commissioners of Irish Education Inquiry, 1826★

Location of pay school	Schoolmaster /schoolmistress Name	Religion of teacher	Description of the schoolhouse	Religion of scholars RC	EC	Pres.	Patronage/ annual support	Scriptures read
Mullagherogery	John Bell	Presbyterian	A thatched house with earthen floor	9		22	Mr Shirley gives 5*l*.	Read; AV
Carrickmaclim	Peter Ward	R. Catholic	A thatched house, the master's own	56	15		None	Read; AV
Greaghadromnisk	James Meighan	R. Catholic	A thatched house	30			Mr Shirley gives 5*l*.	Not read
Cornasassanah	Bernard Ward	R. Catholic	A thatched house	37	1		None	Not read
Carrickadoey	Richard Maguire	R. Catholic	A barn	50			None	Not stated
Carghamore	Owen Sheridan	R. Catholic	A thatched house	52		2	Mr Shirley gives 5*l*.	Read; V.n.s.
Lisirill	John McArdle	R. Catholic	Master's house	38	2		None	Not read
Derrylavan	Nicholas Marran	R. Catholic	A thatched house	30			None	Not read
Carrickmacross	William Gleeson	R. Catholic	A room in the town of Carrickmacross	27	3		None	Not read
Carrickmacross	Mary Gleeson	R. Catholic	A room in a lodging house	27	3		None	Not read
Shancoagh	Michael Coony	R. Catholic	A thatched house	24		11	None	Read; V.n.s.
Lurgans	John Hogan	R. Catholic	A thatched house	42	3		None	Not read
Carrickmacross	Rev. Wm. T. Palmer	Protestant	Good house	4	16		Bath gives 7*l*. 16s. 8d.	Read; AV
Carrickmacross	John McCabe	R. Catholic	An old house intended to be taken down	35	1		None	Not read
Carrickmacross	Patrick McCabe	R. Catholic	A room rented in the town	26	2		None	Not read
Corduffkelly	Owen O'Brien	R. Catholic	Room in own house	18	6		None	Not read
Carrickmacross	Philip Gartlan	R. Catholic	A thatched house	30			None	Not read
Carrickmacross	Bridget Lynden	R. Catholic	Her own house	38	2		None	Not read
Aghalile	John Cassidy	R. Catholic	A thatched house	48			Mr Shirley gives 5*l*.	AV; one scholar
Corduff Mountain	Owen Rush	R. Catholic	A room attached to a chapel	49	1		Mr Shirley gives 5*l*.	Not read
Coraghy	Francis Reilly	R. Catholic	A thatched house rented	15			None	Not read
Corcreeagh	Bernard Larkin	R. Catholic	A barn	46	2		Mr Shirley gives 5*l*.	Not read
Coolfore	Patrick McMahon	R. Catholic	A thatched house	58			None	Not read

*All schools were pay schools; AV: Authorised version; V.n.s.: Version not stated

*Source: Second Report of the Commissioners of Irish Education Inquiry (HC, 1826), Appendix to the Second Report, Appendix No. 22, pp. 458–61.

APPENDIX 3
The Old School in Coolfore
Mrs K. McCahey (née Ward) Alts, Carrickmacross

Not long ago I went to see
A scene of early life
Though in years the time is brief
I went to see my old schoolhouse
But now a school no more
For nigh a hundred years of teaching ends
At the old school in Coolfore

It stands along a winding road
A building tall, austere
And many a youthful heart I'm sure
Had entered it in fear
Erected by the landlord
In oppression days of yore
Yet good Irishmen and women came
To the old school in Coolfore

The river flowing as of yore
Onto the lonely glen
For nature does not change its way
Whatever the whims of men
I stood upon the little bridge
Where oft I stood before
But no boys and girls to join me now
At the old school in Coolfore

Denuded now the countryside
Of boys and girls so young
Taken away from the lanes and fields
To swell the urban throng
How can they love the rural scene
When they cannot see it more
And the bus is death to many a school
Like the old school in Coolfore

Along the road there is little change
In the things I used to know
The honeysuckle smells as sweet
And the old crab trees still grow
But gone from the school are the grey stone steps
And none shall count them more
For a renovated dwelling now
Is the old school in Coolfore

Where are they now the hundreds
Who passed through that school gate
And what in nigh a hundred years
Has been their final fate?
Some are sleeping their last long sleep
Far from their native shore
Many rest at home and many still live
Near the old school in Coolfore

I walk again to the little bridge
There is a gentle Autumn breeze
It mingles with the river's hum
And softly stirs the trees
They echo back my sadness
That now for evermore
There shall be nought but memories
Of the old school in Coolfore

BIBLIOGRAPHY

PRIMARY SOURCES

Commissioners of National Education in Ireland: Annual reports with appendices
Available online at ProQuest UK Parliamentary Papers and/or at UCD
  Library Special Collections, as follows:

Reports of the Commissioners of National Education in Ireland with
  appendices for the following years: 1835, 1836, 1845, 1853, 1847, 1848,
  1852, 1860, 1867, 1870, 1871, 1872, 1873, 1880, 1883, 1895, 1900, 1903,
  1904, 1905, 1907–1908, 1918–1919.

**Commissioners of National Education in Ireland (CNEI):
Miscellaneous reports and correspondences**
Available at National Archives of Ireland (NAI) and/or at Cavan County
Library (CCL) Collections, as follows:

A.J. Crowley Esq. to Commissioners, 24 March 1874, CCL/NE/10/00009.
Circular issued by the Commissioners of National Education in Ireland, to
  teachers of national schools in Ireland regarding attendance at meetings,
  &c., together with correspondence, &c. relative thereto, 4 August 1905
  (Dublin, 1905).
CNEI, Circular from Education Office to district inspectors,
  CCL/NE/10/00001, 9 Jan.1855.
—— Circular from Education Office to district inspectors,
  CCL/NE/10/000109.

—— Circular from Education Office to district inspectors, 1877: Memoranda to be observed in the written examination of teachers, pupil-teachers and monitors, CCL/NE/10/00013.

—— *Reading Book for the use in Female Schools* (Dublin, 1838).

—— Commissioners to J. Simpson Esq., CCL/NE/10/00010.

—— Commissioners to the several district and sub inspectors, 7 March 1855, CCL/NE/10/00010.

—— Education Office to William Bole, Esq., Carrickmacross Female Industrial School, 10 July 1872, CCL/NE/10/00004.

Commission on Manual and Practical Instruction in Primary Schools under the Board of National (Dublin, 1898).

CNEI, Communication to district inspector, 20 May 1875, CCL/NE/10/00012.

Corporal Punishment Book, 'N.' National School, NAI/PRIV1231/10.

Education Office to Samuel Adair, Esq., Carrickmacross Female Industrial School, 10 July 1872, CCL/NE/10/00004.

Education in Ireland (1898a) *Final report 1898* (Dublin, 1902b).

].J. Hazlett to Resident Commissioners of National Education in Ireland, 1 June 1905.

National schools teacher salary book: County Monaghan, vol. 2, roll numbers 8984–14996, 1921–1923, NAI/ED/4/2759.

National Education (Ireland), *New Rules and Regulations 1900–1*, Rule 54.

Registers of summaries of documents relating to administration of national schools: District 24, vol. 2, roll nos. 147–2963, 1857–1888, NAI/ED/2/103.

Teachers employed by the Commissioners of National Education on 31 March 1905, NAI/PCO/10/1/24.

Commissioners of National Education in Ireland: Reports and correspondence with schools

Clontrain national school
CNEI, Queries to be answered by applicants for aid towards the fitting-up of schools, the paying of teachers, and the obtaining of school requisites, signed 10 Jan. 1834, Clontrain school, NAI/ED1/69/42/1.

Coolfore national school
CNEI, Application for aid towards payment of teacher's salary and for supply of books &c., 4/1/1872, application of John Thomas Holland, NAI/ED 1/70.

BIBLIOGRAPHY

—— Coolfore national school, NAI/ED/2/36, roll 4537, folio 179.
—— Coolfore national school, roll 10700, 1870–1875, CCL/NE/10/00032.
—— Coolfore national school, 1874–1879, CCL/NE/10/00039.
—— Coolfore national school, NAI/ED/9/27001/16 and NAI/ED/9/27255.
—— Coolfore national school, 1884, CCL/NE/10/00019.
—— Coolfore national school, Roll, 10700, NAI/ED/2/103, folio 48 and vol. 2, folio 15; file ED 9/1627 and ED 9/27255.
—— Efficiency case 1931–35, NAI/ED12, File no: 27920; Box no: 636.
—— Report upon application for aid towards payment of teacher's salary and for supply of books &c., 20 June 1845, Coolfore, NAI/ED 1/69 No 123.
—— Report upon application for aid towards payment of teacher's salary and for supply of books &c., 10 February 1872, roll no. 10700, report of Mr John Thomas Simpson, NAI/ED1/70.

Corcreagh national school
Education Office to A. Simpson, Esq., Corcreagh, 10 July 1872, CCL/NE/10/00009.
CNEI, Corcreagh national school, NAI, District 24, NAI/roll 9632, folio 31.

Corduff male and female national schools
CNEI, Corduff national school, District 24, rolls 2017, 2018, 13806 and 12807, NAI, folios 17, 18, 53 and 54.
—— Corduff national school, District 24, roll 13806 and 12807, NAI, folios 17,18, 53 and 54.
—— Corduff male national school inspector's marking paper, CCL/NE/10/00039.
—— Education Office to A Simpson, Esq., Corduff female, 24 March 1871, CCL/NE/10/00009.
—— Corduff national school, District 24, roll 13806 and 12807, NAI, folio 17.

Corvally national school
CNEI, Corvally national school, District 24, roll 10706, NAI, folio 49.

Sreenty national school
CNEI, Sreenty national school, District 24, roll 8015, NAI, folio 8.
—— Sreenty national school, NAI/ED/9/27255.

Department of Education: Miscellaneous reports and circulars to schools

Department of Education (DOE), Coolfore/Corduff Staffing Part 1 1928–62, NAI/10700/13806/File no: 19975; Box 430.

—— Efficiency case 1931–35, NAI/ED12/File no: 27920; Box no: 636.

—— *Investment in education: Report of the survey team appointed by the Minister for Education in October 1962*, 1965 (Dublin, 1965).

—— National schools teacher salary book: County Monaghan, volume 2, roll numbers 9130-14845, 1930–32, NAI/ED/4/2768.

—— National schools teacher salary book: County Monaghan, volume 2, roll numbers 10574-15329, 1957–1959, NAI, ED/4/2794.

—— Primary Branch, Circular 9/82, *Circular to Boards of Management and Principal Teachers of National Schools, Re: The Abolition of Corporal Punishment in National Schools* (Dublin, 1982).

Provisional Government of Ireland, National Education, *Programme for Students in Training, Session 1922–23* (Dublin, 1922).

—— *Report of the Department of Education for the School Years 1925–26–27 and the Financial and Administrative year 1925–26* (Dublin, 1928).

—— *Report of the Department of Education for the School Year 1939–40 and the Financial and Administrative year 1939–40* (Dublin, 1940).

—— *Rules for National Schools under the Department of Education*, Rule 130, Part 1 (Dublin, 1965).

Saorstát Éireann, *Report of the Department of Education for the School Years 1925–26–27* (Dublin, 1927).

—— *Schools Reconfiguration for Diversity: Transfer of Patronage of Primary Schools: Information for School Communities* (Dublin, 2022).

House of Commons: Reports and debates

Hansard, 'Leases for schools (Ireland) Bill, Second reading', Volume 264: debated on Tuesday 9 August 1881, cc1732–1733.

—— 'Salaries of teachers in Corcreagh national school', HC debate 30 November 1906 vol. 166 c396.

—— 1803–2005, Commons Sitting, Leighlinbridge National School, HC debate 10 August 1894, Vol 28, cc565–6565.

HC, *Carrickmacross national schools, return exhibiting the amount earned by females attending the central and seven district national schools of Carrickmacross, in Ireland, on combining literary education with industrial instruction* (London, 1854).

First Report of the Commissioners of Irish Education Inquiry (London, 1825).

—— National Education (Ireland) Building Grants, 1 August 1894 (London,

1894).

—— National Schools (Ireland), *Return of the number of pupils examined for results in each school in Ireland under the National Board of Education for the past two years* (London, 1879).

—— National Education (Ireland) Building Grants, 1 August 1894, *Return of applications made between 1 June 1887 and the 31 December 1893, to the Board of Commissioners of National Education in Ireland* (Dublin, 1893).

—— *Practical observations upon the views and tendency of the First Report of the Commissioners of Irish Education Inquiry* (London, 1826).

—— *Report of Mr. F.H. Dale, His Majesty's Inspector of Schools, on Primary Education in Ireland* (Dublin, 1904).

—— *Reports from the Commissioners of the Board of Education in Ireland, 1809–1812* (London, 1812).

—— *Royal Commission of Inquiry into Primary Education (Ireland), Vol. 1 containing the Report of the Commissioners with an Appendix* (London, 1870).

—— *Second Report of the Commissioners of Irish Education Inquiry* (London, 1826).

—— *Twelfth Report from the Commissioners of the Board of Education in Ireland, 1809–1812* (London, 1812).

—— *Vice-Regal Committee of Inquiry into Primary Education (Ireland) 1913* (Dublin, 1913).

—— *Vice-Regal Committee of Inquiry into Primary Education (Ireland) 1913, Final Report of the Committee* (Dublin, 1914).

—— *Vice-Regal Committee of Inquiry into Primary Education (Ireland) Report of the Committee, Volume I* (Dublin, 1918).

Miscellaneous reports

Irish National Teachers' Organisation (INTO), 'Report of the Central Executive Committee for the year 1932–33', *Annual Directory and Irish Educational Yearbook for 1933* (Dublin, 1933).

Society for Promoting the Education of the Poor of Ireland (Society), *First Report of the Society for Promoting the Education of the Poor of Ireland* (Dublin, 1813).

—— *Eighth Report of the Society for Promoting the Education of the Poor of Ireland* (Dublin, 1820).

—— *Ninth Report of the Society for Promoting the Education of the Poor of Ireland* (Dublin, 1821).

Public Records Office of Northern Ireland (PRONI)

PRONI, *Shirley Papers*, Evelyn J. Shirley obituary, *Leamington Spa Courier*, 10

January 1857.
—— *Shirley Papers*, 'Reports by George Sudden on the state of the schools on the Shirley estate, together with an earlier petition, of 1834, from sundry Protestant tenants to E.J. Shirley asking him to contribute towards the cost of building a parish school, and 3 printed copies of a proselytizing school catechism, 1837', PRONI/D3531/C/3/6.
—— PRONI/D3531/C/3/3–4; PRONI/D3531/S/58.

NEWSPAPERS

Anglo-Celt, 29 March 1952; 28 September 1918; 7 March 1959.
Belfast Newsletter, 23 March 1906; 26 March 1906.
Dundalk Democrat, February 1896; 21 September 1896; 2 May 1903; 6 March 1904; 4 February 1905; 7 August 1907; 19 June 1909; 26 June 1908; 27 June 1908; 26 June 1909; 26 November 1932; 1 December 1934; 30 January 1937; 1 May 1937; 29 January 1938; 5 November 1938; 16 April 1966; 25 October 1974.
Evening Herald, 23 June 1908; 18 April 1962.
Freeman's Journal, 20 November 1896; 6 March 1906; 23 June 1908.
Irish Independent, 26 June 1908; 13 October 1956; 10 August 1957.
Irish Press, 10 October 1935.
The Irish Times, 25 August 2015.
Monaghan Argus, 22 May 1954; 18 November 1950.
Newry Examiner and Louth Advertiser, 18 November 1837.
Northern Standard, 16 October 1841; 25 May 1889; 25 July 1908; 19 December 1908; 17 October 1930; 10 December 1937.
Sligo Champion, 29 April 1905.

SECONDARY SOURCES

Books and journal articles
Akenson, Donal H., *The Irish education experiment: The national system of education in the nineteenth century* (London, 2012).
Anonymous, 'Henry Morris' *Journal of the County Louth Archaeological Society*, 11:1 (1945), 13–14.
Beale, George, 'Local education authority administration in Northern Ireland after partition: The early years of the County Down Education Committee 1925–31', *The Irish Journal of Education*, 31 (2000), 5–24.

Brown, Lindsay T., 'The Presbyterians of County Monaghan Part I: The unfolding story', *Clogher Record*, 13:3 (1990), 7–54.

Brown, Martin, McNamara, Gerry & O Hara, Joe, 'Teacher accountability in education: The Irish experiment' in Walsh, *Essays* (2016), pp. 359–81.

Chuinneagain, Sile, 'The politics of equality: Catherine Mahon and the Irish national teachers' organisation, 1905–1916', *Women's History Review*, 6:4 (1997), 527–49.

Conway, Heather, 'Where there's a will: Law and emotion in sibling inheritance disputes', in Heather Conway & John Stannard (eds) *The emotional dynamics of law and legal discourse* (Oxford, 2016), pp. 35–57.

Coolahan, John, 'The daring first decade of the Board of National Education, 1831–1841', *The Irish Journal of Education*, xvii (1983), 35–54.

—— 'The historical development of teacher education in the Republic of Ireland' in Andy Burke (ed.) *Teacher education in the Republic of Ireland: retrospect and prospect* (Maynooth, 2004).

Coolahan, John, Hussey, Caroline & Kilfeather, Fionnuala, *The Forum on Patronage and Pluralism in the Primary Sector: Report of the forum's advisory group* (Dublin, 2012).

Costigan, Lucy & Cullen, Michael, *The strangest genius: The stained glass of Harry Clarke* (Dublin, 2010).

Cullen Owens, Rosemary, *A social history of women in Ireland 1870–1970* (Dublin, 2005).

Daly, Mary E., 'The development of the National School System, 1831–1840' in Art Cosgrave & Donal McCartney (eds), *Studies in Irish history: presented to R Dudley Edwards* (Dublin, 1979), pp. 151–63.

—— 'The Irish Free State and the Great Depression of the 1930s: The interaction of the global and the local', *Irish Economic and Social History*, 38 (2011), 19–36.

Day, Angélique & McWilliams, Patrick, *Counties Cavan, Leitrim, Louth, Monaghan and Sligo (v. 40) (The Ordnance Survey memoirs of Ireland 1830–1840)* (Belfast, 1998).

Devine, Dympna, 'Children: Rights and status in education – a socio-historical analysis', *Irish Educational Studies*, Spring 18:1 (1999), 14–28.

Dickson, David, Pyz, Justyna & Shepard, Christopher (eds), *Irish classrooms and British Empire: Imperial contexts in the origins of modern education* (Dublin, 2012).

Duffy, Patrick J. 'Assisted emigration from the Shirley estate 1843–54', *Clogher Record*, 14:2 (1992), 7–62.

Dowling, Patrick J., *The Hedge Schools of Ireland* (Dublin, 1935).

Fahey, Tony, 'State, family and compulsory schooling in Ireland', *The*

Economic and Social Review, 13:4 (1992), 369–95.

Faulkner, Pádraig, 'Education in the Parish of Dunleer', *Journal of the County Louth Archaeological and Historical Society*, 23:1 (1993), 97–114.

Fealy, Gerard M. & Harford, Judith. 'Nervous energy and administrative ability: The early lady principals and lady superintendents in Ireland', *Journal of Educational Administration & History*, 39:3 (2007), 271–83.

FitzGerald, Garret, 'Estimates for baronies of minimum level of Irish-speaking amongst successive decennial cohorts: 1771–1781 to 1861–1871', *Proceedings of the Royal Irish Academy: Archaeology, culture, history, literature* 84C (1984), 117–55.

—— *Irish Primary Education in the Early Nineteenth Century: An analysis of the first and second reports of the Commissioners of Irish Education Inquiry, 1825–6* (Dublin, 2013).

Gailey, Alan, 'Vernacular dwellings of Clogher Diocese', *Clogher Record*, 9:2 (1977), 187–231.

Harford, Judith, 'The emergence of a national policy on teacher education in Ireland', *Journal of Educational Administration and History*, 41:1 (2009), 45–56.

Higgins, Roisin, Holohan, Carole & O'Donnell, Catherine, '1966 and all that: The 50th anniversary commemorations', *History Ireland*, 14:2 (1996), available online at: https://www.historyireland.com/1966-and-all-that-the-50th-anniversary-commemorations/

Hyland, Aine with Green, Desmond, *A brave new vision for education in Ireland: The Dalkey School Project 1974–1984* (Dublin, 2020).

—— 'The investment in education report 1965: Recollections and reminiscences', *Irish Educational Studies*, 33:2 (2014), 1–17.

Hyland, Cal & Kelly, James, 'Richard Twiss's "A Tour of Ireland in 1775 (London, 1776)": The missing pages and some other notes', in *Eighteenth-Century Ireland/ Iris an dá chultúr*, 13 (1998), 52–64.

Johnston, John I.D., 'Hedge schools of Tyrone and Monaghan', *Clogher Record*, 7:1 (1969), 34–55.

Jordan, Thomas E., 'A great statistical operation: A century of Irish censuses, 1812–1911', *New Hibernia Review*, 1:3 (1977), 94–114.

Kerley, Frances, 'The rise and fall of a village industry: Cornacarrow and Laragh mills, 1775–1925' in Jack Johnson (ed.), *Monaghan: Studies in local history* (Maynooth, 2006).

Larkin, Tom, *Seven generations: Carickatee, a history of gatherings* (Castleblaney, 2021).

Livingstone, Peadar, *The Monaghan story: A documented history of the County Monaghan from the earliest times to 1976* (Enniskillen, 1980).

Logan, John, 'The dimensions of gender in nineteenth-century schooling' in Margaret Kelleher & James H. Murphy (eds), *Gender perspectives in nineteenth-century Ireland: Public and private spheres, society for the study of nineteenth century Ireland 2* (Dublin, 1997), pp. 36–49.

McCormick, Eugene, *The INTO and the 1946 teachers' strike* (Dublin, 1996).

McG, P. (1983) '100 years of education in our local schools', *Corduff Calling* (Carrickmacross, 1983), pp. 111–17.

McManus, Antonia, 'Irish hedge schools and social change' in Deirdre Raftery and Karin Fischer (eds), *Educating Ireland: Schooling and social change, 1700–2000* (Dublin, 2014), pp. 1–21.

—— *The Irish hedge school and its books, 1695–1831* (Dublin, 2004).

—— 'The transformation of Irish education: The ministerial legacy, 1919–1999', in Walsh, *Essays* (2016), pp. 267–96.

McNamee, Brian, 'The "Second Reformation" in Ireland', *Irish Theological Quarterly*, 33:1 (1966), 39–64.

Madaus, George F., Ryan, Joseph P., Kellaghan, Thomas & Airasian, Peter W., 'Payment by results: An analysis of a nineteenth century performance-contracting programme', *The Irish Journal of Education*, 21:2 (1987), 80–91.

Mangione, Thomas, 'The establishment of the model school system in Ireland', *New Hibernia Review*, 7:4 (2003), 103–22.

Mulligan, Kevin, *The buildings of Ireland: South Ulster, Armagh, Cavan and Monaghan* (London, 2013).

Murnane, James H., 'The national school system in County Monaghan', *Clogher Record*, 12:2 (1986), 209–32.

Murphy, Gerard, 'Irish in our schools, 1922–1945', *Studies: An Irish Quarterly Review*, 37:148 (1948), 421–28.

Nowlan-Roebuck, Catherine, 'The Presentation Order and national education in nineteenth-century Ireland' in Raftery & Fischer (eds), *Educating Ireland* (Dublin, 2014), pp. 124–45.

O'Connor, Anne V., 'Education in nineteenth-century Ireland' in Angela Bourke, Siobhán Kilfeather, Maria Luddy, Margaret MacCurtain, Gerardine Meaney, Máire Nic Dhonnchadha, Mary O'Dowd & Clair Wills (eds), *The Field Day anthology of Irish writing: Volume V: Irish women's writing and traditions* (Cork, 2002), pp. 647–66.

O'Brien, Gerard, 'Workhouse management in pre-famine Ireland', *Proceedings of the Royal Irish Academy: Archaeology, Culture, History, Literature*, 86C (1986), 113–34.

O'Ceallaigh, Tadhg, 'Disestablishment and church education', *Studia*

Hibernica, 10 (1970), 36–69.

ÓCeallaigh T.J. & Ní Dhonnabháin, Áine, 'Reawakening the Irish language through the Irish education system: Challenges and priorities', *International Electronic Journal of Elementary Education*, 8:2 (2015), 179–98.

O'Doherty, Teresa & O'Donoghue Tom, *Radical Reform in Irish Schools, 1900–1922: The 'new education' turn* (London, 2021).

O'Donoghue, Tom, 'Stanley's letter: the national school system and inspectors in Ireland 1831–1922 by Patrick F O'Donovan (book review)', *History of Education*, 48:1 (2019), 143–45.

O'Donovan, Patrick F. *Stanley's Letter: The national school system and inspectors in Ireland, 1831–1922* (Galway, 2017).

Ó Grada, Cormac, 'The population of Ireland 1700–1900: A survey', *Annales de Démographie Historique*, (1979), 281–99, available online at: https://www.persee.fr/doc/adh_0066-2062_1979_num_1979_1_1425

Ó hÓgartaigh, Margaret, 'The servants of the nation: Quiet revolutions in education', *Journal of the Armagh Diocesan Historical Society*, 24:2 (2013), 201–35.

O'Flaherty, Enda, *Deserted schoolhouses of Ireland* (Dublin, 2018).

Ó Mearáin, Lorcán, 'Estate agents in Farney: Trench & Mitchell', *Clogher Record*, 10:3 (1981), 405–13.

—— 'Schools in County Monaghan, 1824–1826', *Clogher Record*, 5:1 (1963), 63–95.

Ó Mórdha, Pilib, 'Peter Urson, hedge schoolmaster', *Clogher Record*, 8:3 (1975), 381.

—— 'Notes on education in Currin Parish', *Clogher Record*, 5:2 (1964), 251–62.

O'Toole, Barbara, '1831–2014: An opportunity to get it right this time? Some thoughts on the current debate on patronage and religious education in Irish primary schools', *Irish Educational Studies*, 34:1 (2015), 89–102.

O'Toole, Leah, McClelland, Diane, Forde, Deirdre, O'Keeffe, Suzanne, Purdy, Noel, Säfström, Carl Anders & Walsh, Thomas, 'Contested childhoods across borders and boundaries: Insights from curriculum provisions in Northern Ireland and the Irish Free State in the 1920s', *British Educational Research Journal*, 47:4 (2021), 1021–38.

Parkes, Susan M., *Kildare Place: The history of the Church of Ireland Training College 1811–1969* (Dublin, 2011).

Puirséil, Niamh, *Kindling the flame: 150 years of the Irish National Teachers' Organisation* (2017, Dublin).

Quane, Michael, 'Viscount Weymouth Grammar School, Carrickmacross',

BIBLIOGRAPHY

The Journal of the Royal Society of Antiquaries of Ireland, 86:1 (1956), 27–51.

Quinlan, Timothy, 'Shining light on silence: Corporal punishment as an abuse of power in the Irish school system', *Études Irlandaises*, 46:2 (2021), 85–102.

Redmond, Jennifer & Harford, Judith, '"One man one job": The marriage ban and the employment of women teachers in Irish primary schools', *Paedagogica Historica*, 46:5 (2010), 639–54.

Rogan, Marion, 'Proselytism, priestly opposition and persecution', *Clogher Record*, 23:1/2 (2018–19), 19–40.

Sheehy, Ruth, *The life and work of Richard King: Religion, nationalism and modernism* (Oxford, 2020).

Walsh, Brendan (ed.) *Essays in the History of Irish Education* (London, 2016).

—— 'Teachers' experience of school: First-hand accounts, 1943–1965' in Walsh, *Essays* (2016), pp. 203–33.

Walsh, Thomas, 'The revised programme of instruction, 1900–1922', *Irish Educational Studies*, 26:2 (2007), 127–43.

—— 'The national system of education, 1831–2000' in Walsh, *Essays* (2016), pp. 7–43.

Whelan, Irene, *The Bible war in Ireland: The 'Second Reformation' and the polarization of Protestant-Catholic relations, 1800–1840* (Dublin, 2005).

Unpublished theses

Duggan, Michael, 'Twenty hearts beating as none': Primary education in Ireland, 1899–1922' (PhD, DCU, 2021).

O'Donovan, Bernadette, 'Primary school teachers' understanding of themselves as professionals' (EdD, DCU, 2013).

O'Reilly, Lorraine, 'The development and demise of a landed estate in County Monaghan' (PhD, TCD, 2014).

Rogan, Marion, 'The "Second Reformation" in Ireland, 1798–1861: Case study of Rev. Robert Winning and the Kingscourt District' (PhD, Maynooth University, 2019).

ONLINE SOURCES

Bath and Shirley Schools:
https://nationalinventoryich.chg.gov.ie/carrickmacross-lace-making/
Blackrock baths: 'Gathering Heritage':
https://audioboom.com/posts/6293409-callans-baths-blackrock-co-louth-ireland?playlist_direction=reversed&t=0

Census 1911, NAI: http://www.census.nationalarchives.ie/
Central Statistics Office:
https://www.cso.ie/en/releasesandpublications/ep/p-
1916/1916irl/society/education/
Chief Secretary's Office, *Chief Secretary's Office Registered Papers: Historical Commentary for 1818*:
https://csorp.nationalarchives.ie/context/commentaries.html
Church of Ireland, 'Disestablishment: Free to shape our future':
https://www.ireland.anglican.org/about/welcome-to-disestablishment-150/disestablishment-in-context
Cloughfin National School: https://www.cloughfinns.com/about-us/
Commission on Manual and Practical Instruction in primary schools under the Board of National Education in Ireland: Final Report of the Commissioners:
https://www.dippam.ac.uk/eppi/documents/19608/pages/533530
Corcreagh national school, Ireland Stats:
https://www.irelandstats.com/school/corcreagh-n-s-rollnumber-13811l/
Corvally school, Shanco, County Monaghan, National Inventory of Architectural Heritage: https://www.buildingsofireland.ie/buildings-search/building/41403004/corvally-school-shanco-co-monaghan
Dúchas, *The Schools' Collection*: https://www.duchas.ie/en/cbes
Education: Primary Public Education – National Schools from 1831:
https://www.encyclopedia.com/international/encyclopedias-almanacs-transcripts-and-maps/education-primary-public-education-national-schools-1831
Farrell, Stephen, 'Shirley, Evelyn John, The history of parliament':
https://www.historyofparliamentonline.org/volume/1820-1832/member/shirley-evelyn-1788-1856
Gathering heritage: Danny Hughes:
https://audioboom.com/posts/7341319-conor-hughes-danny-hughes-shop
De LaSalle College: https://www.delasallewaterford.com/college-history/H
Harford, Judith, 'Fifty years on since 'free education', it's time to reflect on who the system really serves', *Irish Times*, 9 April 2017:
https://www.irishtimes.com/news/education/fifty-years-on-since-free-education-it-s-time-to-reflect-on-who-the-system-really-serves-1.3036172
Irvin, Sara, 'Education': *Irish History Live*:
https://www.qub.ac.uk/sites/irishhistorylive/IrishHistoryResources/Sh

ortarticlesandencyclopaediaentries/Encyclopaedia/LengthyEntries/Educ
ation/

Government of Ireland, Irish Statute Book, School Attendance Act 1926:
https://www.irishstatutebook.ie/eli/1926/act/17/enacted/en/print

The History of Parliament, Member biographies: Shirley, Evelyn John
(1788–1856), of Ettington, Warws.; Coolderry and Lough Fea, co.
Monaghan and 11 North Audley Street, Mix:
https://www.historyofparliamentonline.org/volume/1820-
1832/member/shirley-evelyn-1788-1856

Houses of the Oireachtas, Dáil Éireann Debate, 17 November 1922:
https://www.oireachtas.ie/en/debates/debate/dail/1922-11-17/12/

The Irish Aesthete: //theirishaesthete.com/category/farm-house/

Irish Community Archive Network (iCAN), Richard King/Rísteard Ó
Cíonga: Stained Glass Artist/Illustrator:
https://www.ouririshheritage.org/content/archive/people/101_mayo_peo
ple/arts-craft-and-culture/richard-king-risteard-o-cionga-stained-glass-
artist-illustrator

Irish National Schools Trust, 'The Stanley Letter':
http://irishnationalschoolstrust.org/document_post_type/the-stanley-
letter/

Lohan, Rena, 'The archives of the Office of Public Works and their value
for local history', National Archives of Ireland (Dublin, 1994):
https://www.nationalarchives.ie/historical-records/research-guides-
sources/

Mitchell, Phyllis, 'The axing of Carysfort', Education Matters:
https://educationmatters.ie/the-axing-of-carysfort/

ÓCiardha, Éamonn, 'Morris, Henry', Dictionary of Irish Biography:
https://www.dib.ie/biography/morris-henry-a5989

Northern Sound Radio: https://www.northernsound.ie/podcasts/the-
wider-view/monaghan-remembers-ww2-bomb-drop-part-heritage-we
ek-127388

Office of Public Works (OPW) 'Architectural and engineering drawings',
OPW/NAI/5HC/8/1/24:
https://www.nationalarchives.ie/article/behind-the-scenes-heritage-
and-education-opw-national-school-plan/

O'Flaherty, Enda, 'The school house in Ireland: Architecture and meaning –
Part 2': https://endaoflaherty.com/2018/02/23/the-school-house-in-
ireland-architecture-and-meaning-part-2/

—— 'The school house in Ireland: Architecture and meaning – Part 3':
https://endaoflaherty.com/2018/03/01/the-school-house-in-ireland-

architecture-and-meaning-part-3/.

Pine Emilie, Mark Keane, Susan Leavy, *The Industrial Memories Project*, Chapter 4: https://industrialmemories.ucd.ie/ryan-report/report/1-4-14

Pigot & Co's Provincial Directory of Ireland, 1824, Ulster entries, p. 363: https://www.failteromhat.com/pigotu.htm.

Rathnageeragh national school, Co. Carlow: http://www.myshalldrumphea.com/rathnageeragh-ns.htm

Reynolds, Tony, Local History–Corporal punishment in National School: https://reynoldshistorycastleknockblog.wordpress.com/2017/08/18/local-history-corporal-punishment-in-national-school/

Shaun O'Byrne to Tessa Fleming on *Northern Sound Radio*, 21 August 2017: https://www.northernsound.ie/podcasts/the-wider-view/monaghan-remembers-ww2-bomb-drop-part-heritage-week-127388

'Seamus McHugh remembers': https://www.facebook.com/profile.php?id=100064695428381

Scoil Phádraig National School, Corduff: https://www.scoilphadraigcorduff.ie/

'The old schoolhouse, Tullyvrane, Lanesborough, Longford: https://www.buildingsofireland.ie/buildings-search/building/13401708/the-old-schoolhouse-tullyvrane-lanesborough-longford

The turf spade: http://www.pcl-eu.de/virt_ex/detail.php?entry=05

Wilson Philip, 'Warwickshire Yeomanry Gallipoli': https://www.warwickshire-yeomanry-museum.co.uk/gallipolli-history-jpw

Notes

CHAPTER 1

1   Patrick F. O'Donovan, *Stanley's Letter: The national school system and inspectors in Ireland, 1831–1922* (Galway, 2017), p. 10.
2   *Second Report of the Commissioners of Irish Education Inquiry* (House of Commons (hereafter HC), 1826), p. 4. The statistics in the report were for the numbers recorded in the autumn of 1824.
3   The Anglican Church of Ireland was the Established Church at that time, meaning that it was established as the official or state Church. The term 'Established Church' (often abbreviated as EC) was used in official reports up until the disestablishment of the Church of Ireland in 1871.
4   R. Twiss, *A Tour of Ireland in 1775 with a map and a view of the salmon leap at Ballyshannon* (London, 1776). For a discussion on selected contents of the book, see: Cal Hyland and James Kelly, 'Richard Twiss's "A tour of Ireland in 1775 (London, 1776)": The missing pages and some other notes', *Eighteenth-Century Ireland*, 1998, 13, 52–64.
5   Cited by Pádraig Faulkner, 'Education in the Parish of Dunleer', *Journal of the County Louth Archaeological and Historical Society*, 23:1 (1993), 97–114.
6   *Second Report of the Commissioners of Irish Education Inquiry* (1826), p. 37. See also: Lorcán Ó Mearáin, 'Schools in County Monaghan, 1824–1826', *Clogher Record*, 5:1 (1963), 63–95. Ó Mearáin is the former Rev. Monsignor Laurence Marron (Fr 'L'), former parish priest of Carrickmacross. 'Fr L' was a prolific scholar and published several articles on local history under his Irish name. He was a son of Master Patrick Marron of Coolfore national school.
7   In the thirty-year period up to 1821, the population of Ireland had risen from 4.7 million to 6.8 million. See: Cormac Ó Grada, 'The population of Ireland 1700–1900: A survey', *Annales de Démographie Historique* (1979), 281–99, available online at: https://www.persee.fr/doc/adh_0066-2062_1979_num_1979_1_1425 (accessed 13 October 2021).
8   Anne V. O'Connor, 'Education in nineteenth-century Ireland' in A. Bourke S. Kilfeather, M. Luddy, M MacCurtain, G. Meany, M. O'Dowd & C. Willis (eds), *The Field Day anthology of Irish writing: Volume V: Irish women's writing and traditions* (Cork, 2002), 647–66.
9   *Second Report of the Commissioners of Irish Education Inquiry* (1826), p. 18.
10 Cited in John I.D. Johnston, 'Hedge schools of Tyrone and Monaghan', *Clogher Record*, 7:1

(1969), 34–55.

[11] Antonia McManus, 'Irish hedge schools and social change', in D. Raftery and K. Fischer, *Educating Ireland: Schooling and Social Change, 1700–2000* (Dublin, 2014), pp. 1–21.

[12] Cited in P.J. Dowling, *The Hedge Schools of Ireland* (Dublin, 1935), p. 36.

[13] Dowling, *Hedge Schools* (1935), pp. 47–48.

[14] *Chief Secretary's Office registered papers: Historical commentary for 1818*, National Archives of Ireland (hereafter NAI), available online at: https://csorp.nationalarchives.ie/context/commentaries.html (accessed 21 September 2021).

[15] 'Donaghmoine' is the archaic spelling. The modern spelling is Donaghmoyne.

[16] John Logan, 'The dimensions of gender in nineteenth-century schooling', in M. Kelleher and J.H. Murphy (eds), *Gender perspectives in nineteenth-century Ireland: Public and private spheres, society for the study of nineteenth century Ireland 2* (Dublin, 1997), pp. 36–49.

[17] Ulster entries, *Pigot & Co's provincial directory of Ireland* (1824), p. 363. Available online at: https://www.failteromhat.com/pigotu.htm (accessed 27 September 2021).

[18] McManus, 'Irish hedge schools' (2014), pp. 1 and 4.

[19] Dowling, *Hedge Schools* (1935), p. 111. 's.' denotes shilling, 'd.' denotes pence.

[20] Ó Mearáin, 'Schools in County Monaghan' (1963), p. 63.

[21] Dowling, *Hedge Schools* (1935), p. 111.

[22] Cited in Dowling, *Hedge Schools* (1935), p. 47.

[23] Pilip Ó Mórdha, 'Peter Urson, hedge schoolmaster', *Clogher Record*, 8:3 (1975), 381. Ursin was also spelt Urson.

[24] *Second Report of the Commissioners of Irish Education Inquiry* (1826), p. 454.

[25] Pilib B. Ó Mórdha, 'Notes on education in Currin parish', *Clogher Record*, 1964, 5:2 (1964), 251–62.

[26] Ó Mórdha, 'Peter Urson' (1975), p. 381.

[27] Cited in Ó Mórdha, 'Notes on education' (1964), p. 257.

[28] Ó Mórdha, 'Peter Urson' (1975), p. 381.

[29] *Ibid.*

[30] A. McManus, *The Irish Hedge School and its Books, 1695–1831* (Dublin, 2004), p. 118.

[31] Cited in Johnston, 'Hedge schools of Tyrone and Monaghan' (1969), p. 39.

[32] *Ibid.*

[33] *Ibid.* p. 40.

[34] Dúchas, *The Schools' Collection*, available online at: https://www.duchas.ie/en/cbes/4758590 (accessed 20 April 2023).

[35] *Ibid.*, p. 268.

[36] Dowling, *Hedge Schools* (1935), p. 53.

[37] McManus, 'Irish hedge schools' (2014), p. 3.

[38] Cited in McManus, *The Irish Hedge School and its Books* (2004), p. 118.

[39] Johnston, 'Hedge schools of Tyrone and Monaghan' (1969), p. 43.

[40] *Ibid.*

[41] Cited in Dowling, *Hedge Schools* (1935), p. 80.

[42] McManus, 'Irish hedge schools' (2014), p. 5.

[43] *Ibid.*

[44] Cited in Dowling, *Hedge Schools* (1935), p. 124.

[45] *Ibid*, p. 20.

[46] Johnston, 'Hedge schools of Tyrone and Monaghan' (1969), p. 45.

[47] Dowling, *Hedge Schools* (1935), p. 47.

[48] *First Report of the Commissioners of Irish Education Inquiry* (HC, 1825), p. 92.

[49] *Ibid.*

[50] Cited in Johnston, 'Hedge schools of Tyrone and Monaghan' (1969), p. 38.

51 *Ibid.*, citing J. McEvoy 'Statistical Survey of Co. Tyrone (Dublin, 1802).

52 *Second Report of the Commissioners of Irish Education Inquiry* (1826), p. 18.

53 NAI, *Historical Commentaries for 1818*, available online at:
    https://csorp.nationalarchives.ie/context/commentaries.html (accessed 20 January 2022).

54 Mary Daly, 'The development of the national school system, 1831–1840', in A. Cosgrave
    and D. McCartney (eds), *Studies in Irish history: Presented to R Dudley Edwards* (Dublin, 1979),
    pp. 151–63.

55 *Second Report of the Commissioners of Irish Education Inquiry* (1826), p. 17.

56 Catherine Nowlan-Roebuck, 'The Presentation Order and national education in nine-
    teenth-century Ireland', in D. Raftery and K. Fischer (eds), *Educating Ireland* (Dublin, 2014),
    pp. 124–145.

57 *Second Report of the Commissioners of Irish Education Inquiry* (1826), p. 97.

58 *First Report of the Commissioners of Irish Education Inquiry* (1825), p. 90.

59 Daly, 'Development of the national school system' (1979), p. 155.

60 Cited in Dowling, *Hedge Schools* (1935), p. 39.

61 *Ibid.*

62 Society for Promoting the Education of the Poor of Ireland, *Eighth Report of the Society for
    Promoting the Education of the Poor of Ireland* (Dublin, 1820), p. 7. For a detailed history of the
    Society, see: S.M. Parkes, *Kildare Place: The history of the Church of Ireland Training College
    1811–1969* (Dublin, 2011).

63 *First Report of the Society for Promoting the Education of the Poor of Ireland* (Dublin, 1813), p. 4.
    The Society's constitution was based on recommendations made by the Commissioners of
    the Board of Education in Ireland, which reported on the state of education in Ireland in
    the period 1806 to 1812. See: NAI, *Historical Commentaries for 1818*.

64 *Ibid.* Original emphasis.

65 *Second Report of the Commissioners of Irish Education Inquiry* (1826), p. 8.

66 *Ninth Report of the Society for Promoting the Education of the Poor of Ireland* (1820), p. 7.

67 *Second Report of the Commissioners of Irish Education Inquiry* (1826), p. 145.

68 O'Donovan, *Stanley's Letter* (1917), p. 12.

69 *Ibid.*

70 *First Report of the Commissioners of Irish Education Inquiry* (1825), p. 90.

71 *Ibid.*

72 After 2015, along with the Church of Ireland College of Education, St Patrick's Training
    College and the Mater Dei Institute were also incorporated into the Institute of Education
    at Dublin City University.

73 *Reports from the Commissioners of the Board of Education in Ireland, 1809–1812* (HC, 1813), p. 15.

74 Cited in G. FitzGerald, *Irish Primary Education in the Early Nineteenth Century: An analysis of
    the first and second reports of the Commissioners of Irish Education Inquiry, 1825–6* (Dublin, 2013),
    p. 2.

75 *Ibid.*; Dowling, *Hedge Schools* (1935), p. 35.

76 Helena Kelleher Kahn, '"Objects of raging detestation" the charter schools', *History Ireland*,
    19:2 (2011), available online at: https://www.historyireland.com/objects-of-raging-detesta-
    tion-the-charter-schools/ (accessed 18 December 2022); for a detailed report on the charter
    schools and their failings, see *First Report of the Commissioners of Irish Education Inquiry* (1825),
    pp. 5–30.

77 *Ibid.*

78 FitzGerald, *Irish Primary Education* (2013), p. 2.

79 *First Report of the Commissioners of Irish Education Inquiry* (1825), p. 91.

80 *Ibid.*

81 *Ibid.*, p. 89.

CHAPTER 2

[1] Johnston, 'Hedge schools of Tyrone and Monaghan' (1969), p. 36.

[2] *Second Report of the Commissioners of Irish Education Inquiry* (1826), p. 48. Free schools were schools in which no tuition fee was paid.

[3] Ó Mearáin, 'Schools in County Monaghan (1963), p. 64.

[4] *Second Report of the Commissioners of Irish Education Inquiry* (1826), p. 48. The civil parish of Magheross is also more commonly referred to as the parish of Carrickmacross.

[5] Corcreeghagh is more commonly spelt 'Corcreagh'.

[6] Ó Mearáin, 'Schools in County Monaghan' (1963), p. 63.

[7] These numbers were based on the returns to the Commissioners from the Roman Catholic clergy in Magheross parish.

[8] For a discussion on the history of the Presbyterian settlers of County Monaghan, see: Lindsay T. Brown, 'The Presbyterians of County Monaghan, Part 1: The unfolding story', *Clogher Record*, 13:3 (1990), 7–54.

[9] Ó Mearáin, 'Schools in County Monaghan' (1963), p. 64. The Authorized Version of the Bible was the English version of the Christian Bible and was used in Anglican worship. Its use was authorised by an Act of Parliament. The Douai Version was an English version of the Catholic Bible, translated at the Catholic Seminary associated with the University of Douai in France.

[10] *Twelfth Report from the Commissioners of the Board of Education in Ireland, 1809–1812* (HC, 1913), p. 183.

[11] Public Records Office of Northern Ireland (hereafter PRONI), *Introduction: Shirley Papers* (Belfast, 2007), p. 4.

[12] Michael Quane, 'Viscount Weymouth Grammar School, Carrickmacross', *The Journal of the Royal Society of Antiquaries of Ireland*, 86: 1 (1956), 27–51.

[13] The number given by the Protestant clergy was fifty children.

[14] '*l*' denotes the symbol for the English pound (£) and is derived from the Latin *libra*, the historic Roman weight measure.

[15] *Second Report of the Commissioners of Irish Education Inquiry* (1826), p. 460.

[16] Ordnance Survey Ireland (hereafter OSI), available online at: https://osi.maps.arcgis.com/apps/dashboards/d5bdc7daef3e4537b67caa31dfcc42d5 (accessed 6 January 2022).

[17] The Dúchas Folklore Collection includes an essay by Laurence McMahon, a pupil at Coolfore national school in the 1940s, who wrote that the river drains Carragartha Bog; however, the local topography and Google Maps indicates that the river emerges from nearby hills at the extreme north-western part of Coolfore townland that borders Drumgowna townland. See: Dúchas, available online at: https://www.duchas.ie/en/cbes/4758590/4757303 (accessed 7 November 2022).

[18] Dúchas, *The Schools' Collection*, available online at: https://www.duchas.ie/en/cbes/4758590 (accessed 20 April 2023).

[19] *Ibid.*, pp. 270–72. Laurence collected the story from Mrs McMahon of Coolfore, presumably his mother.

[20] 'Evelyn J. Shirley obituary, *Leamington Spa Courier*, 10 January 1857, p. 3.

[21] I. Whelan, *The Bible war in Ireland: The 'Second Reformation' and the polarization of Protestant-Catholic relations, 1800–1840* (Dublin, 2005).

[22] Brian McNamee, 'The "Second Reformation" in Ireland', *Irish Theological Quarterly*, 33:1 (1966), 39–64.

[23] Marion Rogan, 'Proselytism, priestly opposition and persecution', *Clogher Record*, 2018–19, 23: 1/2 (2018–9), 19–40. For a more detailed analysis of this topic, see also M. Rogan, The 'Second Reformation', in 'Ireland, 1798–1861: Case study of Rev. Robert Winning and the

Kingscourt District' (PhD, Maynooth University, 2019).

24 Rogan, 'Proselytism' (2018–19), p. 40.
25 Garret FitzGerald, 'Estimates for baronies of minimum level of Irish-speaking amongst successive decennial cohorts: 1771–1781 to 1861–1871', *Proceedings of the Royal Irish Academy: Archaeology, Culture, History, Literature*, 84C (1984), pp. 117–55.
26 Rogan, 'Second Reformation' (2019), pp. 90 and 97.
27 *Ibid.* p. 88; *Practical observations upon the views and tendency of the First Report of the Commissioners of Irish Education Inquiry*, Appendix II (London, 1826), pp. 94–96.
28 *Ibid.* Original emphasis.
29 *Ibid.*
30 *Ibid.*, pp. 94–100.
31 *Ibid.*, p. 33. See also: *The History of Parliament, Member biographies: Shirley, Evelyn John (1788–1856), of Ettington, Warws.; Coolderry and Lough Fea, Co. Monaghan and 11 North Audley Street, Mix.*, available online at: https://www.historyofparliamentonline.org/volume/1820-1832/member/shirley-evelyn-1788-1856 (accessed 7 April 2022).
32 *Second Report of the Commissioners of Irish Education Inquiry* (1826), 3, ccxiv, pp. 458–63.
33 Rogan, 'Proselytism' (2018–19), p. 35.
34 *Ibid.*, p. 23.
35 *Second Report of the Commissioners of Irish Education Inquiry* (1826), Appendix to the Second Report, Appendix No. 22, pp. 458–61. The spellings of some townland names in Table 2.1 are from the Commissioners' 1826 report and do not correspond with the modern spellings.
36 *Newry Examiner and Louth Advertiser*, 18 November 1837, p. 2. I am grateful to Dr Marion Rogan for alerting me to this source.
37 *Ibid.*
38 *Ibid.*
39 *Shirley papers*, PRONI/ D3531/C/3/3–4.
40 L. O'Reilly, 'The development and demise of a landed estate in County Monaghan' (PhD, TCD, 2014), p. 97.
41 Rogan, 'Proselytism' (2018–19), p. 24; O'Reilly, 'Development and demise' (2014), p. 97.
42 Rogan, 'Second Reformation' (2019), p. 195.
43 Lorcan Ó Mearáin, 'Estate agents in Farney: Trench & Mitchell', *Clogher Record*, 10:3 (1981), 405–13.
44 Cited by Ó Mearáin, 'Estate agents' (1981), p. 407.
45 *Ibid.*, p. 409.
46 James H. Murnane 'The national school system in County Monaghan', *Clogher Record*, 12:2 (1986), 209–32.
47 Ó Mearáin, 'Estate agents' (1981), p. 407.
48 P. Livingstone, *The Monaghan Story: A documented history of the County Monaghan from the earliest times to 1976* (Enniskillen, 1980), p. 203.
49 *Ibid.*, p. 271. The OS map for the years 1834 does not show a schoolhouse in the townland of Greaghlane. However, the school at Corduff Mountain also does not appear on this map; hence, it is likely that the map was recorded earlier, most probably during the 1830s.
50 Rogan, 'Second Reformation' (2019), p. 203.
51 For a detailed study of this conflict, see: Whelan, *Bible war in Ireland* (2005).
52 Livingstone, *The Monaghan Story* (1980), p. 202.
53 Rogan, 'Proselytism' (2018–19), p. 33.
54 Rogan, 'Second Reformation' (2019), p. 251.
55 *Ibid.*, p. 39; Patrick J. Duffy, 'Assisted emigration from the Shirley Estate 1843–54', *Clogher Record*, 14:2 (1992), 7–62.
56 FitzGerald, 'Estimates for baronies', p 135. See also: *The Irish Language Part 1: Decline*, available

online at: https://www.theirishstory.com/2010/09/14/the-irish-language-part-i-decline/ #.Yk3YnjXTVPZ (accessed 6 April 2022).

[57] I am grateful to Dr Marion Rogan for alerting me to this school and to Shirley's role in preventing it from being connected with the Board of National Education.

[58] Commissioners of National Education in Ireland (hereafter CNEI), *Queries to be answered by applicants for aid towards the fitting-up of schools, the paying of teachers, and the obtaining of school requisites, signed 10 Jan. 1834*, 'Clontrain school', NAI/ED1/69/42/1.

[59] *Ibid.*

[60] *Second Report of the Commissioners of Irish Education Inquiry* (1826), pp. 460–61. See also: Murnane 'National school system in County Monaghan' (1986), 209–32.

[61] CNEI, 'Clontrain school', NAI/ED1/69/42/1.

[62] *Ibid.*

[63] Murnane, 'National school system in County Monaghan' (1986), pp. 209–32.

CHAPTER 3

[1] *First Report of the Commissioners of Irish Education Inquiry* (1825), p. 90.

[2] *Ibid.*; FitzGerald, *Irish Primary Education* (2013), p. 2.

[3] Tom Walsh, 'The national system of education,1831–2000', in B. Walsh (ed.), *Essays in the History of Irish Education* (London, 2016), pp. 7–43.

[4] A brief biographical sketch of Lord Stanley is available online at: https://www.oxfordreference.com/display/10.1093/oi/authority.20110803095711766 (accessed 17 November 2021).

[5] The Stanley Letter, available online at: http://irishnationalschoolstrust.org/document_post_type/the-stanley-letter/ (accessed 17 November 2021).

[6] For example, Roman Catholics did not support the schools that the Kildare Place Society supported, because of the Society's insistence that children should read the Holy Scriptures without note or comment.

[7] Walsh, 'National system of education' (2016), p. 10.

[8] John Coolahan, 'The daring first decade of the Board of National Education, 1831–1841', *The Irish Journal of Education*, xvii (1983), 35–54.

[9] *Rules and Regulations of the Commissioners of National Education, and Directions for making Application for Aid towards the Building of School-houses, or for Support of Schools*, Appendix A, *Nineteenth Report of the Commissioners of National Education in Ireland* (HC, 1853), p. 3.

[10] Coolahan, 'Daring first decade' (1983), p. 41. See also: Hansard, 'Leases for schools (Ireland) Bill, Second reading', Volume 264: debated on Tuesday 9 August 1881, available online at: https://hansard.parliament.uk/lords/1881-08-09/debates/dfb31c90-22af-4585-b9c6-6c96e19f70e8/LeasesForSchools(Ireland) Bill (accessed 17 November 2021).

[11] R. Lohan, 'The archives of the Office of Public Works and their value for local history' (NAI, 1994), available online at: https://www.nationalarchives.ie/historical-records/research-guides-sources/ (accessed 18 April 2022).

[12] ' OPW Architectural and engineering drawings', NAI/OPW/5HC/8/1/24, available online at: https://www.nationalarchives.ie/article/behind-the-scenes-heritage-and-education-opw-national-school-plan/ (accessed 18 April 2022).

[13] FitzGerald, *Irish Primary Education* (2013), p. 35.

[14] Daly, 'Development of the national school system' (1979), pp. 151–63.

[15] *Second Report of the Commissioners of National Education in Ireland for the year ending 31st March 1835*, [300], xxxv, (HC, 1835), pp. 15–16.

[16] *Fifteenth Report of the Commissioners of National Education in Ireland for the year 1848*, (HC,

1849), p. 4.

17 Coolahan, 'Daring first decade' (1983), p. 38.

18 *Second Report of the Commissioners of National Education* (1835), p. 3.

19 Cited in Donal H. Akenson, *The Irish Education Experiment: The National System of Education in the Nineteenth Century* (London, 2012), p. 270.

20 Livingstone, *The Monaghan Story* (1980), pp. 270–80.

21 *Ibid.*

22 Cited in Murnane, 'National school system in County Monaghan' (1986), p. 210.

23 *Ibid.*

24 *Ibid.* See also: Sara Irvin, 'Education', *Irish History Live*, available online at: https://www.qub.ac.uk/sites/irishhistorylive/IrishHistoryResources/Shortarticlesandencyclopaediaentries/Encyclopaedia/LengthyEntries/Education/ (accessed 17 November 2021).

25 Coolahan, 'Daring first decade' (1983), p. 41.

26 Daly, 'Development of the national school system' (1979), pp. 155–56.

27 *Ibid.*, p. 156.

28 J. Coolahan, C. Hussey and F. Kilfeather, *The Forum on Patronage and Pluralism in the Primary Sector: Report of the Forum's Advisory Group* (Dublin, 2012), p. 11.

29 Walsh, 'National system of education' (2016), p 16.

30 *Second Report of the Commissioners of National Education* (1835), p. 3.

31 For a detailed discussion on state policy in teacher training, see: Judith Harford, 'The emergence of a national policy on teacher education in Ireland', *Journal of Educational Administration and History*, 41:1 (2009), 45–56.

32 Thomas Mangione, 'The establishment of the model school system in Ireland', *New Hibernia Review*, 7:4 (2003), 103–22.

33 Murnane, 'National school system in County Monaghan' (1986), p. 211.

34 *Ibid.* Today, the model schools at Baileborough and Monaghan are co-educational primary schools with a Protestant ethos, catering, mainly but not exclusively, for children from the Protestant community.

35 *Thirty-eighth Report of the Commissioners of National Education* (HC, 1872), p. 25.

36 Coolahan, 'Daring first decade' (1983), p. 38.

37 *Second Report of the Commissioners of National Education* (1835), p. 5.

38 *Fifteenth Report of the Commissioners of National Education* (1849), p. 8.

39 *Ibid.*, p 19. Original emphasis.

40 *Second Report of the Commissioner of National Education* (1835), pp. 5–6.

41 *Ibid.*, p. 5.

42 Coolahan, Hussey and Kilfeather, *Forum on Patronage* (2012), p. 10.

43 *Fifteenth Report of The Commissioners of National Education* (1849), p. 5.

44 *Commissioners of National Education in Ireland: Circular from Education Office to District Inspectors*, 9 January 1855 (Dublin, 1855), Cavan Library Archives, NE/10/00001.

45 Murnane, 'National school system in County Monaghan' (1986), p. 211.

46 Walsh, 'The national system of education' (2016), p. 17; Mangione, 'Model school system' (2003), p. 120.

47 *Ibid.*

48 Coolahan, Hussey and Kilfeather, *The Forum on Patronage* (2012), p. 10.

49 Margaret Ó hÓgartaigh, '"The servants of the Nation": Quiet revolutions in education', *Journal of the Armagh Diocesan Historical Society*, 24:2 (2013), 201–35.

50 *Ibid.*, p. 234.

51 Murnane, 'National school system in County Monaghan' (1986), p. 211.

52 Coolahan, 'Daring first decade' (1983), p. 47.

[53] *Second Report of the Commissioners of National Education* (1835), p. 10.

[54] *Fifteenth Report of the Commissioners of National Education* (1849), p. 20.

[55] O'Connor, 'Education in nineteenth-century Ireland' (2002), pp. 647–66.

[56] Daly, 'Development of the national school system' (1979), pp. 155–56.

[57] CNEI, *Memoranda to be observed in the written examination of teachers, pupil-teachers and monitors,* Circular from Education Office to District Inspectors (Dublin, 1877), Cavan Library Archives, NE/10/00013.

[58] The Kildare Place Society had developed a school inspectorate system involving teacher observation prior to 1831. The inspectorate system under the national system for school inspection was almost identical to that used by the Society. See: Martin Brown, Gerry McNamara, Joe O Hara, 'Teacher accountability in education: The Irish experiment', in: Walsh (ed.) *Essays* (2016), pp. 359–81.

[59] *Third Report of the Commissioners of National Education in Ireland for the Year 1836,* Appendix, Section II (E), containing 'Inspection of Schools' 1836, in: *Report of the Commissioners of National Education in Ireland from the Year 1834 to 1845, Inclusive, Vol. 1* (HC, 1851), p. 109.

[60] *Fifteenth Report of the Commissioners of National Education,* Appendix IV (1849), p. 4.

[61] *Ibid.*, p. 8.

[62] Cited in Coolahan, 'Daring first decade' (1983), p. 48.

[63] *Fifteenth Report of the Commissioners of National Education* (1849), p. 6.

[64] *Fourteenth Report of the Commissioners of National Education* (1848), p. 115.

[65] *Commissioners of National Education in Ireland: Circular from Education Office to District Inspectors* (undated) Cavan Library Archives, NE/10/000109. At the time, the Commissioners created twelve District Inspectors of the First Class, six Protestant and six Roman Catholic.

[66] *Thirty-seventh Report of the Commissioners of National Education* (HC, 1871), p. 142.

[67] *Ibid.*, p. 184.

[68] *Ibid.*, p. 162.

[69] CNEI, Education Office to Samuel Adair, Esq., Carrickmacross Female Industrial School, 10 July 1872 (Dublin, 1872), Cavan Library Archives, NE/10/00004.

[70] CNEI, Education Office to William Bole, Esq., Carrickmacross Female Industrial School, 10 July 1872 (Dublin, 1872), Cavan Library Archives, NE/10/00004.

[71] *Ibid.*

[72] Murnane, 'National school system in County Monaghan' (1986), p. 212; R. Cullen Owens, *A Social History of Women in Ireland 1870–1970* (Dublin, 2005), p. 22.

[73] *Second Report of the Commissioners of National Education,* Appendix I (1835), p. 11.

[74] Logan, 'Dimensions of gender' (1977), pp. 36–49.

[75] Cullen Owens, *Social History of Women in Ireland* (2005), p. 26.

[76] *Ibid*, p. 23. See also a brief historical case study of Rathnageeragh National School, County Carlow, available online at: http://www.myshalldrumphea.com/rathnageeragh-ns.htm (accessed 25 November 2021).

[77] *Thirty-ninth Report of the Commissioners of National Education in Ireland for the Year 1872,* Appendix E IV (HC, 1873), pp. 274–75.

[78] *Second Report of the Commissioners of National Education* (1835), pp. 5–6.

[79] *Commissioners of National Education in Ireland: Reading Book for the use in female schools* (HC, 1838), available online at: https://babel.hathitrust.org/cgi/pt?id=hvd.32044102787124&view=1up&seq=7&skin=2021 (accessed 30 November 2021).

[80] *Ibid.*, pp. 329–30.

[81] Logan, 'Dimensions of gender' (1977), p. 45.

NOTES

CHAPTER 4

1 Walsh, 'National system of education' (2016), p. 10
2 Murnane, 'National school system in County Monaghan' (1986), p. 210.
3 Livingstone, *The Monaghan Story* (1980), p. 270.
4 Coolahan, 'Daring first decade' (1983), p. 51.
5 Cited in Murnane 'National school system in County Monaghan' (1986), p. 209.
6 *Ibid.*
7 Cited in A. Day and P. McWilliams, *Counties Cavan, Leitrim, Louth, Monaghan and Sligo (v. 40)* (*The Ordnance Survey memoirs of Ireland 1830–1840*) (Belfast, 1998), p. 147.
8 Johnston, 'Hedge schools of Tyrone and Monaghan' (1969), p. 51.
9 *Second Report of the Commissioners of National Education*, Appendix IV (1836), p. 66.
10 Murnane 'National school system in County Monaghan' (1986), p. 212.
11 CNEI, 'Report upon application for aid towards payment of teacher's salary and for supply of books &c.', 20 June 1845, Coolfore (Dublin 1845), NAI/ED 1/69 No 123.
12 Walsh, 'National system of education' (2016), p. 18.
13 Murnane, 'National school system in County Monaghan' (1986), p. 212.
14 Cited in Day and McWilliams, *Ordnance Survey Memoirs* (1998), p. 147.
15 Murnane, 'National school system in County Monaghan' (1986), p. 226.
16 *Ibid.*, p. 225; Livingstone, *The Monaghan Story* (1980), p. 270.
17 Day and McWilliams, *Ordnance Survey Memoirs* (1998), p. 157.
18 Murnane, 'National school system in County Monaghan' (1986), p. 226.
19 *Ibid.*
20 *Fifteenth Report of the Commissioners of National Education* (1849), p. 55.
21 Day and McWilliams, *Ordnance Survey Memoirs* (1998), p. 150.
22 Quane, 'Viscount Weymouth Grammar School' (1956), p. 45.
23 *Ibid.*
24 Murnane, 'National school system in County Monaghan' (1986), p. 226. See also *Nineteenth Report of the Commissioners of National Education in Ireland for the Year 1852* (HC, 1853), p. 599.
25 *Ibid.*, p. 140.
26 Patrick J. Duffy, 'Assisted emigration from the Shirley estate 1843–54', *Clogher Record*, 14: 2 (1992), 7–62. See also: See: Trevor McClaughlin, Stephanie James and Simon O'Reilley, 'Migration to Australia mid-nineteenth century; emigration from the Shirley estate at the time of the famine', *Clogher Record*, 20:2, (2010), 287–334.
27 Gerard O'Brien 'Workhouse management in pre-famine Ireland', *Proceedings of the Royal Irish Academy: Archaeology, Culture, History, Literature*, 86C (1986), 113–34.
28 *Ibid.*, p. 123.
29 *Fifteenth Report of the Commissioners of National Education* (1849), p. 8.
30 O'Donovan, *Stanley's letter* (2017), p. 48.
31 *Twentieth Report of the Commissioners of National Education*, p. 627.
32 *Ibid.*, p. 658.
33 *Nineteenth Report of the Commissioners of National Education* (1853), p. xxvi.
34 T. Kennedy, and W.K, Sullivan, *On the industrial training institutions of Belgium and on the possibility of organising an analogous system in connection with the national schools of Ireland* (Dublin, 1855), p. 53.
35 Murnane, 'National school system in County Monaghan' (1986), p. 210. Based on district model schools, the agricultural school was essentially a national school for training in agricultural methods.
36 *Ibid.*, p. 53.

235

[37] *Ibid.*, p. 54

[38] *Appendix to the nineteenth report of the Commissioners*, Report of Mr Eugene A. Conwell (1852), p. 14.

[39] Cited in Kennedy & Sullivan, *On the industrial training institutions* (1855), p. 54.

[40] *Nineteenth Report of the Commissioners of National Education* Appendix G (1853), pp. 6–15.

[41] *Ibid.*, p. 6. *Guipure* is a coarse large-patterned lace with a net background. *Appliqué* is decoration in needlework made by cutting pieces of one material and applying them to the surface of another.

[42] *Nineteenth Report of the Commissioners of National Education*, Vol. 2, Appendix G, 'Reports of district inspectors of industrial schools' (1853), pp. 6–15.

[43] *Ibid.*

[44] *Carrickmacross National Schools, Return exhibiting the amount earned by females attending the Central and seven District National Schools of Carrickmacross, in Ireland, on combining Literary Education with Industrial Instruction* (HC, 1854), p. 269.

[45] *Nineteenth Report of the Commissioners of National Education*, Appendix G (1853), p. 15.

[46] Murnane, 'The National school system in County Monaghan' (1986), p. 213.

[47] *Ibid.* A brief history of the Bath and Shirley lace schools is available online at: https://nationalinventoryich.chg.gov.ie/carrickmacross-lace-making/ (accessed 23 November 2021).

[48] *Thirty-ninth Report of the Commissioners of National Education in Ireland for the Year 1872*, Appendix E IV (HC, 1873), p. 275.

[49] *Fiftieth Report of the Commissioners of National Education in Ireland for the Year 1883*, Appendix C, Appendix F (HC, 1884), p. 202.

[50] Day and McWilliams, *Ordnance Survey Memoirs* (1998), p. 150.

[51] *Ibid.*

[52] O'Reilly, 'Development and demise' (2014), p. 97.

[53] *Ibid.* Table adopted from O'Reilly.

[54] Samuel Lewis, 'A topographical directory of Ireland: Carrickmacross, 1837', available online at: https://www.libraryireland.com/topog/C/Carrickmacross-Farney-Monaghan.php (accessed 23 November 2021). Corduffkelly was also written as 'Corduff Kelly' and 'Corduff (Kelly)'.

[55] 'Reports by George Sudden on the state of the schools on the Shirley estate, together with an earlier petition, of 1834, from sundry Protestant tenants to E.J. Shirley asking him to contribute towards the cost of building a parish school, and 3 printed copies of a proselytising school catechism, 1837', Shirley Papers, PRONI, D3531/C/3/6.

[56] Lisdoonan is in the parish of Donaghmoyne, but on the Shirley estate.

[57] O'Reilly, 'Development and demise' (2014), p. 96. The schools connected with the Board of National Education were Carrickmacross Boys, Carrickmacross Girls, Carrickmacross Workhouse School, and the Carrickmacross Central Female Industrial School.

[58] Today Terrygarvan is spelt Tiragarvan. Previously, it comprised two adjacent townlands, Terrygarvan and Mullaghboy; the Terrygarvan part adjoined the Shercock Road, whereas the Mullaghboy part adjoined the Aghalile Road, and now forms part of Beagh townland. I am grateful to M.F. Kerley for this information. In the report of 1848, Corduff National School was listed as 'Corduff Chapel'.

[59] *Fifteenth Report of the Commissioners of National Education*, Appendix XX (1849), pp. 55–56.

[60] 'Reports by George Sudden', 1847, *Shirley Papers*, D3531/C/3/6.

[61] In addition to Mr Crilly and Mrs Crilly, there were two other teachers at Lossets school, Mr Fegan and Mr Duffy.

[62] The 'Salt Water' is possibly a reference to Blackrock seaside village in Co. Louth.

[63] Stephen Farrell, 'Shirley, Evelyn John', *The History of Parliament*, available online at: https://www.historyofparliamentonline.org/volume/1820-1832/member/shirley-evelyn-

1788-1856 (accessed 22 September 2022).
64 *Northern Standard*, 16 October 1841.
65 The present national school at Corcreagh/Raferagh was erected in 1890.
66 Cited in O'Reilly, 'Development and demise' (2014), pp. 98–99.
67 *Twelfth Report of the Commissioner of National Education*, Appendix XVII (1846), p. 49.

CHAPTER 5

1 Coolahan, 'Daring first decade' (1983), p. 51.
2 *Ibid*. See also: Thomas E. Jordan, 'A great statistical operation: A century of Irish censuses, 1812–1911', *New Hibernia Review*, Autumn, 1:3 (1997), 94–114.
3 Murnane, 'National school system in County Monaghan' (1986), p. 209.
4 *Fifteenth Report of the Commissioners of National Education* (1849), p. 55.
5 CNEI, 'Report upon application for aid towards payment of teacher's salary and for supply of books &c.', 20 June 1845, Coolfore, NAI/ED 1/69 No 123.
6 *Ibid*.
7 OSI, available online at: https://osi ie/products/professional-mapping/historical-mapping/ (accessed 16 December 2021).
8 *Shirley Papers*, PRONI/D3531/S/58.
9 CNEI, 'Report upon application for aid', Coolfore, 1845, NAI/ED 1/69 No 123.
10 *Ibid*.
11 The *Twelfth Report of the Commissioners of National Education* recorded 112 pupils, eighty-six males and thirty-four females for September 1845; see *Twelfth Report of the Commissioner*, Appendix XVII (1846), p. 51.
12 Coolahan, 'Daring first decade' (1983), p. 4.
13 *Nineteenth Report of the Commissioners of National Education in Ireland for the Year 1852, with Appendices*, 'Return of the religious denominations of the children on the rolls for six months ending 31st March 1852 – County of Monaghan' (HC, 1853), p. 333 and pp. 139–40. This number included several male and female schools located in the same schoolhouse.
14 *Ibid*., p. 141.
15 *Ibid*., p. 333.
16 *Shirley Papers*, 'Reports by George Sudden', 1837, PRONI/D3531/C/3/6.
17 Murnane, 'National school system in County Monaghan' (1986), p. 210.
18 *Nineteenth Report of the Commissioners of National Education*, Appendix B (1853), pp. 279–81 and pp. 324–29.
19 *Ibid*., p. 280.
20 *Ibid*., p. 279.
21 *Ibid*., p. 281.
22 *Ibid*., p. 327. An endowed school is one that was endowed with funds, such as money or property by its founders, and was established for charitable purposes.
23 *Ibid*.
24 *Ibid*.
25 *Ibid*.
26 *Ibid*., p. 329.
27 *Twelfth Report of the Commissioner of National Education*, Appendix XIX (1846), p. 116.
28 *Ibid*.
29 See Murnane 'National school system in County Monaghan' (1986), p. 228.
30 CNEI, Coolfore national school, Roll 4537, NAI/ED/2/36, folio 179.
31 In addition to Coolfore national school, the Report of the Commissioners of National Edu-

cation for the year 1852 listed two other schools in the north of the county that were struck off; these were the schools at Tydavnet and at Dartry-house, a girls' school.

[32] Murnane, 'National school system in County Monaghan' (1986), p. 210.

[33] *Nineteenth Report of the Commissioners of National Education*, Appendix (1853), p. 140. In Co. Monaghan at that time, the majority of the children (10,392) were Roman Catholic. As obtaining in earlier years, Presbyterians (1,463) outnumbered Protestants (1,206).

[34] *Second Report of the Commissioners of Irish Education Inquiry* (1826), p. 4.

CHAPTER 6

[1] Coolahan, Hussey and Kilfeather, *Forum on Patronage and Pluralism* (2012), p. 1.

[2] Thomas McGrath, 'Education: Primary public education – National schools from 1831', available online at: https://www.encyclopedia.com/international/encyclopedias-almanacs-transcripts-and-maps/education-primary-public-education-national-schools-1831 (accessed 19 January 2022).

[3] *Thirty-seventh Report of the Commissioners of National Education* (1871), p. 15.

[4] Tadhg ÓCeallaigh, 'Disestablishment and church education', *Studia Hibernica*, 10 (1970), 36–69.

[5] *Ibid.*, p. 41. The majority (54,200) of the children on the rolls of the Society were in Ulster.

[6] *Thirty-fourth Report of the Commissioners of National Education* (1868), p. 16.

[7] *Royal Commission of Inquiry into Primary Education (Ireland), Vol. 1 containing the Report of the Commissioners with an Appendix* (hereafter *Powis Commission*) (HC, 1870), p. 13.

[8] Walsh, 'The national system of education, 1831–2000' (2016), p. 11.

[9] *Ibid.*

[10] *Powis Commission* (1870), p. 223. These numbers were based on returns collected in June 1868. The Commissioners of National Education listed 151 'convent and monastic schools' in 1870.

[11] While some of the private schools were categorised as 'hedge schools', the Powis Commission could not estimate the precise number of such schools. The monastery schools were schools run by religious brotherhoods, most notably the Congregation of the Christian Brothers.

[12] *Powis Commission* (1870), p. 258. The highest average attendance was in Ulster, with thirty-four being the average in that province.

[13] *Thirty-seventh Report of the Commissioner of National Educations* (1871), p. 5. Ulster had the highest number of schools (2,523), while Connaught had a little over one thousand schools (1,089).

[14] Church of Ireland, 'Disestablishment: Free to shape our future', available online at: https://www.ireland.anglican.org/about/welcome-to-disestablishment-150/disestablishment-in-context (accessed 29 December 2021).

[15] Ó Ceallaigh, 'Disestablishment and church education' (1970), p. 46.

[16] *Ibid.*, p. 45.

[17] *Ibid.*, p. 68. The Society continues in this role to the present day.

[18] *Powis Commission* (1870), p. 229.

[19] *Thirty-seventh Report of the Commissioners of National Education* (1871), p. 260.

[20] *Ibid.*, p. 185.

[21] *Ibid.*

[22] *Powis Commission* (1870), p. 253.

[23] *Appendix to the Sixty-seventh Report of the Commissioners for National Education for the Year 1900*, Report of Mr A Purser, Chief Secretary (1901), p. 18. Mr Purser was writing in 1900.

[24] *Thirty-seventh Report of the Commissioners of National Education*, Appendix D, Report of Mr

Macaulay (1871), p. 222.
[25] *Ibid.*
[26] *Ibid.* Appendix D, Report of A.J. Simpson, p. 276.
[27] *Ibid.*
[28] *Ibid.*, Appendix C, Report of J.G. Fleming, p. 193.
[29] *Ibid.*, Appendix D, Report of Mr MacSheehy, pp. 321–22.
[30] *Ibid.*, Report of Mr Bradford, p. 283.
[31] *Ibid.*
[32] *Ibid.*, Report of Mr Fitzgerald, p. 343
[33] *Ibid.*, Report of Mr Roantree, p. 274.
[34] *Powis Commission* (1870), p. 293.
[35] *Ibid.*, p. 388.
[36] Bernadette O'Donovan, 'Primary School Teachers' Understanding of Themselves as Professionals' (PhD, Dublin City University, 2013), p. 23.
[37] *Powis Commission* (1870), p. 293.
[38] George F. Madaus, Joseph P. Ryan, Thomas Kellaghan and Peter W. Airasian, 'Payment by results: An analysis of a nineteenth century performance-contracting programme', *The Irish Journal of Education*, 21:2 (1987), 80–91.
[39] The country was divided into sixty districts at that time.
[40] *Thirty-seventh Report of the Commissioners of National Education* (1871), p. 32.
[41] *Ibid.*, Appendix D, Report of Mr Eardley, p. 260.
[42] *Ibid.*, Report of Mr J.G. Fitzgerald, p. 343. Original emphasis.
[43] *Ibid.*, Report of Mr Wood, p. 251.
[44] *Ibid.*, Report of Mr Bradford, p. 283.
[45] *Ibid.*, Report of Mr Nesbit, p. 258.
[46] *Ibid.*, Report of Mr Barrett, p. 267.
[47] *Ibid.*, Report of Mr Baldwin, p. 387. Justus von Leibig was a German chemist who developed theories about nutrients and manufacturing in agriculture.
[48] *Ibid.*
[49] This figure was based on a census of schools, 25 June 1868.
[50] *Thirty-seventh Report of the Commissioners of National Education*, Appendix D, Report of Mr Hamilton (1871), p. 237.

CHAPTER 7

[1] CNEI, 'Report upon application for aid towards payment of teacher's salary and for supply of books &c.', Coolfore school, 1/1/1872 (Roll no. 10700), Report of Mr John Thomas Simpson, NAI/ED1/71/70/2.
[2] *Ibid.* 'Application to the Commissioners of National Education for aid towards payment of teacher's salary and supply of requisites', Application of John Thomas Holland, 4/1/1872, NAI/ED/71/70/1.
[3] CNEI, Coolfore school, Cavan Co. Library, 1872, NE/10/00032. The 'old' Carrick to Ballybay road is known locally as the Aghalile Road.
[4] *Ibid.*, Application of John Thomas Holland, NAI/ED/71/70/1.
[5] *Ibid.* Ballaghnagearn (Ballynagearn) was a school in the neighbouring parish of Magheracloone, also on the Shirley Estate. E.P. Shirley was the patron of both Ballaghnagearn and Sreenty schools.
[6] CNEI, Coolfore school, Roll no. 10700, Cavan County Library, NE/10/00032, 1870–1875.
[7] The school at Laragh was connected with the Board of National Education and was built for the children of the millworkers who worked at the Laragh flax mill. For a brief summary

of key events at Laragh National School, see T. Larkin, *Seven generations: Carickatee, a history of gatherings* (Castleblaney, 2021), pp. 49–50. See also: Mary Frances Kerley, 'The rise and fall of a village industry: Cornacarrow and Laragh mills, 1775–1925', in J. Johnson (ed.), *Monaghan: Studies in Local History* (Maynooth, 2006), pp. 7–26.

[8] CNEI, Application of John Thomas Holland, NAI/ED/71/70/1.

[9] I am grateful to Mr M. Ward, Coolfore, for providing me with access to the plaque. The date 1871 on the plaque references the fact that the schoolhouse was newly constructed in that year.

[10] I am grateful to Kevin Mulligan, local architectural historian, for his helpful comments and advice on the design of the Coolfore schoolhouse, including his observation on the casement windows and his description of the gabled windbreak, which he notes is common to most vernacular houses, and is not deep enough to form a separate space.

[11] Here again, I acknowledge Kevin Mulligan's contribution to the textual descriptions of the schoolhouse design. For an analysis of vernacular dwellings in the region, see: Alan Gailey, 'Vernacular dwellings of Clogher Diocese', *Clogher Record*, 9:2 (1977), 187–231. See also: K. Mulligan, *The Buildings of Ireland: South Ulster, Armagh, Cavan and Monaghan* (London, 2013), p. 68.

[12] See the image of Edgeworthstown schoolhouse, available online at: https://stanleysletter.com/ (accessed 24 January 2023). See also 'The old schoolhouse, Tullyvrane, Lanesborough, Longford', available online at: https://www.buildingsofireland.ie/buildings-search/building/13401708/tullyvrane-lanesborough-longford (accessed 28 February 2023).

[13] See, for example, 'The Irish Aesthete', available online at: https://theirishaesthete.com/category/farm-house/ (accessed 7 March 2022).

[14] See, for example, Killymarly national school in north Co. Monaghan, available online at: https://endaoflaherty.com/2016/06/29/killymarly-national-school-killymarly-townland-co-monaghan/ (accessed 26 January 2023).

[15] E. O'Flaherty, *The deserted schoolhouses of Ireland* (Dublin, 2018).

[16] *Thirty-ninth Report of the Commissioners of National Education* (1873), pp. 21 and 26.

[17] Principal teachers were classified according to three classes, First, Second, and Third. Each class was further divided into a first and second 'division' and assistants were also classified under these two divisions.

[18] CNEI, 'Salary case', Minute Form B, NAI/ED 9/1627.

[19] CNEI, Coolfore National School, roll 10700, Cavan County Library, NE/10/00032, 1870–1875.

[20] CNEI, 'Teachers employed by the Commissioners of National Education on 31 March 1905', available online at: https://www.nationalarchives.ie/article/list-of-teachers-employed-by-the-commissioners-of-national-education-on-31-march-1905/ (accessed 21 February 2022).

[21] Fr Laurence Marron, *Family Tree: The Marron-Callan Family* (undated), p. 3. I am grateful to Brian Flanagan for providing me with information on the genealogy of the Marron family.

[22] 'Carrick Teacher's success', *Dundalk Democrat, c.* 21 September 1896.

[23] CNEI, 'Teachers employed: J McTernan–May,' NAI/PCO/10/1/23. The same record shows that John Marron trained at Coolfore national school.

[24] Cloughfin NS, available online at: https://www.cloughfinns.com/about-us/ (accessed 22 February 2022).

[25] The National Census of 1901 includes Mr Marron in the returns for Co. Waterford, where he was listed as an 'elementary teacher' and a boarder at Newtown House, which was attached to the De La Salle Training College.

[26] Our Lady of Mercy Teacher Training College, Baggot Street, Dublin, later moved to Carysfort in Blackrock, in south Co. Dublin. It was an all-female training college.

27 Mrs Mee is also included in the list of teachers in service in 1905; see: CNEI, 'Teachers employed: Mayers-SMorris_Redux', NAI/PCO/10/1/24. The census of 1901 lists Mary Mee aged thirty-two of Greaghnaroog townland.

28 CNEI, Coolfore NS, NAI/ED/2/103, folio 48 and vol. 2, folio 15; File: ED 9/1627 and ED 9/27255.

29 *Ibid.*, Coolfore NS, NAI/ED/2/103, folio 48.

30 *Ibid.*, vol. 2, folio 15.

31 *Appendix to Thirty-ninth Report of the Commissioners of National Education* (1873), p. 500.

32 CNEI, Coolfore NS, Cavan County Library, NE/10/00039, 1874–1879.

33 National Schools (Ireland), *Return of the number of pupils examined for results in each school in Ireland under the National Board of Education for the past two years* (HC, 1879), p. 41.

34 *Appendix to Seventieth Report of the Commissioners of National Education* (1904), pp. 188–89.

35 *Northern Standard*, 25 May 1889, p. 3.

36 CNEI, Corcreagh National School, District 24, Roll 9632, Folio 31.

37 CNEI, 'Communication to district inspector, 20 May 1875', Cavan County Library, NE/10/00012, 1875.

38 'County Monaghan sensation', *Evening Herald*, 23 June 1908, p. 1; 'National teacher shot', *Freeman's Journal*, 23 June 1908, p. 1.

39 *Evening Herald*, 23 June 1908, p. 1.

40 *Freeman's Journal*, 23 June 1908, p. 1.

41 *Ibid.*

42 For example: 'A County Monaghan sensation', *Nenagh Guardian*, 24 June 1908; 'A County Monaghan sensation', *Cork Examiner* 23 June 1908, p. 5; 'Serious shooting at Carrickmacross', *Sunday Independent*, 28 June 1908, p. 8; 'A County Monaghan sensation: Teacher shot', *Freeman's Journal*, 23 June 1908.

43 *Northern Standard*, 27 June 1908.

44 *Irish Independent*, 26 June 1908, p. 6.

45 'Carrickmacross shooting case', *Northern Standard*, 19 December 1908, p. 1.

46 Heather Conway, 'Where there's a will: Law and emotion in sibling inheritance disputes', in H. Conway & J. Stannard (eds), *The Emotional Dynamics of Law and Legal Discourse* (Oxford, 2016), pp. 35–57.

47 *The Anglo-Celt*, 29 March 1952, p. 9.

CHAPTER 8

1 CNEI, 'Commissioners to the several district and sub inspectors', 7 March 1855, Cavan Library Archives, NE/10/00010.

2 CNEI, 'Commissioners to J Simpson Esq.' Cavan Library Archives, NE/10/00010.

3 'Seamus McHugh remembers', available online at: https://www.facebook.com/profile.php?id=100064695428381 (accessed 28 September 2022).

4 *Forty-seventh Report of the Commissioners of National Education*, Report of district inspectors (1881), p. 58. Mr Skeffington was the father of Francis Sheehy-Skeffington, who married Hannah Sheehy. Both were radical nationalists in the early twentieth century.

5 *Ibid.*

6 *Fiftieth Report of the Commissioners of National Education*, Appendix F (HC, 1884), p. 197.

7 Cited in O'Reilly, 'Development and demise' (2014), pp. 98–99.

8 Livingstone, *The Monaghan Story* (1980), p. 203.

9 The incident was later described by Fr Smollen of Donaghmoyne in 1869.

10 Cited in O'Reilly, 'Development and demise' (2014), pp. 98–99.

11 CNEI, 'Inspector's marking paper, Corduff male national school', Cavan Library Archives, NE/10/00039; Murnane, 'National school system in County Monaghan' (1986), p. 226.

12 CNEI, Corduff national school, District 24, Rolls 2017, 2018, 13806 and 12807, NAI, Folios 17, 18, 53 and 54. The original roll numbers for the boys' and girls' schools were 2107 and 2108, respectively.

13 *Twelfth Report of the Commissioner of National Education*, Appendix XVII (1846), p. 51. The named trustees were the Most Rev. James Donnelly, Bishop of Clogher, Rev. Peter Birmingham and Rev. Patrick Callan of Carrickmacross.

14 *Ibid.*

15 CNEI, Corduff national school, NAI, Folio 17.

16 CNEI, National Education (Ireland) Building Grants, 1 Aug. 1894, 'Return of applications made between 1 June 1887 and the 31 December 1893', p. 5.

17 CNEI, Corduff national school, NAI, Folio 17.

18 In the Census of 1901, Michael Nulty, national schoolteacher, is recorded as being aged thirty-one, which suggests that he was aged about sixteen years when appointed.

19 Census 1911, NAI, available online at: http://www.census.nationalarchives.ie/pages/1911/Monaghan/Drumgurra/Corduff/ (accessed 1 April 2022).

20 CNEI, Corduff national school, NAI, Folio 17.

21 CNEI, Education Office to A Simpson, Esq., Corduff female, 24 March 1871, Cavan Library Archives, NE/10/00009.

22 *Belfast Newsletter*, 23 March 1906, p. 2; *Dundalk Democrat*, 1 February 1896, p. 4; *Freeman's Journal*, 20 November 1896, p. 5.

23 *Dundalk Democrat*, 24 September 1904, p. 9. See also: *Dundalk Democrat*, 1 February 1896, p. 4; *Belfast Newsletter*, 26 March 1906, p. 11; *Freeman's Journal*, 6 March 1906, p. 2.

24 *Ibid.*

25 CNEI, Corduff national school, NAI, Folio 17, 18, 53 and 54. The school roll number was 13806.

26 Clogher Diocesan Archives, 'Pastors' report to the Bishop of Clogher', 30 March 1951.

27 *Ibid.*, 'Report of Fr L. Marron', 18 May 1967.

28 Scoil Phádraig national school, Corduff, available online at: https://www.scoilphadraigcorduff.ie/ (accessed 4 August 2022).

29 Murnane, 'National school system in County Monaghan' (1986), p. 226

30 *Fifteenth Report of the Commissioners of national Education* (1849), pp. 55–56.

31 Murnane, 'National school system in County Monaghan' (1986), p. 226.

32 The school roll number was 8015, in District 24.

33 CNEI, Sreenty National School, District 24, Roll 8015, NAI, Folio 8.

34 P. McG, '100 years of education in our local schools', in *Corduff Calling* (Corduff, 1983), pp. 111–17.

35 *Twenty-seventh Report of the Commissioners of National Education, Vol. II*, Appendix E (1861), p. 71.

36 Cited in P. McG, '100 years of education' (1983), p. 116.

37 CNEI, Sreenty national school, NAI, Folio 8.

38 *Ibid.*

39 The Teachers' Act required that a male teacher, having reached sixty-five years, should retire and a female should retire at age sixty.

40 CNEI, Sreenty national school, NAI, Folio 8.

41 *Ibid.*, Sreenty NS, NAI, ED/9/27255.

42 *Ibid.*

43 By 1910, the Shirley estate was sold to the tenants in line with the land reforms of the late nineteenth and early twentieth centuries.

[44] Clogher diocesan archives, 'Pastors' report to the Bishop of Clogher', 30 March 1951.

[45] *Ibid.*, Report of Fr L. Marron, 18 May 1967.

[46] *Dundalk Democrat*, 25 October 1974.

[47] I am grateful to Mr Brian McDermott for this information.

[48] *Dundalk Democrat*, 8 October 1988.

[49] The official spelling is 'Corcreeghagh'.

[50] O'Reilly, 'Development and demise' (2014), pp. 98–99.

[51] P. McG, '100 years of education' (1983), p. 47.

[52] CNEI, Education Office to A Simpson, Esq., Corcreagh, 10 July 1872, Cavan Library Archives, NE/10/00009.

[53] CNEI, National Education (Ireland) Building Grants, 1 August 1894, p. 5.

[54] *Hansard,* 'Salaries of teachers in Corcreagh National School', *HC Debate 30 November 1906 vol. 166 c396*, available online at: https://api.parliament.uk/historic-hansard/commons/1906/nov/30/salaries-of-teachers-in-corcreagh (accessed 4 April 2022).

[55] 'Seamus McHugh remembers', available online at: https://www.facebook.com/profile.php?id=100064695428381 (accessed 28 September 2022).

[56] Clogher Diocesan Archives, 'Report of Fr L. Marron: Raferagh school', 18 May 1967.

[57] Corcreagh national school, Ireland Stats, available online at: https://www.irelandstats.com/school/corcreagh-n-s-rollnumber-13811l/ (accessed 5 August 2022).

[58] Brown, 'Presbyterians of County Monaghan, Part I' (1990), p. 20.

[59] Rogan, 'Proselytism' (2018–19), p. 20.

[60] Rogan, The "Second Reformation" (2019), p. 57. Many headstones at the little churchyard at Carrickmaclim bear the family names of several former local merchants and shop owners in Carrickmacross, such as Eakin, Reed, and Hanna.

[61] Brown, 'Presbyterians of County Monaghan' (1990), p. 37.

[62] Rogan, 'Proselytism' (2018–19), p. 29. See also Rogan, *The 'Second Reformation'* (2019), pp. 25–33.

[63] PRONI, *Shirley Papers,* 'Reports by George Sudden', D3531/C/3/6, 1837.

[64] The schoolhouse remains standing as a private dwellinghouse.

[65] National Inventory of Architectural Heritage, Corvally School, Shanco, Co. Monaghan, available online at: https://www.buildingsofireland.ie/buildings-search/building/41403004/corvally-school-shanco-co-monaghan (accessed 26 April 2022).

[66] I am grateful to John Braden for this information. Ardragh church was built between 1865 and 1870.

[67] *Thirty-ninth Report of the Commissioners of National Education,* Appendix G (1873), p. 500.

[68] CNEI, A.J. Crowley Esq. to Commissioners of National Education, 24 March 1874, Cavan Library Archives, NE/10/00009.

[69] CNEI, Registers of summaries of documents relating to administration of national schools: District 24, Vol. 2, roll numbers 147–2963, 1857–1888, NAI/ED/2/103.

[70] *Thirty-ninth Report of the Commissioners of National Education,* Appendix G (1873), p. 500.

[71] CNEI, Corvally national school, District 24, Roll 10706, NAI, Folio 49.

[72] *Ibid.*

[73] *Irish Independent*, 24 December 1951, p. 10.

[74] *Irish Independent*, 13 October 1956, p. 15; *Irish Independent*, Monday, 10 August 1957, p. 16. The acronym JAM refers to junior assistant mistress.

[75] CNEI, National school teacher salary book: County Monaghan, volume 2, roll numbers 10574–15329, 1957–1959 NAI/ED4/2794.

[76] I am grateful to Mavis Pepper for this information.

CHAPTER 9

[1] *Sixty-seventh Report of the Commissioners of National Education* (1901), pp. 12–13. Three-quarters of all the pupils enrolled were Roman Catholic and the remainder were distributed about equally between Protestants and Presbyterians, and the average daily attendance was 62 per cent.

[2] *Appendix to the Seventieth Report of the Commissioner of National Educations* (1905), p. 98. The Patrician Brothers (official title: the Brothers of St Patrick) commenced teaching at the Carrickmacross Boy's National School in 1902.

[3] *Ibid.*, p. 16.

[4] Harford, 'The emergence of a national policy' (2009), p. 55. In 1903, there were five Catholic teacher training colleges; these were St Patrick's College, Drumcondra; Our Lady of Mercy College, Carysfort, Dublin; De La Salle College, Waterford; St Mary's College, Belfast; and Mary Immaculate College, Limerick. In addition, there was one Protestant college, the Church of Ireland College, Kildare Place, Dublin, and one mixed-denominational college, the Central Training College at Marlborough Street.

[5] This can be explained, in part, in the fact that two of the Catholic training colleges were for females only.

[6] Harford, 'The emergence of a national policy' (2009), p. 55.

[7] F.H. Dale, *Report of Mr. F.H. Dale, His Majesty's Inspector of Schools, Board of Education, on Primary Education in Ireland* (Dublin, 1904), p. 53.

[8] *Ibid.*, p. 86.

[9] *Ibid.*, p. 87.

[10] After 1900, under Rule 173f, training in a recognised college was an essential condition for appointment as a principal in an Irish national school.

[11] Dale, *Report of Mr. F.H. Dale* (1904), p. 37.

[12] M. Duggan, '"Twenty hearts beating as none": Primary education in Ireland, 1899–1922' (PhD, Dublin City University, 2021), p. 157.

[13] *Ibid.*

[14] For a detailed discussion of the response to Rule 127(b), see Duggan, 'Twenty hearts' (2021), pp. 153–66.

[15] The new class of teacher was formerly employed as manual instructresses after 1900.

[16] *Seventy-second Report of the Commissioners of National Education* (Dublin, 1906), p. 20.

[17] Duggan, 'Twenty hearts' (2021), p. 32.

[18] *Powis Commission* (1870), p. 293.

[19] *Seventieth Report of the Commissioners of National Education* (1905), p. 33.

[20] *Sixty-second Report of the Commissioners of National Education* (1901), p. 8.

[21] Thomas Walsh, 'The revised programme of instruction, 1900–1922', *Irish Educational Studies*, 26:2 (2007), 127–43.

[22] *Ibid.*, p. 130.

[23] In Ireland, Fröbel's ideas would later influence the development of primary teacher training, when the Congregation of Dominican Sisters founded Fröbel College of Education at Sion Hill, Dublin, in 1943. Fröbel College of Education was re-established as the Department of Primary and Early Childhood Education at Maynooth University in 2013.

[24] Walsh, 'The revised programme' (2007), p. 128.

[25] Commission on Manual and Practical Instruction in Primary Schools under the Board of National Education in Ireland (1898a), *Final report 1898* (Dublin, 1898); CNEI, (1902b), available online at: https://www.dippam.ac.uk/eppi/documents/19608/pages/533530 (accessed 4 June 2022); *Sixty-seventh Report of the Commissioners of National Education, Appendix, Section II (F): Revised programme of Instruction in National Schools* (Dublin, 1901), pp. 66–96.

26 *Commission on Manual and Practical Instruction* (1898), pp. 2–4.
27 *Ibid.*, p. 68.
28 *Sixty-seventh Report of the Commissioners of National Education, Revised programme* (1901), p. 3.
29 *Ibid.*, p. 4.
30 *Ibid.*, p. 9
31 Walsh, 'The revised programme' (2007), pp. 132–34.
32 *Ibid.*, p. 134.
33 *Ibid.*, p. 136.
34 Dale, *Report of Mr. F.H. Dale* (1904), p. 91.
35 Walsh, 'The revised programme' (2007), p. 140.
36 *Seventieth Report of the Commissioners of National Education* (1905), p. 17.
37 *Ibid.*, pp. 107 and 114.
38 Duggan, 'Twenty hearts' (2021), p. 50; Walsh, 'The revised programme' (2007), p. 139.
39 Duggan, 'Twenty hearts' (2021), p. 51; Walsh, 'The revised programme' (2007), p. 132.
40 Duggan, 'Twenty hearts' (2021), p. 253.
41 *Seventieth Report of the Commissioners of National Education* (1905), pp. 33 and 101.
42 Walsh, 'The revised programme' (2007), p. 140.
43 *Ibid.*, 2 May 1903.
44 *Ibid.*
45 T.J. Ó Ceallaigh and Áine Ní Dhonnabháin, 'Reawakening the Irish language through the Irish education system: Challenges and priorities', *International Electronic Journal of Elementary Education*, 8:2 (2015), 179–98.
46 Duggan, 'Twenty hearts' (2021), p. 108.
47 CNEI, *National Education (Ireland), New Rules and Regulations 1900–1*, Rule 54 (Dublin, 1901), p. 9. The other optional subjects listed under Rule 54 were French, Latin, Mathematics and Instrumental Music.
48 Duggan, 'Twenty hearts' (2021), p. 125.
49 *Ibid.*, p. 126; Ó Ceallaigh and Ní Dhonnabháin, 'Reawakening the Irish language' (2015), p. 181.
50 *Appendix to the Seventy-fourth Report of the Commissioners of National Education*, Report of Mr D. Lehane, Inspector in Irish instruction (1908), p. 160.
51 *Ibid.*, Report of Mr D. Mangan, Examiner and Inspector of Irish instruction, p. 112.
52 *Ibid.*, p. 113.
53 *Ibid.*, p. 167.
54 Ó Ceallaigh and Ní Dhonnabháin, 'Reawakening the Irish language' (2015), p. 182.
55 Duggan, 'Twenty hearts' (2021), p. 127.

CHAPTER 10

1 For a discussion on teacher accountability, see: Brown, McNamara and O'Hara, 'Teacher accountability' (2016), pp. 359–81.
2 For a detailed study of the history of the INTO see Niamh Puirséil, *Kindling the flame: 150 years of the Irish National Teachers' Organisation* (Dublin, 2017).
3 *Dundalk Democrat*, 4 February 1905, p. 10. The Teachers' Pension Fund, into which teachers contributed, was established in 1879, but declared insolvent in 1897.
4 Sile Chuinneagain, 'The politics of equality: Catherine Mahon and the Irish national teachers' organisation, 1905–1916', *Women's History Review*, 6:4 (1997), 527–49.
5 *Sixty-seventh Report of the Commissioners of National Education* (1901), p. 22.
6 *Appendix to the Sixty-seventh Report of the Commissioners of National Education*, Report of Mr

A Purser (1901), p. 20.

7   *Dundalk Democrat*, 7 August 1907, p. 15.

8   *Ibid.*, 1 February 1896, p. 8.

9   *Seventy-second Report of the Commissioners of National Education* (1906), p. 5.

10 *Dundalk Democrat*, 27 June 1908, p. 13.

11 *Hansard 1803–2005*, Commons sitting, Leighlinbridge National School, HC Debate 10 August 1894 Vol. 28 cc565–6565; see also: County Carlow Ireland Genealogy Projects, available online at: http://igp-web.com/Carlow/Leighlinbridge_NS_1.htm (accessed 6 April 2022).

12 Duggan, 'Twenty hearts' (2021), p. 168.

13 *Dundalk Democrat*, 26 June 1908, p. 13.

14 *Vice-Regal Committee of Inquiry into Primary Education (Ireland) 1913, Final Report of the Committee* (Dublin, 1914).

15 Duggan, 'Twenty hearts' (2021), p. 191.

16 *Vice-Regal Committee of Inquiry into Primary Education, Volume I* (1918).

17 *Ibid.*, p. 21.

18 *Dundalk Democrat*, 19 June 1909, p. 14.

19 *Ibid.*

20 Cited in *Dundalk Democrat*, 26 June 1909, p. 14. The veracity or otherwise of Mr Farmer's claim could not be verified.

21 CNEI, *Circular issued by the Commissioners of National Education, Ireland, to teachers of national schools in Ireland regarding attendance at meetings, &c., together with correspondence*, &c. relative thereto, 4 August (Dublin, 1905).

22 *The Sligo Champion*, 29 April 1905.

23 CNEI, J.J. Hazlett to Resident Commissioners of National Education in Ireland, 1 June 1905.

24 CNEI, Rule 94 III.

25 CNEI, Circular (1905), p. 3.

26 Mary E. Daly, 'The Irish Free State and the Great Depression of the 1930s: The interaction of the global and the local', *Irish Economic and Social History*, 38 (2011), 19–36.

27 *Ibid.*, p. 34.

28 Irish National Teachers' Organisation (INTO), Report of the Central Executive Committee for the year 1932–33', *Annual Directory and Irish Educational Yearbook for 1933* (Dublin, 1933), pp. 7–33.

29 Jennifer Redmond and Judith Harford '"One man one job": The marriage ban and the employment of women teachers in Irish primary schools', *Paedagogica Historica*, 46:5 (2010), 639–54.

30 INTO, Report of the Central Executive Committee, pp. 17–18.

31 Cited in Redmond and Harford, 'One man one job' (2010), p. 643.

32 Eugene McCormick, *The INTO and the 1946 Teachers' Strike* (Dublin, 1996).

33 *Ibid.*, pp. 42 and 44.

34 *Ibid.*, p. 1.

35 Duggan, 'Twenty hearts' (2021) p. 195. In this context, Duggan uses 'fiefdom' metaphorically to denote the Church's self-appointed control and dominion over the national school system.

36 Barbara O'Toole, '1831–2014: An opportunity to get it right this time? Some thoughts on the current debate on patronage and religious education in Irish primary schools', *Irish Educational Studies*, 34:1 (2015), 89–102.

37 F. Lane (FL), interview with author, 11 December 2021.

38 Examples of these challenges included student activism at University College Dublin and women's campaigning for access to birth control. For a discussion on this period, see: Brian

Girvin, 'Contraception, moral panic and social change in Ireland, 1969–79', *Irish Political Studies*, 23:4 (2008), 555–76.

[39] *Appendix to the Fortieth Report of the Commissioners of National Education*, Appendix D, 1875, p. 473.

[40] Walsh, 'Revised programme' (2007), p. 128.

[41] Tony Fahey, 'State, family and compulsory schooling in Ireland', *The Economic and Social Review*, 13:4 (1992), 369–95. See also: Government of Ireland, Irish Statute Book, School Attendance Act 1926, available online at: https://www.irishstatutebook.ie/eli/1926/act/17/enacted/en/print (accessed 28 May 2022).

[42] *Ibid.*, p. 376.

[43] *Sixty-seventh Report of the Commissioners of National Education* (1901), p. 12.

[44] *Ibid.*, Appendix, Report of Mr E. Dowling, p. 4. Original emphasis.

[45] *Dundalk Democrat*, 2 May 1903.

[46] Dale, *Report of Mr. F.H. Dale* (1904), p. 53.

[47] *Sixty-seventh Report of the Commissioners of National Education*, Appendix (1901), p. 5.

[48] Dale, *Report of Mr. FH. Dale* (1904), p. 90.

[49] *Ibid.*, p. 57.

[50] *Vice-Regal Committee of Inquiry into Primary Education (Ireland)*, Minutes of evidence with Appendices, Evidence of T.P. O'Connor (Dublin, 1913), p. 113.

[51] Houses of the Oireachtas, Dáil Éireann Debate, 17 November 1922, available online at: https://www.oireachtas.ie/en/debates/debate/dail/1922-11-17/12/ (accessed 28 May 2022).

[52] Fahey, 'State, family and compulsory schooling' (1992), p. 376.

[53] Walsh, 'The National System of Education' (2016), p. 29.

[54] Dympna Devine, 'Children: Rights and status in education – a socio-historical analysis', *Irish Educational Studies*, 18:1 (Spring, 1999), 14–28.

[55] *Ibid.*, p. 16.

[56] *Ibid.*, p. 17.

[57] *Rules and Regulations of the Commissioners of National Education in Ireland*, 1904, Rule 190, Part IX, p. 127.

[58] CNEI, *Corporal Punishment Book, 'N' National School*, NAI/PRIV1231/10 (name of school anonymised).

[59] *Appendix to Seventy-first Report of the Commissioners of National Education in Ireland* (1904), p. 9.

[60] Department of Education, *Rules for National Schools under the Department of Education* (1965), Rule 130, Part 1 (Dublin, 1965), p. 74.

[61] *Ibid.*

[62] Emilie Pine, Mark Keane, Susan Leavy, *The Industrial Memories Project*, Chapter 4, available online at: https://industrialmemories.ucd.ie/ryan-report/report/1-4-14 (accessed 5 July 2022).

[63] CNEI, *Corporal Punishment Book*, Sources on Education, NAI.

[64] Corporal punishment is a complex topic; hence a detailed discussion of the social, ethical or legal dimensions of the topic is outside the scope of the present discussion. See for example: Timothy Quinlan, 'Shining light on silence: Corporal punishment as an abuse of power in the Irish school system', *Études Irlandaises* [Online], 46:2 (2021), 85–102.

[65] Tony Reynolds, *History of Castleknock: Local History–Corporal punishment in National School*, available online at: https://reynoldshistorycastleknockblog.wordpress.com/2017/08/18/local-history-corporal-punishment-in-national-school/ (accessed 4 July 2022).

[66] Quinlan, 'Shining light on silence' (2021), p. 90.

[67] *Irish Press*, 10 October 1935, p. 7.

[68] *Ibid.*

[69] Brendan Walsh, 'Teachers' experience of school: First-hand accounts, 1943–1965', in Walsh (ed.) *Essays* (2016), pp. 203–33. Brendan Walsh, a historian of education, collected secondary schoolteachers' own accounts of the use of corporal punishment in the period 1943–65.

[70] Department of Education Primary Branch, Circular 9/82, *Circular to Boards of Management and Principal Teachers of National Schools, Re: The Abolition of Corporal Punishment in National Schools* (Dublin, 1982).

CHAPTER 11

[1] George Beale, 'Local education authority administration in Northern Ireland after partition: The early years of the County Down Education Committee 1925-31', *The Irish Journal of Education*, 31 (2000), 5–24.

[2] Duggan, 'Twenty hearts' (2021), p. 247.

[3] *Ibid.*

[4] CNEI, 'Teachers employed by the Commissioners of National Education on 31 March 1905', NAI/PCO/10/1/24.

[5] Lawerence J. was ordained a priest in 1927 and later became Monsignor L. Marron, a prominent Catholic priest in the Diocese of Clogher and a noted historian. Census 1911, NAI, available online at: http://www.census.nationalarchives.ie/pages/1911/Monaghan/Drumgurra/ Drumgowna/ (accessed 1 April 2022); Fr L. Marron, *Family Tree: The Marron-Callan Family* (undated). I am grateful to Brian Flanagan for sharing this source with me.

[6] *Evening Herald*, 18 April 1962, p. 2.

[7] CNEI, Coolfore national school, NAI/ED/9/27001/16.

[8] The Commissioners recorded the school roll number 366 against Mr Marron's name, the roll number of the Patrician Monastery School, Carrickmacross.

[9] CNEI, Coolfore national school, NAI/ED/9/27255. King's scholars were prospective teachers who took the King's scholarship examination, and if successful, were called to one of the teacher training colleges, such as Marlboro Street or St Patrick's College, Drumcondra.

[10] *Ibid.*

[11] *Ibid.*

[12] Among the named trustees were Emily Jean Shirley (née Macdonald), who was S.E. Shirley's widow, Major Harry Colquhoun MacDonald and Colonel Charles George Heathcote

[13] Gibbings died some few years later in May 1908. See *Northern Standard*, 25 July 1908, p. 4. Mr Pierce remained as the school manager until the patronage of the school was transferred to Catholic diocesan trustees in 1921.

[14] For a discussion of this period, see O'Reilly, 'Development and demise' (2014), pp. 242–44.

[15] CNEI, Coolfore national school, NAI/ED/2/103, folio 48.

[16] CNEI, Sreenty national school, NAI/ED/9/27255.

[17] Philip Wilson, 'Warwickshire Yeomanry Gallipoli', available online at: https://www.warwickshire-yeomanry-museum.co.uk/gallipolli-history-jpw (accessed 10 May 2022).

[18] CNEI, Coolfore national school, NAI/ED/9/27255.

[19] *Ibid.*

[20] *Ibid.*

[21] *Ibid.*, Coolfore national school, NAI/ED/2/103, folio 15.

[22] *Ibid.*, Coolfore national school, NAI/ED/9/27255.

[23] *Ibid.*

[24] Timothy W. Guinnane and Ronald I. Miller, 'The limits to land reform: The Land Acts in

Ireland, 1870–1909', *Economic Development and Cultural Change*, 45:3 (1997), 591–612.

[25] Fr McKenna died in 1916. See *Anglo-Celt*, 28 September 1918, p. 5.

[26] CNEI, 'National schools teacher salary book: County Monaghan, volume 2, roll numbers 8984–14996', 1921–1923 NAI/ED/4/2759.

[27] *Ibid.*

[28] *Ibid.*

[29] Clogher Diocesan Archives, Episcopal Visitation, 23 April 1922. Episcopal visits occurred every three years. I am grateful to Dr Gary Carville, who provided documentary materials from the Clogher Diocesan Parish Records.

[30] *Ibid.*

[31] *Ibid.*

[32] At Corduff male school it was 65 per cent, at Corduff female school it was 62 per cent, and at Corcreagh school it was 67 per cent

[33] *Northern Standard*, 25 October 1946, p. 1.

[34] *Dundalk Democrat*, 5 November 1938, p. 2.

[35] *Dundalk Democrat*, 30 January 1937, p. 2.

[36] *Dundalk Democrat*, 1 December 1934, p. 2.

[37] Lucy Costigan and Michael Cullen, *The Strangest Genius: The stained glass of Harry Clarke* (Dublin, 2010).

[38] Monsignor Finnegan was also the Dean of Clogher and a former President of St Macartan's College, the diocesan seminary.

[39] Monsignor Finnegan also commissioned the building of the Holy Family Hall in the town.

[40] For a detailed study of King and his work, see Ruth Sheehy, *The life and work of Richard King: Religion, Nationalism and Modernism* (Oxford, 2020).

[41] King designed the Kevin Barry commemorative window at University College Dublin and completed several other commissions for church windows in Ireland and abroad.

[42] Leagh O'Toole, Diane McClelland, Deirdre Forde, Suzanne O'Keeffe, Noel Purdy, Carl Anders Säfström & Thomas Walsh, 'Contested childhoods across borders and boundaries: Insights from curriculum provisions in Northern Ireland and the Irish Free State in the 1920s', *British Educational Research Journal*, 47:4 (2021), 1021–1038; T. O'Doherty and T. O'Donoghue, *Radical Reform in Irish Schools, 1900–1922: The 'new education' turn* (London, 2021), p. 13.

[43] *Ibid.*

[44] Walsh, 'The national system of education' (2016), p. 16.

[45] *Ibid.*, p. 32; O'Doherty and O'Donoghue, *Radical Reform* (2021), p. 13.

[46] Saorstát Éireann, *Report of the Department of Education for the School Years 1925–26–27* (Dublin, 1927), p. 17.

[47] Walsh, 'The national system of education' (2016), p. 12.

[48] The Society is a Pontifical Mission Society aimed at coordinating support for the pastoral and evangelising activities for Catholic missionaries.

[49] *Dundalk Democrat*, 30 January 1937, p. 2.

[50] *Ibid.*

[51] *Dundalk Democrat*, 16 April 1966, p. 11.

[52] Gerard Murphy, 'Irish in our schools, 1922–1945', *Studies: An Irish Quarterly Review*, 37:148 (1948), 421–28.

[53] *Ibid.*, p. 422.

[54] *Dundalk Democrat*, 26 November 1932, p. 5.

[55] *Monaghan Argus*, 18 November 1950, p. 2.

[56] The Society is a Pontifical Mission Society aimed at coordinating support for the pastoral and evangelising activities of Catholic missionaries.

57 *Dundalk Democrat*, 30 January 1937, p. 2.
58 *Ibid.*, 1 May 1937, p. 2.
59 *Northern Standard*, 10 December1937, p. 10.
60 *Dundalk Democrat*, 29 January 1938, p. 2.
61 *Northern Standard*, 21 January 1938, p. 2.
62 Dúchas, *The Schools' Collection*, available online at: https://www.duchas.ie/en/cbes (accessed 28 June 2022). The original children's manuscripts are retained at the University College Dublin Archives.
63 The pupils who wrote essays on the subject of 'Old schools' were: Laurence McMahon (Coolfore), James Murtagh (Legghimore), James Dowdall (Killarue), Brian Keenan (Greagh-drumitt) and Margaret Shankey (Rakeragh).
64 Dúchas, *The Schools' Collection*, p. 269.
65 *Ibid.*, pp. 274–75.
66 *Ibid.*, p. 247.
67 *Ibid.*, p. 287.
68 *Ibid.*, pp. 285–86; 329–30; 331–34.
69 *Ibid.*, pp. 348–49.
70 Sappers were military engineers.

CHAPTER 12

1 Ó Ceallaigh and Ní Dhonnabháin, 'Reawakening the Irish language' (2015), p. 182. See also Antonia McManus, 'The transformation of Irish education: The ministerial legacy, 1919–1999', in Walsh (ed.), *Essays* (2016), pp. 267–96.
2 Éamonn ÓCiardha, 'Morris, Henry', *Dictionary of Irish Biography*, available online at: https://www.dib.ie/biography/morris-henry-a5989 (accessed 11 August 2022). See also: Anon, Henry Morris, *Journal of the County Louth Archaeological Society*, 11:1 (1945), 13–14.
3 National Education, *Programme for Students in Training, Session 1922–23* (Dublin, 1922), pp. 12–13.
4 *Ibid.*, p. 134.
5 McManus, 'The transformation of Irish education' (2016), p. 267.
6 CNEI, 'Teacher salary book', 1921–1923, NAI/ED/4/2759.
7 For periods during 1921, Master James Marron was on sick leave and Mr James Daly, who had acted as a substitute principal at Ashburton national school, was appointed during Marron's absence. Ashburton was located on the former Bath estate.
8 CNEI, 'Teacher salary book', 1921–1923, NAI/ED/4/2759.
9 Mr Cooney was born on 15 September 1895.
10 Department of Education (Hereafter DOE), NAI/ED12/Efficiency case 1931–35, File no: 27920; Box no: 636.
11 *Ibid.*
12 *Ibid.*
13 *Ibid.* Original emphasis.
14 *Northern Standard*, 17 October 1930, p. 2.
15 *Monaghan Argus*, 22 May 1954, p. 3.
16 M. Ward (MW), interview with author, June 2022.
17 P. Gilsenan (PG), interview with author, 20 July 2022.
18 DOE, Teacher salary book, volume 2, roll numbers 9130-14845, 1930–32, NAI/ED/4/2768.
19 DOE, 'Staffing Part 1 1928–62 (Coolfore/Corduff)', NAI/10700/13806, File no: 19975; Box 430.

[20] John Coolahan, 'The historical development of teacher education in the Republic of Ireland', in A. Burke (ed.), *Teacher Education in the Republic of Ireland: Retrospect and Prospect* (Maynooth, 2004), pp. 3–1.

[21] *Ibid.*

[22] National Education, *Programme for Students* (1922–23), p. 38.

[23] *Ibid.*

[24] Pádraic Ó Brolcháin was an Irish volunteer during the 1916 Rising and was a contributor to several publications, including the *United Irishman* and the *Catholic Bulletin*.

[25] Phyllis Mitchell, 'The axing of Carysfort', *Education Matters*, available online at: https://educationmatters.ie/the-axing-of-carysfort/ (accessed 28 June 2022).

[26] *Ibid.*

[27] I am grateful to Gerard and Rosie Callan for providing me with access to Miss Rushe's personal papers. (The papers are uncatalogued.)

[28] M. Nulty (MN), interview with author, 20 June 2022.

[29] This practice was not uncommon among girls who were educated in convent schools. Enfante de Marie could also denote membership of the Confraternity of the Child of Mary.

[30] Merriam-Webster dictionary, available online at: https://www.merriam-webster.com/dictionary/noblesse%20oblige (accessed 5 July 2022).

[31] Miss Rushe, personal papers.

[32] J. Meehan (JMe), interview with author, 7 August 2022. MW interview.

[33] MW interview.

[34] PG interview.

[35] Fergus Lane (FL) interview with the author, 11 December 2021.

[36] Mary Byrne (MB) interview with author, 28 March 2022.

[37] The phrase was a request to the pupils to go to their classroom upstairs. The literal translation is 'Up with you'.

[38] Bernard Fealy (BF) interview with author, 29 January 2022.

[39] At the time of her appointment, she was Miss Caitlín Ní Chearnacháin.

[40] MB interview; Joseph Callan (JC) interview with author, 22 March 2022; MN interview.

[41] JC interview.

[42] MB interview.

[43] FL interview; 'go maith', 'an-mhaith', 'míshásúil' translate, respectively, as: 'good', 'very good', and 'unsatisfactory'.

[44] *Ibid.*

[45] FL interview.

[46] MN interview.

[47] DOE, *Report of the Department of Education for the School Years 1925–26–27 and the Financial and Administrative year 1925–26* (Dublin, 1928), p. 27. The Division also included parts of Leitrim, Meath, and Louth.

[48] DOE, *Report of the Department of Education for the School Year 1939–40 and the Financial and Administrative year 1939–40* (Dublin, 1940), p. 8.

[49] *Anglo-Celt*, 7 March 1959, p. 4.

[50] *Ibid.*

[51] DOE, *Report for the School Year 1939–40*, p. 39.

[52] *Anglo-Celt*, 7 March 1959, p. 4.

[53] DOE, *Investment in education: Report of the survey team appointed by the Minister for Education in October 1962* (Dublin, 1965). The acronym OECD denotes The Organisation for European Cooperation and Development. For a discussion of the development of the OECD report, see: Áine Hyland 'The investment in education report 1965: Recollections and reminiscences', *Irish Educational Studies*, 33:2 (2014), 1–17.

[54] Judith Harford, 'Fifty years on since "free education", it's time to reflect on who the system really serves', *Irish Times*, 9 April 2017, available online at: https://www.irishtimes.com/news/education/fifty-years-on-since-free-education-it-s-time-to-reflect-on-who-the-system-really-serves-1.3036172 (accessed 26 June 2022).

[55] *Ibid.*

[56] Alice Lavery (née Murtagh) (AL) interview with author, 15 November 2021.

CHAPTER 13

[1] MB interview.

[2] The full list of the oral history participants is included in Appendix 1.

[3] Colloquially, a 'street' is a farmyard, and a 'brae' refers to a steep incline on a road. The name 'Tumelty' is spelt 'Tumulty' in the Coolfore roll book.

[4] Josephine Marron (JMa) interview with author, 15 April 2022.

[5] MB interview.

[6] Pronounced locally as 'Nail's Brae and known locally as 'the Becka Brae'. These townlands were home to the Crosby, Keenan, Gilsenan, Cunningham, Fealy, Farrell and Nelson families and two Murtagh families.

[7] JMe interview.

[8] *Ibid.*

[9] JMa MN, PWd interviews.

[10] JC interview.

[11] MB interview.

[12] Patrick Wallace (PWc) interview with author November 2022.

[13] AL interview.

[14] Bernard McGinnity (BMcG) interview with author, 25 March 2022, and MN, JMe, PG, MB, interviews.

[15] PG, AL interviews.

[16] Roisin Higgins, Carole Holohan and Catherine O'Donnell '1966 and all that: The 50th anniversary commemorations', *History Ireland*, available online at https://www.historyireland.com/1966-and-all-that-the-50th-anniversary-commemorations/ (accessed 7 September 2022).

[17] FL interview.

[18] 'Cigire' is the Irish translation of inspector.

[19] MW, MN interviews.

[20] AL interview.

[21] FL interview.

[22] PG interview.

[23] JMa, MB, interviews.

[24] MW interview.

[25] The pupil in question was the author.

[26] MN interview.

[27] PG interview.

[28] MW interview.

[29] JMe interview.

[30] *Ibid.* See also: 'Cures', *Duchas Irish Folklore Collection*, available online at: https://www.duchas.ie/en/cbes/5084100/5040700/5084419?ChapterID=5084100 (accessed 9 September 2022). 'Winkers' are the eye screens attached to the bridle of a donkey or horse to prevent it from seeing to the side.

[31] *Anglo-Celt*, 7 March 1959, p. 4.

[32] MN, PG, interviews.
[33] JC interview.
[34] PWd interviews.
[35] BMcG, MW interviews.
[36] MN interview.
[37] JMa AL, interviews.
[38] JMe interview.
[39] MB interview
[40] MW interview.
[41] *The Argus*, 22 May 1954, p. 3.
[42] PG interview
[43] JMe interview.
[44] PG interview.
[45] MW interview.
[46] MN, JJC interviews.
[47] MB interview.
[48] AL interview.
[49] BF interview.
[50] AL interview.
[51] JMa interview.
[52] PWd, MB interviews.
[53] AL, JJC, MW interviews.
[54] AL interview.
[55] *Ibid.*
[56] PWd, MB interviews.
[57] BF interview.
[58] PWc interview.
[59] BF interview.
[60] JC interview
[61] AL interview.
[62] JMa interview.
[63] PG interview.
[64] MB, PWd interviews.
[65] JJC interview.
[66] BMcG interview.
[67] JJC interview.
[68] MW interview
[69] *Ibid.*
[70] JJC interview. The team had earlier played at 'the Pope's Field' at Drumgowna.
[71] BF, JJC, interviews.
[72] *Ibid.* Cassius Clay later converted to Islam and became Mohammed Ali.
[73] MN interview.
[74] MB, PWd interviews.
[75] MB, PWd PWc interviews.
[76] BF interview.
[77] MW interview.
[78] 15 August also marked the Catholic Festival of Our Lady of the Harvest.
[79] PWd interview.
[80] MW interview. For a brief oral history of the Blackrock baths, visit: 'Gathering Heritage', available online at: https://audioboom.com/posts/6293409-callans-baths-blackrock-co-

louth-ireland?playlist_direction=reversed&t=0 (accessed 6 September 2022).
81 For a brief oral history of Danny Hughes, visit: 'Gathering heritage', available online at: https://audioboom.com/posts/7341319-conor-hughes-danny-hughes-shop (accessed 6 September 2022).
82 *Ibid.*
83 *Ibid.*
84 Although the Belfast shipyards were the target of the bombing raids on Belfast, much of the city was destroyed.
85 Shaun O'Byrne to Tessa Fleming on *Northern Sound Radio*, 21 August 2017, available online at: https://www.northernsound.ie/podcasts/the-wider-view/monaghan-remembers-ww2-bomb-drop-part-heritage-week-127388 (accessed 4 September 2022). See also Frank McNally, 'An Irishman's diary', *The Irish Times*, 25 August 2015, p. 15.
86 *Ibid.*
87 *Ibid.*
88 *Ibid.* The German's had earlier bombed a creamery in County Wexford that was exporting butter to England.
89 PWc interview.
90 A description of the turf-cutting slane is available online at: http://www.pcl-eu.de/virt_ex/detail.php?entry=05 (accessed 5 September 2022).
91 JMa interview.
92 MB interview.

CHAPTER 14

1 Enda O'Flaherty, 'The school house in Ireland: Architecture and meaning – Part 2', available online at: https://endaoflaherty.com/2018/02/23/the-school-house-in-ireland-architecture-and-meaning-part-2/ (accessed 7 March 2022).
2 O'Flaherty, *Deserted schoolhouses* (2018); Enda O'Flaherty, 'The School House in Ireland: Architecture and Meaning – Part 3', available online at: https://endaoflaherty.com/2018/03/01/the-school-house-in-ireland-architecture-and-meaning-part-3/ (accessed 7 March 2022).
3 D. Dickson, J. Pyz and C. Shepard (eds) *Irish classrooms and British Empire: Imperial contexts in the origins of modern education* (Dublin, 2012), p. 1.
4 O'Donovan, *Stanley's Letter* (1917), p. 353. The Education Act of 1998 obliged the state to provide education for everyone and emphasised, among other things, inclusivity and equality of access to education, including those with a disability or special educational needs.
5 *Ibid.*
6 For a comparative analysis of women's education and nursing education, see Gerard M. Fealy and Judith Harford '"Nervous energy and administrative ability": The early lady principals and lady superintendents in Ireland', *Journal of Educational Administration & History*, 39:3 (2007), 271–83.
7 O'Donovan, personal communication, February 2023.
8 Cullen Owens, *Social History of Women in Ireland* (2005), p. 22.
9 *Ibid.*, p. 28.
10 FitzGerald, *Irish Primary Education*, pp. 2 & 42. For A brief summary of the process of the disestablishment of the Established Church in Ireland is available online at: https://www.ireland.anglican.org/about/welcome-to-disestablishment-150/disestablishment-in-context (accessed 21 December 2021).
11 Akenson, *The Irish Education Experiment* (2012), p. 270.

[12] Tom O'Donoghue, 'Stanley's letter: The national school system and inspectors in Ireland 1831–1922 by Patrick F. O'Donovan' (book review), *History of Education*, 4:1 (2019), 143–45.

[13] Citizens' Information, 'Admissions policies in primary and secondary schools', available online at: https://www.citizensinformation.ie/en/education/the_irish_education_system/admissions_policies_in_primary_and_secondary_schools.html (accessed 20 December 2022).

[14] For a detailed history of the prototype educate together school, see: A. Hyland and D. Green, *A Brave New Vision for Education in Ireland: The Dalkey School Project 1974–1984* (Dublin, 2020).

[15] Educate Together, *Annual Report 2021* (Dublin, 2021).

[16] Department of Education, *Schools Reconfiguration for Diversity: Transfer of Patronage of Primary Schools: Information for School Communities* (Dublin, 2022).

Index